D1580549

ESSAYS
*in the History of
Community & Youth Work*

Edited by Ruth Gilchrist, Tony Jeffs & Jean Spence

YOUTH • WORK • PRESS

WITHDRAWN

YOUTH • WORK • PRESS

LIVERPOOL JMU LIBRARY

3 1111 00921 9427

Avril Robarts LRC

Liverpool John Moores University

Published by

**Supporting and improving
work with young people**

17–23 Albion Street
Leicester
LE1 6GD.
Tel: 0116.285.3700.
Fax: 0116.285.3777.
E-mail: nya@nya.org.uk
Website: http://www.nya.org.uk

ISBN 0 86155 245 8
Price £16.95

© February 2001

Editor: Denise Duncan
Cover design: Ruth Gilchrist

The views expressed and the terms used are the authors' own and do not necessarily
represent the views of the National Youth Agency.

Typeset by Avon DataSet Ltd, Bidford on Avon, Warwickshire B50 4JH.
(www.avondataset.com)

Y O U T H • W O R K • P R E S S

is a publishing imprint of the National Youth Agency

Contents

Acknowledgments

This book grew out of a conference on the History of Community and Youth Work held at Ushaw College, Durham in November 1998. The conference took place thanks to the generous support of the journal *Youth and Policy* and the Community and Youth Work Studies Unit at the University of Durham. Without the willingness of both organisations to put their trust in the ability of the organisers to deliver, neither book nor conference would have materialised. Both the journal and the unit therefore deserve the unreserved thanks of the editors.

Along the way we have received considerable help from Angela Emerson who tirelessly tied up the administrative ends for the conference and managed to sort out the manuscript on a number of occasions. Also from Jill Flowers who has made sense of our editorial changes and produced clean copies of chapters that have delighted editors and contributors alike.

Andy Hopkinson at Youth Work Press has encouraged us to stick to the task with patience and we trust he will not be unduly disappointed with the final document.

Finally, we would like to thank the contributors for their good humour, support and willingness to meet deadlines. It goes without saying that without their commitment this book would not have appeared.

Ruth Gilchrist, Tony Jeffs and Jean Spence
Durham 2000

ESSAYS
in the History of Community & Youth Work

WW1 soldier from Sunderland Waits' Rescue Agency

Henry Morris

GFS campsite

Pearl Jephcott

Jane Nassau-Senior (GFS)

George Williams (YMCA)

Strays and Waifs building

YMCA Newcastle

Impington Village College

Thomas Auld

Mrs Townsend, founder of the GFS

Josephine Macalister Brew

Lady Badn-Powell

Waits' Rescue Agency, Sunderland

Who's who on the cover.

Contributors

Crescy Cannan is senior lecturer in social policy at the University of Sussex. She has a long-standing interest in the history of social welfare and in social activists and movements. She is currently working on environmentalism and its relationship to community developments and to social policy.

Keith Cranwell is coordinator for playwork and childhood studies at Thurrock College.

Bernard Davies has been involved in youth and community work for over 40 years – as practitioner, manager, trainer, policy-maker, researcher, writer and trade unionist. His two-volume *History of the Youth Service in England* was published by Youth Work Press in 1999. Currently he is a part-time freelance consultant.

Ray Fabes, former youth worker with a voluntary organisation, has been involved in the education and training of youth and community workers at De Montfort University, Leicester for 27 years where he is currently research fellow specialising in rural issues.

Ruth Gilchrist is a development worker for the Newcastle YMCA, currently responsible for the student project at Newcastle College. She is an editor of the journal *Youth and Policy*.

Cathy Hawkes is a research associate at the Department of Sociology, Liverpool University. Her special interests lie in the area of community work.

John Holmes is currently head of community, play and youth studies at the University of Birmingham, Westhill. He has a background in youth work, community work and adult education.

Tony Jeffs teaches in the community and youth work studies unit in the Department of Sociology and Social Policy, Durham University. He is an editor of the journal *Youth and Policy*.

Bert Jones is the former head of the youth and community work department NEWI Wrexham, a training consultant with the Wales Youth Agency and an advocate of young people and the youth service.

Ian McGimpsey was until recently a student at Durham University. He now works at Toynbee Hall, London, combining a developmental role with researching and writing about the settlement movement.

Carolyn Oldfield is an information officer at the National Youth Agency and part-time research student at the University of Warwick.

John Rose is a qualified and practising youth worker, assistant chief executive at the Wales Youth Agency and a Rhondda Valley socialist.

Margaret Simey is an honorary senior research fellow in the Department of Sociology, Liverpool University. She has a long experience of youth and community work.

Alison Skinner is an information officer at the Centre for Social Action, De Montfort University, Leicester.

Mark K. Smith is the Rank research fellow and tutor at the YMCA George Williams College, London.

Jean Spence teaches in the community and youth work studies unit in the Department of Sociology and Social Policy, Durham University. She is an editor of the journal *Youth and Policy*.

Annmarie Turnbull is a tutor for Turning Point at Goldmiths College, London.

Tom Wylie has been chief executive at the National Youth Agency, Leicester since 1996. He was an HMI from 1979 to 1996. Born and educated in Belfast, he worked there as a teacher and voluntary youth worker.

Introduction

Ruth Gilchrist, Tony Jeffs and Jean Spence

Over half of the chapters in this book are based on workshop papers presented during the History of Youth and Community Work conference held at Ushaw College, Durham in November 1998. That weekend, organised by the editors of *Youth and Policy,* emerged from our concern that youth and community workers are in danger of losing their 'repertory of the past'. The intentions of both the conference and this book are to help secure this repertory. We are keen to establish the significance of the history of the profession, not only for its own sake, but also because it is a valuable aid to the critical understanding of practice from a number of perspectives.

Firstly, to pay due homage to those who went before is important as a means of situating and recognising our own theory and practice. To acknowledge and record the contribution of individuals and groups who created and nurtured organisations and forms of practice upon which subsequent generations have built is to value the work in general. There is much to celebrate regarding past achievements within this enclave of social policy. Community and youth workers and their organisations have initiated important forms of intervention and helped focus the public gaze on previously hidden manifestations of need.

For over two centuries our predecessors have made an incalculable contribution to the sustenance of social movements and to the formation of policy. Failure to catalogue this bequest has cost practitioners dearly. On the one hand it has led to a superficial arrogance which suggests that only in the current generation do we have the appropriate understanding or methodologies to enable us to respond adequately to the needs and demands of local communities and their young people. On the other hand it has fuelled an insecurity and an unwarranted tendency towards self-deprecation – a 'we are only community and workers' attitude. Workers surely need to wrap around themselves and their work the confidence that flows from a consciousness of earlier achievements; an élan that kindles innovation, sustains independence of thought and banishes both unfounded arrogance and humility in our dealings with other professionals. The contribution of history should never be lightly dismissed. Christopher Hitchens in a virtuoso article on the life and work of the historian, activist and revolutionary C. L. R. James reminds us that just what it can bequeath is not least its ability to provide 'an affirmation of the unguessed-at capacity of an educated working class' (Hitchens, 1993, 326).

Secondly, reflecting upon historical achievements and failures helps us lay down markers;

guides to a better understanding of what we do and why we do it. Our approach to the history of community and youth work must therefore amount to more than a pandering to sentimental nostalgia. Serious and sustained attention to what went before will aid the formation of clearer and more robust theory. It will provide a vantage point from which we can interrogate contemporary practice and hopefully formulate more appropriate policy.

Widespread failure to pay due attention to our history has at times fatally hindered the formulation of useful theory and effective policy. It has made us a prey to fashion, encouraged intellectual indolence and led to a tendency to uncritically accept off-the-peg policies which in recent years, have been usually imported from the United States. Politicians and policy makers, too keen to sell themselves through an appeal to 'newness', too obsessed with catching floating voters to care about the abiding strengths within our own professional practices or to learn about possibilities and problems from history, are ferried ceaselessly across the Atlantic. Off they go, hoping to steal an idea, to lift a community initiative which they can then sell as their own unique and new approach. Bewildered practitioners, unaware of the solidity of their own traditions, find themselves on shifting sands in the face of this onslaught. Alternatively, because of the absence of a strong and distinctive professional identity, community and youth workers are frequently subject to the imposition of policy borrowed from other welfare sectors.

Both approaches have unacceptably high failure rates. The result is that we scamper with mind numbing rapidity from policy initiative to policy initiative as politicians, advisers and workers seek to put clear water between themselves and last week's brilliant idea transformed into today's embarrassing disaster. Managers and politicians almost invariably sail majestically on. Youth and community workers move out as funding is redirected into yet another initiative elsewhere. Only the young people and communities whose lives the policies were meant to improve remain *in situ* to co-exist with failure, to live with the 'policy blight' bequeathed them. Movement and change in the contemporary climate become ends in themselves fostering an environment where innovation is all, where reflection is feared and where theory is dismissed as irrelevant ideology, as tired, outdated and a threat to progress.

To exhibit a sense of history, to refer to what went before is now almost tantamount to announcing treasonable intent. Yet how we might have benefited from a longer view! If only, as we rush to embrace curfews, we had paused in the United States to look at the long history not only of their use but of their abandonment there. If only, as we plough scarce resources and energy into youth parliaments and similar ventures supposed to involve young people in mainstream political activity, we had a history of the virtually identical initiatives launched in the 1940s and 1950s to guide us. Not only would we have a clearer idea of why this work has once again become 'flavour of the month' but also why the current initiatives are just as likely to fail as their predecessors did. If only, before we squandered money on Foyers which could have been used to provide the housing young people need and want, we had had access to a history of the rise and demise of similar programmes elsewhere. If only, as we launch ourselves into creating a Connexions Service on the basis of the back-of-the-envelope musings of some tame adviser, we had a history of the disastrous attempt to monitor and register young people during the last war to warn us of the pitfalls lurking around the corner. Of course we are not naïve enough to imagine that such histories would have halted the headlong rush of the policy lemmings. However, historical understanding might enable participants to engage in debates that are more informed and more informing on those rare occasions when they are allowed to discuss policy. It would certainly foster a more critical application of policy and enable workers and participants to understand that the inevitable failures that so often follow the implementation of half-considered initiatives, are rooted in structural inadequacies and not in their own short-comings.

This leads us to our third justification for an investment of time and energy in recording, unearthing and publicising the history of community and youth work: it helps to inoculate us against official lying and bluff. Knowledge of history is a powerful weapon in the hands of those seeking to strip away the humbug and cant with which so much policy is bubble-wrapped. This is particularly true of that history which speaks of the realities of everyday experience in organisations in local communities. For that reason it is crucial to document the disasters, follies and fripperies of recent years such as City Challenge, Garden Festivals and the Millennium Volunteers, to ensure that they are not mistaken for community and youth work. Such programmes, strong on style but wanting on substance, can foster a deep cynicism, a conviction that nothing works, everything new a mere variation on a failed theme. For that reason we have to take a broad sweep. We must unearth success as energetically as we seek to expose incompetence and failure. Examples of both abound and each in their own way equips us with the confidence to voice alternatives and defend those aspects of theory and practice which need to be defended. Getting the balance right is crucial but rarely easy.

Building up the reserves

Compared to some areas of welfare the history of community and youth work is under-documented but there is still much for which to be grateful. A number of excellent histories of national organisations exist. For example, with respect to national organisations there are Kadish (1995) on the Jewish Lads' and Girls' Brigade; Springhall (1983) on The Boys' Brigade; Drakeford (1997) on the Kibbo Kift or the Green Shirts – a youth movement linked to the Social Credit Movement; Heath Stubbs' (1926) account of the origins of the Girl's Friendly Society (GFS); Davies (1973) on the Welsh language youth organisation, the Urdd; Russell and Russell (1932) on the Lads' Clubs; and Dawes (1975) and Eagar (1953) on the Boys' Clubs.

Also on hand are some valuable historical studies of community programmes and agencies: for example, Bagwell (1987) on the West London Mission; Glasby (1999; 2000) on the Birmingham Settlement; Loney (1983) on the Community Development Programme; Briggs and Macartney's (1984) history of Toynbee Hall; Mappen (1985) on the Women's Industrial Council; Robertson Scott's (1925) account of the early years of the Women's Institute; and Barber (1960) on the Roland House Settlement. Besides a plentiful supply of hagiographies we have a restricted number of substantive biographies of key figures such as

Baden Powell (Jeal, 1989); George Williams (Binfield, 1973); Octavia Hill (Bell, 1942; Darley, 1990) and Henriques (Loewe, 1976). Lastly we have a limited number of histories of youth work (Davies, 1999a, 1999b; Jeffs, 1979), community work and workers (Popple, 1995; Vincus, 1985), and young people (see, for example, Davin, 1996; Hendricks, 1990).

The texts mentioned hardly comprise an exhaustive bibliography. Rather they are identified to illustrate the flavour of the material on offer and provide possible jumping-off points for those new to the topic. It is nevertheless possible from the brief overview to ascertain the remaining gaps. These are substantial and beckon future chroniclers to take up the challenge. Firstly, in order to acquire a clearer understanding of the development of youth and community work we urgently need research into the histories of individual projects and programmes, studies of clubs and groups which have survived and prospered over many years. We are currently being swamped by evaluation reports and accounts of short-term initiatives. Unfortunately most of these are concocted to furnish post-hoc justification for funding received or to decorate the begging bowl being raised to attract future income. They have limited value for those seeking at some future date to comprehend contemporary practice. What we lack is a range of accounts such as that of Rose (1998) that chronicle the saga of a club or of community groups; narratives conveying the dynamics of change alongside the continuities, that recount the ebbs and flows and resilience in the life of a project; accounts that bestow an insight into the endurance of workers and programmes thereby offering up an understanding of the interventions that work over decades.

Secondly, where are the 'bottom-up' histories? Where are the accounts that endeavour to unearth the experiences of members and project users, of local activists and volunteers, that relate their understanding of practice and responses to it? Practitioners and academics alike would benefit enormously from the emergence of a vibrant tradition that transferred the gaze from policy formation and the experiences of workers to that of the community beyond. At the other end of the spectrum we would profit considerably from the compilation of insider histories that turned the spotlight on the hidden processes of policy making. We need biographies of key individuals to be set beside analytical accounts of how policy has been formulated and enacted. More accounts such as those of Bunt's *Years and Years of Youth* (1990), would offer an entrée into a world that for no good reason has remained concealed. The records are there to be plundered: perhaps all that is needed are the resources, enthusiasm and encouragement for the process to commence.

The stories of community and youth organisations large and small deserve to be told and the experiences of members, workers and affiliates preserved. Historical self-awareness is a prerequisite for the long-term survival of a profession and a discipline which has a great deal to contribute to the well-being of local communities. It is of course important to engage in debates about professionalism, about theoretical frameworks and about philosophical underpinnings. However, unless such debates are located within historical processes, unless they are grounded within a substantive body of practice and thought, they will become nothing more than airy words to be blown adrift when the next 'new' issue is raised by a policy initiative implemented from above. The generational amnesia from which the work has suffered has not only led to much wasted effort in constantly being forced to re-invent theory and practice, but it has exposed the work to the vagaries of the latest trend. Who now remembers the important issues which were raised in the debates in the 1970s about 'professionalism'? Who now remembers why youth workers thought it was important to be labelled 'workers' rather than 'leaders' and how that related to the problem of professionalism? The time and thought which went into such reflections, the knowledge which we can glean from them about our current dilemmas, is entirely wasted if we reject the significance of history. In such a condition, community and youth work is vulnerable at best to colonisation and at worst it is risking its demise as a process which prioritises the interests of people in local communities. This book is intended as a contribution towards the fuller realisation of the importance of our past in the maintenance of the integrity of our present. Hopefully it will encourage a new generation of practitioners to write as well as make history. If it does then in some measure the contributors will feel recompensed for their hard work.

Bibliography

Bagwell, P. S. (1987). *Outcast London: A Christian response*. London, Epworth.

Barber, D. H. (1960). *The House on the Green*. London, Roland House.

Bell, E. Moberly (1942). *Octavia Hill*. London, Constable.

Binfield, C. (1973). *George Williams and the YMCA*. London, Heinemann.

Briggs, A. and Macartney, A. (1984). *Toynbee Hall: The first hundred years*. London, Routledge and Kegan Paul.

Bunt, S. (1990). *Years and Years of Youth*. Croydon, Pro Juventus Publishing Consortium.

Darley, G. (1990). *Octavia Hill: A life*. London, Constable.

Davies, B. (1999a). *From Voluntaryism to Welfare State: A History of the Youth Service in England Vol. (1) 1939–1979*. Leicester, Youth Work Press.

Davies, B. (1999b). *From Thatcherism to New Labour: A History of the Youth Service in England Vol. (2) 1979–1999*. Leicester, Youth Work Press.

Davies, G. (1973). *The Story of Urdd 1922–1972*. Aberystwyth, Cwni Urdd Gobaith Cymru.

Davin, A. (1996). *Growing Up Poor: Home, school and street in London 1870–1914*. London, Rivers Oram Press.

Dawes, F. (1975). *The Cry From the Streets: The Boys' Club Movement in Britain from the 1850s to the present day*. London, Wayland.

Drakeford, M. (1997). *Social Movements and Their Supporters: The Green Shirts in England*. London, Macmillan.

Eager, W. McG. (1953). *Making Men*. London, University of London Press.

Glasby, J. (1999). *Poverty and Opportunity: 100 years of the Birmingham Settlement*. Studley, Brewin Books.

Glasby, J. (2000). '100 Years of the Birmingham Settlement' in R. Gilchrist and T. Jeffs (eds) *Settlements, Social Change and Community Action: Good neighbours*. London, Jessica Kingsley.

Heath-Stubbs, M. (1926). *Friendship's Way*. London, Girl's Friendly Society.

Hendricks, H. (1990). *Images of Youth: Age, class, and the male youth problem 1880–1920*. Oxford, Clarendon Press.

Hitchens, C. (1993). *For the Sake of Argument*. London, Verso.

Jeal, T, (1989). *Baden-Powell*. London, Hutchinson.

Jeffs, A. (1979). *Young People and the Youth Service*. London, Routledge and Kegan Paul.

Kadish, S. (1995). *'A Good Jew and a Good Englishman': The Jewish Lads' and Girls' Brigade 1895–1995*. London, Vallentine Mitchell.

Loewe, L. L. (1976). *Basil Henriques*. London, Routledge and Kegan Paul.

Loney, M. (1983). *Community Against Government*. London, Heinemann.

Mappen, E. (1985). *Helping Women at Work: The Women's Industrial Councils 1889–1914*. London, Hutchinson.

Popple, K. (1995). *Analysing Community Work*. Milton Keynes, Open University Press.

Robertson Scott, J. W. (1925). *The Story of the Women's Institute Movement*. Idbury, The Village Press.

Rose, C. (1998). *Touching Lives: A personal history of Clapton Jewish Youth Centre. 1946–1973*. Leicester, Youth Work Press.

Russell, C. and Russell, L. (1932). *Lads' Clubs: Their history, organisation and management*. London, A. & C. Black.

Springhall, J. (1983). *Sure and Steadfast: A history of the Boys' Brigade 1833 to 1983*. London, Collins.

Vincus, M. (1985). *Independent Women: Work and community for single women 1850–1920*. London, Virago.

A club tea party from the 1940s

Chapter one

Struggling Through the Past: Writing youth service history

Bernard Davies

Rewriting history

I made my first sortie into writing youth work history over 30 years ago when I began to draft 'the history chapter' for *The Social Education of the Adolescent*, the book I co-authored with Alan Gibson (Davies and Gibson, 1967, Chapter 2). (In what follows I, of course, write only for myself.) As I did so, two very naïve thoughts struck me.

One was that the histories of youth work and youth organisations on which I was relying, though valuable as sources of 'the facts', took largely as given the ideologies and the politics of the times with which they were dealing (for example, Evans, 1965; Percival, 1951; Russell and Rigby, 1908; Wilson, 1959). Some very different kinds of historical writing have appeared since (for example, Blanch, 1979; Bunt and Gargrave, 1980; Dyhouse, 1981, 104–114; Jeffs, 1979; Smith, 1997; Spence, 1998; Springhall, 1977; Williams 1988, Chapter 1). Most of the available texts then, however, started from the at least implicit premise that the organisation or practice under consideration was 'a good thing'. The historical task thus became to establish or confirm past and current credentials. With youth work and youth organisations in effect seen as floating free and self-contained in their environment, the world, it seems, was their oyster.

For someone brought up in a strong left-wing tradition, such a starting point just did not ring true. I assumed significant connections between two phenomena which these histories largely kept separate: the personal suffering and degradation which the early youth workers set out to relieve; and the *systematic* (rather than merely personal) economic exploitation and social injustice which, however ameliorated, remains inherent in a capitalist society. Rather belatedly and slowly, I came to realise how little the histories I was using accorded with my 'gut' as well as intellectual understanding of the origins of any such social movements.

My second naïve train of thought at that time was that, despite their ostensibly a-political stance, these histories were run through with powerful ideological and political messages, most of which I rejected. In particular by operating on, and so implicitly reinforcing, notions of unblemished upper-class altruism directed at the poor, they posited a social structure which I did not recognise.

Thus, while in their accounts the traumas faced by working-class young people came, in structural terms, from nowhere, the solutions being offered by usually highly privileged philanthropists were presented as the self-evident product of the best of British society. Later I needed to come to terms, too, with the absence of crucial gender and race perspectives within this kind of analysis. In these histories, the possibility was never really entertained that, at the very least, the altruistic and the exploitative expressions of power – especially the power to define the nature and causes of 'social problems' and their 'proper' solutions – might be subtly but intimately interrelated.

Historical absences

One of the insights released by these discoveries was how far we now work with a dominant and given notion of youth work. This is taken to be self-evidently synonymous with what goes on in a youth service made up largely of the major national voluntary organisations and state sponsored youth centres and projects.

Yet such commonsense definitions impose blinkers on historical writing which may blank out crucial stretches of the territory. 'Absences', when noticed, can explain or illuminate as much as the 'presences' on which we are permitted or encouraged to concentrate. This weakness of critical appraisal within youth work's historiography thus prevents us from actively looking for and then naming other hidden (or written–out) versions of the practice.

Just occasionally and transiently, these have surfaced. Peter Keunstler, for example, one of the most critical and systematic thinkers ever to give time to youth work and the youth service, pointed in his 1950s study of voluntary youth leadership to 'the magnificent "self-help" record of the trade unions and friendly societies'. This he saw as clear evidence that the 'lower orders were indeed capable of high standards of social organisation and leadership' (Keunstler, 1953, 49). How far were these qualities actually applied to youth work? What precisely did youth work mean in this context? What did it achieve? Answers to such questions, in addition to providing material on under-explored areas of work with young people, might also challenge our perceptions of the familiar and the taken-for-granted.

Beyond objectivity – and consensus

Critical history, however, involves more than operating as the innocent asking: Why does this or that event or development *not* appear? Or, why even when it does is it so little considered or valued? More positively, it needs also to apply a range of conceptual tools for probing what has actually been accepted and done.

Such frameworks are to a significant degree bound to reflect the values and beliefs of the analyst. These show up in the very choice to provide, not just an account of past events within unquestioned parameters, but an explicit *critique* of those parameters and so, almost unavoidably, of the society which has helped set them. Such a perspective therefore moves beyond the assumption, usually unarticulated, that all or most of what is decided and done within a society emanates from a consensus among its citizenry about what is good, proper, needed, urgent. The underpinning premise of a critical history is that a range of *sceptical* questions need to be asked, some of them fundamental, about all these and many other dimensions of that society's development.

A crucial corollary to abandoning a consensual model of society in historical writing is the recognition that, within that society, there will exist significant differences of *interests*. These, rooted in often basic differences of value and priority, generate a range of *conflicting* motivations, aims and demands – for example, over social policy. Given that the society continues to adhere and function, some operational resolutions to these conflicts have clearly been found, suggesting that processes of *negotiation* have occurred during which the different interests have, to varying degrees, made pragmatic but also probably some principled compromises.

However, the different interests rarely enter this political process with equal degrees of *power*. Indeed, because some groups within the society have significantly greater control than others over its resources and advantageous leverage on its decision-making machinery, the institutions which result are likely disproportionately to reflect their interests rather than those of the less/least powerful. At certain points in the history of industrial societies over the past century and a half, some of the latter have come together – through trade unions, for example, through their own political parties and through community organisations – in order to strengthen their role in such 'negotiations'. However, such 'oppositional' movements have rarely altered established distributions of power radically or permanently, not least because they (and especially their leadership) have repeatedly been incorporated into existing power structures and so have largely ceased to challenge these balances fundamentally.

Even within these limits, however, the construction and shape of what we now know as the youth service has, over time, been substantially determined by such *struggles,* puny though they may look when set within the grander political scheme of things. The result has been purposes, form and ways of operating which, far from being straightforward or one-dimensional, contain deeply built-in *contradictory* pulls and pushes. Thus, service planners and practitioners have a mandate *both* to help young people to individual development and self-realisation *and* to prepare them for roles – as family members, workers, citizens – which are in significant ways prescribed and circumscribed.

Over the past decade, this mandate within the youth service has been complicated further by a statement of purpose agreed at a national (ministerial) conference in 1990. As well as reaffirming long-established, more individualistic, purposes, this also endorses collective outcomes – by, for example, asserting the need to embrace and nurture shared identities based on gender, race and sexual orientation. The conflicting pressures which those operating at youth work's cutting edge so often experience very directly, far from being aberrations or the result of mere absences of mind, are thus integral and essential elements of the youth service's institutional location within this society.

Though they may persist for long periods, such balances – shifted by changing economic and political conditions – are not set in stone, resulting at times in further confusions for actors struggling to perform their already testing roles. Yet the negotiations and compromises may over time open up niches for inserting some alternative responses to – even perhaps to some extent subverting – those normally endorsed by more dominant societal interests. For those who come after, in comparison to those offered by more consensual accounts of history, they also provide more credible and *usable* explanations of how something like youth work and the youth service have come to be what they are. In particular, they assume that this past has been constructed, not by the mystery of impersonal forces driven by inevitability, but by *human agency* – by the choices and decisions made by men and women, individually and collectively, and by their acceptance of responsibility for the outcomes.

Consensus in the history of the youth service

The decisive moment for the formation of the youth service as a distinguishable state institution came in 1939: indeed, one interpretation of its creation is that, far from being a far-sighted initiative, it constituted a knee-jerk reaction to the unknown conditions of total war. Contrary to what consensual historians sometimes suggest, these did not give birth to an immediate and seamless national unity – strikes still occurred during the war, for example, while motives remained varied and often contradictory. Nonetheless, at this moment powerful interests certainly converged, generating, for example, a concern to reach and engage 'the youth of the nation'.

This was most concretely expressed in a series of government circulars and reports. Ultimately it was (just about) embodied in a major piece of legislation, the 1944 Education Act, though even this, it is important to recall, was in part the product of labour movement struggle over many decades. By the end of the war one outcome of these policies was a youth service to which all key interests gave at least rhetorical support.

One other relatively consensual period in the history of youth work and the youth service can be identified – the decade ushered in by the Albemarle Report (1960). The support for the service during the 1960s and the advances which flowed from this are usually simply attributed to the report itself and the well argued case made by an influential committee led by a skilful political operator.

Yet, though these words on paper were not without their effect, they were as much the product of their time as a significant influence on it. Albemarle happened in part because, once again, crucial and in some respects novel dimensions of 'the youth problem' – a post-war population 'bulge' now reaching its teens, rising levels of delinquency, the ending of National Service for young men – again generated broad agreement across key interest groups that something needed to be done. This was particularly reinforced by emerging perceptions of a distinctive – and, it was presumed, rebellious – teenage culture resulting in a widening generation gap.

Underlying all this were broader economic and ideological changes and the more optimistic social philosophy these generated. An apparently affluent never-had-it-so-good society did much to suppress concerns about threatening social divisions, to the point where, for example, Britain was said to have become a classless society. Its main intrinsic flaws having been eliminated, major political initiatives or forms of economic restructuring were, it was assumed, no longer required. With its newly recognised professions of psychiatry, social work, teaching, careers advice and even (according to Albemarle) youth work in the van, the welfare state was increasingly left to motivate people to take the fullest advantage of the new opportunity society. Where this failed, the task then became one of social engineering solutions to the residual, merely personal and interpersonal problems of individuals, families or, at their broadest, 'deprived communities'.

The limits of consensus

Such periods of consensus on the youth service did not last long. Post-war austerity quickly reminded the nation that the Dunkirk spirit had not actually eliminated the material fissures within its social and economic structures. Even before the end of the affluent 1960s, poverty and the social divisions that went with it had been rediscovered. Throughout this latter period, too, Britain was rapidly being transformed into a multi-racial society. This was judged by large sections of the 'host' population as in effect fracturing the social fabric in very damaging ways – reactions which in turn required the minority communities to take up liberationist stances. By the early 1970s, liberation movements had also emerged among women, disabled people and gay men and lesbians, in the process identifying social division as integral to, and as running very deep within, British society.

Indeed, one interpretation of youth service development over the 60 years of its construction is that an agreed commitment to its expansion – even its maintenance at existing levels – has been the exception rather than the rule. The experience of war and a passing experience of relative prosperity in the 1960s briefly generated some consensual support for it. Even in these periods, however, commitment could be shaky. Thus a backbench amendment was required to persuade the Government that the crucial Section 53 of the 1944 Education Act should place a *duty* on LEAs to provide 'adequate facilities for recreation and social and physical training (by) cooperating with any (appropriate) voluntary societies or bodies' (Dent, 1947, 56). Even in the 1960s large discrepancies existed in local authority expenditure on the service.

Outside these two periods, which at most totalled some 15 years, gains were rare and, as economic and political conditions became less favourable, even these had constantly to be defended, sometimes desperately. In the years immediately after the war, basic questions were still being asked in influential quarters about whether a separate state-sponsored institutional base for youth work was needed at all. In 1948, for example, an independent research body asked:

> First, does it (the youth service) tend to disrupt family life? Secondly, does it isolate youth, so that youngsters do not grow easily and naturally into membership of the adult community?

Thirdly, does it lead to an undesirable separation of boys and girls at a crucial stage in their emotional lives? (Political and Economic Planning, 1948, 298)

On the premise that county colleges and compulsory part-time further education would shortly be established, it also openly debated whether the service could remain as important as it had by then become (Political and Economic Planning, 1948, 302). The debates continued well into the 1950s with a report for the King George Jubilee Trust noting 'serious doubts as to the purpose of the youth service in these days of full employment and the claims it can make on the already over-pressed resources of the State and local authorities' (King George Jubilee Trust, 1955, 102).

Whether for principled or financial reasons, by the later 1940s and for most of the 1950s, those representing youth service interests thus found themselves dealing with state functionaries and their ministers whose 'definite policy (was) not to advance' the youth service (Potts, 1961, 16). All proposals for improvements – such as for national machinery to negotiate workers' pay and conditions – were stalled or simply rejected. Serious losses were also recorded – no separate national advisory council, youth service building curtailed, reduced grant aid to national voluntary organisations, closed full-time youth work courses and fewer students in training, the number of full-time workers in post falling between 1948 and 1954 from 1800 to 700.

In some decisive and lasting ways Albemarle did turn this decline around: indeed, without this relatively brief resurgence of state commitment to it, we would probably by now have forgotten that a youth service ever existed or even what was meant by the term. Nonetheless, by the early 1970s, faced with a Report, *Youth and Community Work in the 70s* (Fairbairn-Milson, 1969) which actually dared to ask questions about the nature of society, the Secretary of State for Education (one Margaret Thatcher) and her civil servants again washed their hands of the service. Not only did they peremptorily reject all the main recommendations of the report itself. They again abolished its advisory council – something which has happened four times in the service's 60-year history. They also proposed that its resources and expertise be targeted on 'areas of high social need' – a policy which acquired harder and harder edges over the following three decades.

Even before Thatcher became prime minister in 1979, the post-war welfare settlement was already crumbling, particularly under the economic pressures generated in the middle of the decade by huge increases in oil prices and an International Monetary Fund loan which imposed draconian controls on public expenditure. In 1976, for example, Thatcher's Labour predecessor James Callaghan launched a 'great education debate' whose barely concealed message was that the person-centred educational values, for long at the heart of youth work as well as much other educational provision, were rapidly going out of fashion.

For Thatcher herself, however, especially as she gained confidence (and won three consecutive elections), the assault on such 1960s permissiveness and on the state education and welfare institutions which had encouraged it was a core strategic objective. By youth workers and other welfare state practitioners, this was experienced most directly (and so was most simply explained) as a policy of 'cuts'. However, the Thatcher project was much more ambitious. It sought radical shifts in *political* priorities and ways of operating and in the state's control of these activities. Equally important, it aimed to change popular understandings of and beliefs about welfare, why social problems occurred and how these should be tackled. Here, it put its faith in the capacity of market forces to provide solutions, thereby defining cuts as much more than mere economic necessities. No less crucial, these were to embody the basic *social* principles summed up in Thatcher's stated credo: there is no such thing as society – only individuals and families.

During the 1970s, new financial constraints, though at the time painful and seen as damaging, largely meant slower rates of growth or, at worst, standstill. Into the 1980s, however, real reductions in the state's financial commitment to the youth service occurred as the block grant to local authorities was steadily reduced and rate-capping introduced. In addition, major pieces of educational legislation were passed with resource implications for the service which, though indirect, were in many respects even more undermining. These laid new responsibilities on LEAs, particularly to implement a national curriculum for schools. Local management of schools and procedures for them to opt out of local authority control altogether concentrated LEAs' minds on keeping heads and governing bodies sweet. The result by the early 1990s was, as one speaker put it in a House of Lords debate, that 'when an LEA is short of cash, it plunders the youth service'.

Fighting back from above

At best therefore the youth service's development has been two-steps-forward-one-step-back. Indeed, the rest of this paper seeks to demonstrate that it has only survived because, with varying degrees of strength, unity and effectiveness, pressure has been maintained against its reduction or even elimination – and for improvements which key dominant interests within and without the service would never otherwise even have considered.

In the immediate post-war period, such advocacy and campaigning on behalf of the service was probably at its weakest and least organised. It was heavily reliant on philanthropic bodies striving to use their insider influence to 'fix' things, and by fledgling trade unions which, at stages divided among themselves, barely survived anyway. Even so, some pressure was maintained. In due course, this showed up in House of Commons Select Committee reports which lambasted the Ministry of Education for its deliberate neglect of the service and at least one broadly sympathetic House of Lords debate. The Government's decision to set up the Albemarle Committee was also in part the result (Smith, 1997).

From the 1970s onwards, the Albemarle effect began to wear off rapidly, in the process ending the political consensus on a youth service sustained by the state at viable levels. In comparison to what had happened in the 1950s, the resistance to the attacks which followed was more coherent and focused, for much of the period operating through a Youth Service Partners Group.

This brought together some strange bed-fellows. They included the national voluntary youth organisations which, as well as in some cases acting independently, became much better organised and invigorated politically after their standing conference converted itself into a National Council (NCVYS). 'The voice of youth' was provided – not always entirely credibly – by the National Youth Assembly and the British Youth Council (BYC). The latter, restructured in mid-1966, was particularly forceful in advancing its own openly political agendas in the later 1970s, especially under the leadership of its radical chair, Peter Mandelson. The professional associations of youth officers and youth workers were also active participants in the partnership, with the latter becoming a union (CYWU) in 1982 and then 10 years later affiliating to the TUC. Finally, until its own forced reorganisation in 1983 (and even to some extent after) the National Youth Bureau used its role as secretariat to the group to make its own indirect and sometimes direct lobbying and campaigning contribution.

Running alongside these activities from the late 1970s, through the 1980s and into the 1990s was a Youth Affairs Lobby. The strength and effectiveness of this certainly ebbed and flowed. Nonetheless, often three or four times a year young people presented to sympathetic MPs their concerns both about the youth service as such and their experience of political issues – unemployment, police harassment, the problems of rural living, the needs of gay and lesbian young people. Supported by a liaison group, the lobby also provided an additional form of collective action for some national youth service bodies.

As organisations and personnel changed, the Partners Group had ceased to function by the end of the 1980s. It was succeeded by a National Youth and Community Work Alliance which by the mid-1990s had become the United Kingdom Youth Work Alliance. This was made up of 15 youth work bodies which again included NCVYS, BYC and CYWU as well as what was by then the National Youth Agency (NYA) and the Standing Conference of Principal Youth and Community Officers (SCPYCO). Formed in 1995, this set out to give a vital interest group a stronger collective voice in the political arena.

Over these 20 years and in particular during the Thatcher and post-Thatcher periods, the impact of much of this pressure group activity was often hard to discern. However, though the 1970s experience of working through a national advisory body (the Youth Service Forum) turned out to be particularly uninspiring, during the decade some (for the youth service) high-profile events were mounted. In 1977 the Youth Charter 2000 Conference and a series of follow-up events, though flawed in their actual execution, brought together on a national stage a number of leading political figures including two former prime ministers. Most notable between 1973 and 1980, however, were the four private members bills, aimed at strengthening the service's statutory basis. At a time when the first Thatcher Government was still finding its feet, the last of these caused enough of a parliamentary furore to force the DES into conceding yet another review of the service.

During the 1980s, legislation which would strengthen the legislation on which the service rested remained a high priority for pressure group activity. Though with even less chance of success than its predecessors, another private members bill was tabled in the Commons, and at various stages MPs and peers were persuaded to table amendments to major education legislation going through Parliament. Despite its creator, Sir Keith Joseph's, palpable lack of enthusiasm, the DES was also pressured in the later 1980s into establishing a National Advisory Council for the Youth Service (NACYS) which youth service interests were able to use more constructively than they had the 1970s Youth Service Forum.

The 1990s saw such pressure maintained. Using a decision by Warwickshire to in effect wind up its statutory youth service as a test case on its legal position, in 1992 CYWU took the council to the High Court. Though the judgement went against it, the judge commented sharply on the lack of clarity in the existing legislation and the failure of successive governments to set standards by which an 'adequate' service could be measured. In 1994 these questions were addressed directly by a Sufficiency Working Party (1994) whose report made the case for strengthened legislation. This was followed two years later by *Agenda for a Generation*, a United Kingdom Youth Work Alliance publication which set out the minimum conditions and arrangements for an effective youth service (United Kingdom Youth Work Alliance, 1996). As by the mid-1990s a Labour Government became a realistic prospect, pressure was maintained on the party's Youth Task Force so that, by the time it won the 1997 General Election, the service had won a number of what seemed like firm commitments to its future development.

If proof was needed that no natural progressive commitment to the youth service existed, however, it was provided by the first two years of the Labour Government. Placing young people at the heart of its 'joined-up' strategy for tackling 'social exclusion', New Labour seemed intent on constructing a national youth policy. Yet, for the youth service the only concrete outcome of these two years was not the new legislation which had been promised, but an audit of its resources and policies. Indeed, with the service's leverage on power apparently no greater than it had been under Conservative governments, the need for continued organisation and pressure was again very clearly demonstrated.

Fighting back from below

This struggle was not just a top-down process, however. Indeed, some of the interventions on the national stage – for example, through the Youth Affairs Lobby and also through Parliamentary lobbies organised by CYWU, BYC and others in the 1980s and 1990s – were in part evidence of grass-roots organising.

Such bottom-up pressure was also highly significant in its own right, especially from the 1970s onwards when both community activism and a range of liberation movements injected new surges of energy and effectiveness. Both also illustrate how far youth work and the youth service were part of wider social movements and social policy developments.

The resultant contradictions repeatedly emerged – for example, through Urban Aid projects (introduced in the late 1960s to improve services to deprived communities); in the Home Office's Community Development Projects of the early 1970s; and even in Manpower Services Commission initiatives such as the Community Programme in the early 1980s. Though intrinsically flawed, not least because of the short-term nature of the funding on offer, these all helped to stimulate or underpin forms of local community activism, some focused on work with young people. Operating 'in and against the state', for over two decades these elements of the independent voluntary sector thus added significantly to youth work provision.

The other key impetus for such struggle – often more noticeable and noticed – were the efforts of a range of oppressed groups to confront the oppressions they were experiencing and in the process strengthen their collective identities and effectiveness. Within the youth service as an institution, as within most individual youth work organisations, little was conceded to them without a fight. Taking national liberation movements as their inspiration and resource, key interest groups within the service thus had to press unrelentingly to move on provision from usually taken-for granted positions which kept them largely powerless and often invisible, if not actually excluded.

Though perhaps unintentionally, the Hunt Report *Immigrants and the Youth Service*, (Hunt, 1967) constituted one of the clearest official statements of state policy which had this effect, particularly by insisting that all youth service facilities should aim at 'integrating' Black and white young people. It thus denied and devalued the efforts of ethnic minority communities both to give their young people some respite from their everyday experiences of racism and to encourage collective pride and strength.

By 1982 the Thompson Report (DES, 1982) was calling the Hunt doctrine 'naïve'. Nonetheless, considerable energy had to be committed to breaking out of the integrationist trap it had imposed or endorsed and especially to getting state support (including funding) for separate provision for Black and Asian young people, staffed by trained and qualified Black and Asian workers. Much of the burden of struggling for this fell to Black groups themselves. By the end of the 1970s a Black Youth and Community Workers Association had emerged which, itself putting pressure on CYWU, helped bring a Black caucus into existence within the union. (From the mid-1980s a women's and a gay and lesbian workers' caucus were also operating within CYWU.) In the early 1990s a Black Workers Conference prepared responses to the Ministerial Conference initiative for a core curriculum for the service, with effects which were perhaps most clearly seen in a statement of purpose explicitly endorsing 'the celebration of diversity' and of the need to challenge racism.

Also with traceable links to wider liberation movements, other groups have parallel (and indeed sometimes overlapping) records of exerting pressure in order to get youth work and the youth service to address the needs of marginalised young people. During the later 1970s, for example, enthusiastic responses to a series of 'Boys Rule Not OK' conferences by women workers adopting explicit feminist perspectives helped generate organised demands for the development of separate work with girls and young women. By 1983 this had produced a National Organisation for Work with Girls and Young Women (NOW) as well as a wide range of publications and local and regional networks and events.

These kinds of self-help efforts to organise on behalf of work with gay and lesbian young people also date back at least to the 1970s. The first gay youth groups – in London and on Merseyside – established themselves in 1976, to be followed before the end of the decade by a National Joint Council for Gay Teenagers. These developments ran alongside the emergent organisation of gay and lesbian youth workers. A gay workers' group, formed in 1976, spearheaded a Sexual Awareness in the Youth Service Campaign as well as demanding, and getting, explicit recognition within CYWU. By the late 1980s and into the 1990s it had led to a National Association of Lesbian and Gay Youth Workers. Throughout much of the 1980s, BYC continued to advocate in favour of more responsive policies and provision for gay and lesbian young people, on occasions putting its own continuing state funding and internal stability at risk.

Though a radical liberation movement among disabled groups also developed in the 1970s, its practical and political impact within the youth service is harder to trace. Even so, as early as 1974 one youth worker, describing himself as 'physically impaired', was drawing inspiration from what was by then happening in the field of race relations and pointing to 'the deprived group coming to take more control over its own destiny'. Occasionally such ideas burst onto the national youth service scene as when trainees on DES-funded apprentice schemes in the late 1980s withdrew from a national conference because arrangements for disabled delegates were inadequate.

Campaigning on behalf of one other 'excluded' group – rural young people – though hardly 'liberationist' in its ideology or methods, also attracted the attention of committed activists. From the 1970s to the 1990s this relied mainly on a series of research and action projects sponsored by NAYC, NYB/NYA and others which repeatedly highlighted the special problems of young people in rural areas and of bringing youth work services to them and proposed strategies and approaches for dealing with these.

Must struggle succeed?

Identifying and valuing these struggles in these ways is not to argue that all – even most – were effective. Defeats (certainly as defined by the campaigning groups themselves) are often easier to discern than victories.

- The appointment to the Thompson Review Group of a Black member came only as a very late – and it seemed tokenistic – afterthought, while in 1984 a NCVYS report, confirming much other evidence within the service, was still painting a picture of voluntary sector complacency in engaging Black young people.
- Work with young women experienced significant local set-backs, as when the London Union of Youth Clubs dismissed its field work officer in 1980, in part because the newsletter she was producing was 'too women's libbish'. It also suffered major national losses, with the closure in 1987 by NAYC of its Girls Work Unit and the winding up of NOW in 1994.
- Clause 28 of the 1988 Local Government Act which prohibited 'the promotion of homosexuality' in schools did significant knock-on damage to youth work provision for gay and lesbian young people.
- Though, significantly, *not* publishing reports on work with Black and gay and lesbian young people, in 1988 and 1989 the National Advisory Council did produce highly critical commentaries on the state of youth work with girls and young women, with disabled young people and in rural areas. Such outspokenness

may well have helped to seal its fate as soon as it had completed its three-year experimental period.

Nor are significant absences, or at least weak points, in these struggles hard to find. Most striking is the virtual disappearance of *class* as an organising focus within the service. Where it did concentrate minds, what usually was emphasised were the failings of working-class young men – their aggressiveness, their territoriality, their denial of feeling. Class experiences of inequality, injustice and exploitation – within the judicial system, by the police or at work – were rarely specifically identified or tapped for the political (or indeed curricular) impetus they might provide.

A second weak link in the efforts at organised pressure and resistance in the development of youth work was the fitful ways (at best) in which young people – Albemarle's fourth partner – were engaged. Youth councils had their (passing) popularity, at least among policy makers: in the flush of democratic enthusiasm after the defeat of totalitarianism in the late 1940s; after renewed endorsement by the Thompson Report in the 1980s; under New Labour's rediscovery of community participation in the 1990s. However, with their usually adult-inspired agendas and adult-conceived structures, these initiatives repeatedly fail to generate wide enthusiasm or motivation among young people. They were hardly designed anyway to provide them with critical political platforms for advancing youth work or the youth service within local or national policy-making.

The purpose of this paper has not been to present a simplistic or idealist account of brave and successful struggles against unrelentingly perverse forces determined to do down young people and that form of institutional provision we call the youth service. It has been rather to make the case that any advances that this provision has made over its 60-year history – indeed, its very survival – are to a significant degree the result of committed individuals and groups acting collectively, organising, pressuring, campaigning – acting 'politically'.

This may seem a rather limited and obvious conclusion to be drawing from so many words. Nonetheless, my own journeys through the history of youth work and of youth organisations have suggested that too often explanations of events rely on 'the inevitability of altruism'. In the end, however, practice and institutions are made by people – men and women who act intentionally, individually but especially in concert, who take responsibility for what they do – and who assume that they are operating in a society whose balance of (often powerful) interests are unlikely for very long to be in their favour.

Bibliography

Blanch, M. (1979). 'Imperialism, nationalism and organized youth', in John Clarke, Chas Critcher and Richard Johnson (eds), *Working Class Culture: Studies in history and theory.* London, Hutchinson. pp 103–120.

Bunt, S. and Gargrave, S. (1980). *The Politics of Youth Clubs.* Leicester, National Youth Bureau.

Davies, B. and Gibson, A. (1967). *The Social Education of the Adolescent.* London, University of London Press.

Dent, H. C. (1947). *The Education Act of 1944.* London, University of London Press.

DES (1969). *Youth and Community Work in the 70s*, (Fairbairn-Milson). London, HMSO.

DES (1967). *Immigrants and the Youth Service*, (Hunt Report). London, HMSO.

DES (1982). *Experience and Participation: Report of the Review Group on the Youth Service in England*, (Thompson Report). London, HMSO.

Dyhouse, C. (1981). *Girls Growing up in Late Victorian and Edwardian England*. London, Routledge and Kegan Paul, pp 104–14.

Evans, W. M. (1965). *Young People on Society*. Oxford, Basil Blackwell.

Keunstler, P. (1953). *Voluntary Youth Leaders*. London, University of London Press.

King George Jubilee Trust (1955), *Citizens of Tomorrow,* (Part IV). London, Odhams.

Jeffs, T. (1979). *Young People and the Youth Service*. London, Routledge and Kegan Paul.

Ministry of Education (1960). *Youth Service in England and Wales*, (Albemarle Report). London, HMSO.

Percival, A. C. (1951). *Youth Will be Led: The story of the voluntary youth*. London, Collins.

Political and Economic Planning (1948). *The Service of Youth Today*. London, PEP.

Potts, D. (1961). *Some Notes on the History of the National Association of Youth Leaders and Organisers*. Manchester, National Association of Youth Leaders and Organisers.

Russell, C. and Rigby, L. (1908). *Working Lads Clubs*. London, MacMillan and Co.

Smith, D. (1997). 'The eternal triangle – youth work, the youth problem and social policy', in *The Challenge of the Future: Towards the new millennium for the youth service*. Lyme Regis Dorset, Russell House Publishing.

Spence, J. (1998). 'Lily Montague: A Short Biography'. *Youth and Policy*, No 60, Summer, pp 73–83.

Springhall, J. (1977). *Youth, Empire and Society: British youth movements 1883–1940*. London, Croom Helm.

Sufficiency Working Party (1994). *Planning for a Sufficient Youth Service: Legislation and funding for the youth service – a consultative paper*. Sufficiency Working Party.

United Kingdom Youth Work Alliance (1996). *'Agenda for a Generation' – building effective youth work*. Edinburgh, Scottish Community Education Council.

Williams, L. O. (1988). *Partial Surrender: Race and resistance in the youth service*. London, New York, The Falmer Press.

Wilson, J. S. (1959). *Scouting Round the World*. London, Blandford Press.

W·A·Y·C

The youth service in Wales

Chapter two

Early Development of the Youth Service in Wales 1830–1917

Bert Jones and John Rose

Migrants physically strong as youth, and perhaps with the bloom of the country in their cheeks, fell an easy prey to excessive labour in cruelly dangerous conditions, the diseases of the noisome courts and undrained industrial villages, and whose lungs already infested with the dreaded consumption, were soon poisoned by the foul air of collieries, mines, quarries and foundries.
(Jones, 1992, 46)

The process of intervention into the lives of young people has inevitably reflected the needs emerging from a range of social, political, cultural and religious trends (HMSO, 1982, Para: 1.3). Understanding the deep and sometimes complex sociological currents of society gives some clarity to those systems put in place to deal with 'the problems of the young'. To consider these problems in isolation from the wider context of society is to fail to understand the synthesis between the raft of social issues that together help shape the identity of a national state. So Wales in the 19th century, undergoing an accelerating and turbulent period of industrial and social change, presented a backcloth against which the experiences of young people began to touch the conscience of social reformers of the time.

Following the impact of rapid industrialisation, with its attendant population explosion, came a host of social issues – poverty, housing, health, social malaise and, more stridently expressed, the undermining of traditional Welsh community life, its culture and its language. A new critical consciousness began to grow, a new awareness of people and their place in the social system; leading the concerns were the emerging trade union movement and the clergy. While the Chartist movement in Wales in the early 1800s, and the inspiration of the Merthyr Rising in 1831 against the exploitation of workers is revered, it is the church which became more insistent in pursuing its vision of a cultural Wales. While agreeing with Williamson (1996) that the origins of informal work with young people are in the early Victorian period, early concerns were for the wide community rather than specifically for the young. The potential for social revolution in the South Wales valleys, the competition for allegiance to particular religious denominations and the drive towards the protection of the Welsh language and traditional culture had deeper meanings than the welfare of young people.

While the nonconformist denominations towered over the religious landscape of Wales, both in town and country, there was intense rivalry with the Roman Catholic Church. Following Pope Gregory XVI's decision in 1840 to reorganise the Catholic Church, in England and Wales clergy adopted a community development approach in their strategy. Dr Thomas Brown, Vicar Apolistic of the Welsh District in 1840 declared that the church building should emphasise 'its educational use, being as important as its religious raison d'être' (Jenkins and Smith, 1988, 33).

Young people were a particular target group, although the problems of poverty and the demands of industry were clearly recognised. Father Carroll comments on his efforts to bring informal education to the young people of Merthyr Tydfil and Tredegar in 1842:

> I keep up two day schools (60 children) — the children of both sexes are employed to pick and pile minerals or coal. They are removed about 7 years of age, which early removal generally deprives them of all taste for instruction.

(Ibid, 38)

For the nonconformists the roots of the social problems of mid-Victorian Wales rested in a loss of community, one based on Welsh language and traditional culture, the absence of which caused the people to be 'degenerate in body and mind' (ibid). The Bishop of Llandaff, in 1827, Charles Summer compared the social order in Merthyr Tydfil to that in 'the heart of Africa' maintaining it was characterised by 'brutality, chauvinism and malice . . . the dark trinity that ruled many families in south-east Wales at the end of the 19th century' (op cit, 84).

Despite a romanticisation by a vocal moral leadership within the traditional nonconformist sector that marriage and allegiance to the expressed culture was the solution to a degenerate lifestyle, profound pressures and tensions existed in every family. Wives were abused and beaten, abandoned and battered. Together with exploitation in the workforce young people were living in anguished poverty for most of the 19th century in working-class Wales. Contemporary phrases in youth work — socially excluded, disadvantaged, disaffected — seem pale in comparison when set beside the private stresses and sorrows of life in 1860 Merthyr Tydfil.

Yet within this dismal picture there were glimmers of light that would lead, towards the end of the 1800s and early 1900s, to a more compassionate and caring attitude towards young people. The Aberdare Parish Church in 1886 commented on the church's responsibility to take care of the poor and overcrowded populations, and the flourishing Church Associations with clothing, shoe and maternity clubs — as well as the coffee tavern movement seen as a relatively safe alternative to the public house (Jones, 1992, 97).

Such initiatives began to become more philanthropic with greater emphasis on care rather than the spiritual needs of young people. While the moral brigade still criticised the people for their 'savage ways' a more caring social scientist attitude commented sympathetically on the negative effects of poor living standards upon the lives of young people (Jones, 1992). Even the report of the enquiry into education in Wales published in 1847, while not able to resist referring to the working class as 'ignorant, depraved and barbarous', contributed to a new social consciousness about young people in Wales.

An emerging philanthropic approach, particularly towards young people, was being nurtured in the unique social, industrial, political and cultural melting pot of urbanised Wales.

The roots of a youth service were beginning to embed themselves in our social structure, some of these roots retaining the dogma that characterised the nature of the religious, military and social influences of the time. Against this backdrop the accelerating shape of youth services from the late 1870s can be best understood.

An historical overview

The early youth service history in both England and Wales has been described by Butters and Newell (1978), Jeffs (1979) and Smith (1988), as a time when work with young people was characterised by both appalling social and employment conditions and by rapid social and political change caused by the development of an industrialised, urban society. At this time it is claimed (Jones, 1997) that many specific parts of Wales were subjected to social change of unprecedented speed, unlike England where industrialisation was based on a long history of craftsmanship. Characteristic of this rapid social change was the population explosion – in the period between 1861 and 1911 the population in Glamorgan rose from 317,712 to 1,120,910, an increase of 253 per cent. It was also a very young population who had to be 'socialised into working for their livings at very tender ages' (Jones, 1988, 2).

For the youth service these demographic changes clearly polarised provision into two distinct categories that still exist in a recognisable form in Wales today. The first of these, urban youth work, is located in areas of high density population such as the industrialised valleys of south Wales and north east Wales, the second, rural youth work is delivered in the sparsely populated areas of mid, north and west Wales. In this rapidly changing environment the growth of the non-Welsh population, particularly from the south west of England and Ireland, produced a racial division within the industrial areas (Williams, 1950) that gave rise to serious social problems that had no parallel in England. Within this context the role of youth work was described (Jeffs, 1979; Davies, 1986) as being concerned with the rescue and rehabilitation of young people, including the teaching of basic education. This approach they claimed resulted in youth work being delivered through a wide range of settings including Sunday schools, the Ragged Schools Union, the Young Men's Christian Association, and benevolent institutions including Dr Barnardo's Homes (Pate, 1972; Evans, 1965). While this research does reflect to some extent on the circumstances in Wales, it does not consider or understand the significant and in some instances unique, changes taking place in Wales. These were concerned with a number of interrelated tensions including:

- rapid industrial expansion;
- the system of local government in Wales;
- the effects on the Welsh language as a result of immigration;
- educational developments;

- the comparative weakness of the middle class; and
- the importance of the Welsh nonconformist movement as a predominantly working-class religion.

This religious difference was markedly different at least until well into the second half of the 19th century (Davies, 1965; Davies, 1994) from its predominantly middle-class equivalent in England (Brown, 1988). It is recognised (Davies, 1994) that these circumstances were relevant at a time of growth within the history of nonconformist religion in Wales and that its power would enter into decline at the start of the 20th century. The effect during that time, however, and the influence of a particular religious approach on the lives of young people in Wales was crucial in a number of different ways. Education in the view of many nonconformist ministers was an enabling process for young working-class people to improve themselves within the existing structure of society. This approach brought with it a particular emphasis with regard to education including the belief, particularly among the Unitarians and Quakers, on the equal role and more radically the equal intellectual ability of women (Watts, 1980). Nonconformist religion also developed an approach described as having a deeply rooted community base that saw many of its buildings used for a wide variety of events including 'educational activities, lectures, eisteddfodau, concerts, adult classes, penny readings and meeting places to discuss politics' (Evans, 1989, 80).

This was in direct contradiction to Anglican dogma, which saw education as a means of instructing young people as to their certain role in society (Fieldhouse, 1996). Differences from England can also be identified with regard to the social structure within Wales recognised by Jones (1981) and Davies (1965) as having a weak or virtually non-existent middle class, which needed to develop to a point where it would be powerful enough to 'break the monopoly of power possessed by the proprietorial class' (Jones, 1981, 48).

These structural differences between Wales and England were also identified by Williams who stated that Welsh society was identified by its 'distinctive class division lacking a vigorous urban bourgeoisie' (1950, 16). Support is given to this analysis by the research of Brennan et al (1954, 63) who claims that south Wales had proportionately fewer families in the middle-class income range which they calculated as being '79.5 per cent working class and 20.5 per cent middle class against 31.5 per cent middle class in England'. Evans (1936) spoke of the scattered elements of the middle class in Wales located as a disparate group in the south and east of Wales and made up of professional rather than mercantile classes. It was also recognised (Williams, 1950) that Welsh society became polarised with the iron masters with their origins in the English middle class, becoming allied through marriage and association with the gentry and Anglicanism. While the Welsh speaking tenant farmer and industrial worker became increasingly nonconformist, the result of this polarisation was the marginalisation of the Welsh workman who 'never finds his way into the office. He may become an overseer or a contractor, but this does not take him out of the labouring and put him in the administering class' (ibid, 246). The repercussions of this weak Welsh social structure within the rapidly emerging, highly populated industrial south and north east, had obvious implications for philanthropic activities related to young people that had in the main been carried out by that group in England (Barnett and Barnett, 1909). In the Welsh context this had been identified as a problem by Jones who claimed that the beneficiaries of capitalism in Wales soon distanced themselves 'from their victims the poor' (1988, 4). Jones also recognised that Wales had its millionaires but:

> The spending of private fortunes on public causes was not one of the characteristics features of their lifestyle; and the towns and surrounding villages of north and south Wales reflected not the riches of the industrialists but the relative poverty and deprivation of the workforce.
> (Ibid)

This was in direct contrast to the situation in England where it is claimed that: 'many distinguished men and women in the leisured and professional classes worked for social reform at this time, and the second half of the nineteenth century saw some remarkable developments' (Evans, 1965, 4).

The effects of this for young people in Wales was an exclusion from, in a large number of areas, the influence of many of the philanthropic organisations so easily recognised in England. This is not to suggest that provision was even across the whole of England. In comparison to Wales there was what appeared to be an embryonic corporate provision focused on young people. Among these initiatives was the YMCA formed in London in 1844 and the YWCA formed in 1846 through the efforts of Lady Kinnaird and Emma Roberts, who was also the driving force behind the development of clubs for girls. The first of these opened in Bristol in 1881 and was used as a model for the further expansion and development of local federations of Girls' Clubs (Evans, 1965). Baden Powell founded the Boy Scout Association in 1907 and the Girl Guides in 1910. This was followed in 1924 by the Youth Department of the Co-operative Movement which was formed at the same time as the National Association of Boys' Clubs in London (Eager, 1953). In England many other philanthropists such as Lord Shaftesbury, Doctor Barnardo, Elizabeth Fry and Octavia Hill had also influenced work with young people. This included the setting up of the East End Juvenile Mission and the Society for Improving the Conditions of the Labouring Classes (Barnett and Barnett, 1909; Eager, 1953).

In comparison few attempts were being made in Wales to introduce youth organisations which reflected a specific Welsh context. Ifan ab Owen Edwards introduced Urdd y Delyn as a children's organisation in 1896 but it failed 10 years later. In 1911 Mallt Williams introduced a new movement called Byddin Cymru (The Wales Army) whose purpose was designed to show the young people of Wales how best to serve their country with the priority being their defence of the Welsh language. This organisation also failed and ceased to exist after 1918, a victim it is claimed of the problems associated with the Great War (Davies, 1973). This failure to develop a national youth organisation in Wales continued until 1922 when the Urdd Gobaith Cymru was formed by Ifan ab Owen Edwards for the purpose of 'creating an undefiled Wales for the benefit of the world and of humanity' (ibid, 14). Despite a sharply focused purpose related to the Welsh language, it became one of the most successful youth organisations in the UK, in terms of numbers. The success of such narrowly focused organisations, which for a large part of their formative years either refused to accept non-Welsh speaking members, or to segregate them when they did, could be seen perhaps as a clear indicator of the paucity of opportunity for many young people in Wales, a phenomenon that may still be found in Wales today. It can be argued with some authority that many of the organisations formed in England did move to Wales but they did so with an apparent attitude that they were only moving into another part of the English domain and as such they gave little attention to the social, political, industrial and religious conditions existing in Wales at this time (Rose, 2000).

However, even when these philanthropic organisations did venture into Wales, their presence was in general of a much more limited nature and later in time than similar developments in England. Examples of this would include the multi-denominational YWCA which had only 14 centres in Wales in 1935 with 1,247 members, or the Girl Guides who had during the same period 21,145 members which was only 4.6 per cent of the membership in England (Rooff, 1935). They also often brought with them added tensions that were focused on both language and religion that suggest that the presence of many of these organisations may not have been as welcome in Wales as they were elsewhere. The Girls' Friendly Society (1875), Boy Scouts Association (1907) and the Girl Guides (1910) were appropriate examples of the potential for tension between imported English-based English-speaking youth organisations with their affiliation to the Anglican Church and their targeted audience of Welsh young people, many of whom spoke Welsh as a first language and who were clearly associated with a nonconformist background.

In the late Victorian period commercial leisure enterprises with a few exceptions, such as cinema and dancing, were also slower developing in the emerging industrialised areas of Wales, as was the opportunity for many young people to participate in them because of the strict influence of religious organisations and the accepted social norm of containing working-class young women within the home. The patterns of employment also involved a large number of young workers entering industry from an early age (Williams, 1950) as well as relatively lower levels of affluence among the very broad base of working-class people which precluded them from involvement in much commercialised leisure activity. This led, in the opinion of the writers, to a restricted concept of both adolescence and leisure time.

Within the emerging industrialised environment it was claimed (Jones and Pool, 1971) that the new urban workers were subjected to appalling conditions at work while their families faced filth and overcrowding in their homes. It is recorded (Evans, 1988) that the Rhondda valleys were polluting the environment with some 3,000 tons of human excrement a year and Blaenau Ffestiniog described as a naturally healthy environment was a man-made death trap with an increase in mortality rate four times higher than similar rural areas. Merthyr Tydfil was described by Rammell (1850) as being almost entirely without drainage, with the total absence of a public water supply described as the 'crowning evil' (ibid, 34). Work conditions were also harsh, influencing the attitude of workers towards the social and political problems directly affecting their lives. It is claimed: 'They were herded together in extreme discomfort and brutalised by long hours of heavy and dangerous work. In winter the miners only saw the sun on Sunday' (Williams, 1950, 232).

As a result the Welsh coal-fields, with their rapidly expanding population were the centre of many social disturbances in the first half of the 19th century described as a *'frontier society'* characterised by:

> *. . . monstrous black iron works and the smoke filled valleys. Up on the hillsides the 40,000 ironminers and colliers lived in their grey barracks, with their diseased and poverty stricken families . . . Poverty was not a novel experience for these people but the relationship between them and their employers was.*
>
> (Jones, 1988, 140)

> *Fast moving social changes and the resulting tensions were also a time of growing awareness of the need to introduce a more clearly defined state controlled education service as a method of social control that was able to 'capture . . . the patterns of thought, sentiment and behaviour of the working class'.*
>
> (Davies 1986, 18)

The need for this politically motivated intervention was caused by the growing concern of central government that young working-class people, caught up in radical social change, did not have the necessary respect for existing social structures, middle class order or for the church-taught ideals of 'honesty, chastity, industry, and familiar order' (Butters and Newell, 1978, 40). As the state interest in education grew, driven by a need to introduce both social control and to develop an adequately prepared workforce more able to contribute to a rapidly developing industrialised society, a number of government reports were produced. In 1839 a Committee of Council for Education was formed to promote four principle objectives for normal and modern schools, namely religious, moral and general instruction and the development of habits in industry. A report was also produced in 1847 on the state of education in Wales. It highlighted both the poor level of elementary education and the equally poor moral state of the population (MacClure, 1973). The report, which caused outrage, was seen by many in Wales as part of a wider campaign by the central government in London to devalue both the Welsh language and nonconformist religion, which were identified as having an overly significant influence on education in Wales (Evans, 1975). Credit was given within the report, however, to the importance of the education delivered through the Sunday school where it is claimed (Jones, 1997) that 20 per cent of the population of Wales attended with 50 per cent of that number being able to read the scriptures. Jones claims that the 1847 report stated that the Dissenting Sunday Schools were considerably more effective than the Anglican Church inasmuch as they also provided opportunities for family spiritual improvement. This report also identified what was described as:

> *The complexities of the relationship between religion, class, economic structure, and education which were key to a school system which, in England and Wales, was increasingly perceived as being inadequate for a new society. Education was linked with social cohesion, right religion and economic competence.*
>
> (Jones, 1997, 20)

Political focus on the youth service had to wait until the second decade of the 20th century to be recognised, and then only as a government response to the perceived weakness of young people to become adequate soldiers or industrial workers in an increasingly competitive and growing global economy. The effect of this situation for young people in the second half of the 19th century and for the first two decades of the 20th century was involvement in the continuing community driven activities initiated and managed by local people within the confines of radical nonconformist influence. Working-class young people isolated in most instances from the emerging philanthropic organisations in England and from any government legislation or intervention were influenced by both contemporary working-class culture and by a particular religious approach. Central to this developing working-class culture was the growth and impact of the trade union movement with its working-class solidarity and strengthening links with socialism and later the Labour Party.

Major changes that had the power to affect the lives of young people continued during the period 1860–70. The 1870 Education Act was approved (MacClure, 1973) empowering school boards to make attendance compulsory in their areas. It also attempted to achieve a better balance between church-based education and growing state intervention. Social life in Wales at this time was confronted with a clear dichotomy – the choice was either the public house or religious establishments:

Social variety and amenities, the contrast between the church and the world were very marked. There was no middle way for those who did not want the church or chapel on the one hand, or the public house on the other, for those were the only social centres available to the majority of inhabitants of these industrial districts.
(Dent, 1969, 141)

Young people who were denied access to the public house were directed through lack of choice to spend their leisure time either in the confines of religious institutions or on the streets or mountains, both made dangerous by the ravages of industrialisation. The influence of religion was also having an impact on the social life of the population in a more diverse way (Evans, 1989) through the active encouragement of what was described as 'diwylliant y werin', the culture of ordinary people. This development, Evans claims, was possible at this time because of a number of key factors including the growth of the temperance crusade that focused the religious denominations on a moral panic relating to alcohol abuse, an issue supported by industrialists who were keen to promote local cultural activities as an alternative to a drunken and unreliable workforce. Employers also believed that an involvement in these activities by their workforce would be preferable to involvement in extreme and violent activities. Complementing these developments which had met with a variety of success was the construction of a number of libraries in a number of the main industrial towns including Dowlais (1852), New Tredegar (1873), Merthyr Vale (1880), Blaina (1884), Blaenavon (1883), Cwmtillery (1884) and Tredegar (1890) (Francis, 1976). Their importance was not significant, however, until they were supported by the miners themselves through a poundage payment allowing for maintenance and expansion so they eventually became established as miners institutes which were transformed into:

Real social centres for the workers, and in one case at least, were supplied with accommodation for women also. Before the end of the century and until recent times they were flourishing social clubs for the workers providing entertainment and recreation as well as cultural activities in the form of library facilities and public lectures.
(Davies, 1965, 144)

It was also claimed (Evans, 1989, 263) that a number of evening schools were introduced through the Llanelli, Hafod and Kilvey Copperworks and the mining areas of Rhondda and Aberdare. Their purpose was the promotion of attendance at day school, to prepare candidates for examination, promote technical instruction and encourage improving leisure-time activities for the workers. These schools were not popular, however, because 'the labouring classes showed little enthusiasm for them. One reason for this was that most people were too exhausted to think of attending classes after a hard day's labour at the mines' (Ibid).

Nevertheless, education was the main focus, and the Aberdare Report (HMSO, 1881) was concerned to examine the existing facilities for secondary and higher education. A comprehensive document, it focused on what were considered to be two key aspects of Welsh society with the capacity to affect the education of young people. These were associated with the importance of both the concept of Welsh nationality and the crucial role of the Welsh language, and the influence of nonconformist religion which was still seen as radical and having a deep suspicion of the state ecclesiastical system. Education debate and legislation continued with the introduction of the 1889 Welsh Intermediate Act responsible for the development of the state system of secondary education considered necessary because of the 'lamentable state of Welsh secondary education' (Evans, 1975, 62). It was claimed that this had been caused by the continuing strength of nonconformist religion and its opposition to endowed grammar schools with their strong established Church connection. 1889 also saw the elections for the new local authorities resulting in the domination of the Liberal Party which gained 63 per cent of the seats and which controlled 12 of the 13 Welsh counties (Morgan, 1981). This development was followed by the introduction of the Central Welsh Board (1896), which coordinated the elements of secondary education and assumed responsibility for inspection, and the 1899 Board of Education Act which amalgamated the Education Department, the Department of Science and Art and the Charity Commission. The Act also saw the establishment of an associated Consultative Committee to advise the board on any educational matters referred to it.

At this time informal education, in the sense that it was outside school, was happening in Wales and had been identified by Pate (1972). The YMCA in St Mary Street in Cardiff was providing three bible classes every week as well as lectures, debates, classes in French, elocution and book-keeping. This type of curriculum activity reinforced the statement by Fieldhouse (1996, 22) that the YMCA 'attracted a lower middle-class rather than working-class clientele'. During this time it was suggested that 'boys' welfare facilities of a social and cultural character slowly came to be regarded as the responsibility of the churches' (Pate, 1972, 80). Although Pate further claimed that the inevitable social centre of the young miner was the ice cream shop or occasional visits to the miners' institute to play table games in an unsupervised way that made them unpopular with the older members. Pate also suggested that 'his recreation consisted of efforts determined by the natural instincts of boys for such games as could be played in the street, or in the case of older boys on any odd patch of ground, particularly on a mountain slope or on a slag or rubbish tip' (Ibid).

There is no difficulty identifying the context within which young people lived in Wales between the 1830s to the start of the 1920s, a period influenced primarily by the interaction between nonconformist religion and industrialisation and the associated growth in trade unionism and the Labour Party. There is also little doubt about the purpose of those altruistic organisations and individuals that came into contact with the young working class in Wales. They were in a general sense driven to promote a particular religious, political or social perspective such as preparation for an increasingly technological industry or the physical defence of the British Empire, the protection of the Welsh language or a rural way of life. This was underpinned by the need to control young people and to inculcate them into middle-class norms.

Also at about this time in Wales a number of issues relating to young people were synthesising, and there began to emerge an embryonic method of working with juveniles that can be recognised as youth service provision. Among these issues was the growing awareness by central government of the poor physical condition of young people, and of the need to develop a more appropriately educated workforce to combat increased industrial competition from other nations. There was also the continuing belief by those in authority that there was a need to control and indoctrinate the mass of young working-class people who were perceived as being out of control. It is the last issue above all others that has shaped the philosophical base of youth work and the process of youth service delivery. The consequence of the developments from the 1830s to the end of the Great War for informal work with young people in Wales was the almost total lack of either a corporate, strategic or holistic provision.

What was achieved, however, was the growing involvement of English-based national voluntary youth organisations. These were almost invariably associated with the Anglican Church with an apparent disinterest in the sensitivities of the Welsh language, the importance of nonconformist religion and the social tensions caused by the consequences of rapid industrial growth. It was also a time that provided the political foundation for life in Wales through the birth and growth of the Labour Party which gradually became the voice of working-class people in Wales as the power of the nonconformist religions began to weaken. The end of the Victorian period with its trauma for Welsh communities and their young people brought a new hope with the publication of the Lewis Report (HMSO, 1917). This report made some comments of importance to the potential development of an emerging youth service. These were presented as a series of questions asking if it was possible to remove the adolescent from economic exploitation and into the social conscience. This, the report claimed, would require a shift in perception, from one that saw the juvenile as a wage earner to one that saw the juvenile as a workman and citizen in training – contemporary ideas before their time, to be resurrected in the lifelong learning debate of the 1990s.

Bibliography

Barnett, S. A. and Barnett, H. O. W. (1909). *Towards Social Reform*. London, Unwin.

Boyne, G. A., Griffiths, P., Lawton, A. and Law, J. (1991). *Local Government in Wales*. York, Joseph Rowntree Foundation.

Brown, K. D. (1988). *A Social History of the Nonconformist Ministry in England and Wales 1800– 1930*. Oxford, Clarendon Press.

Butters, S. and Newell, S. (1978). *Realities of Training*. Leicester, National Youth Bureau.

Brennan, T., Cooney, E. W. and Pollins, H. (1954). *Social Change in South East Wales*. London, Watts.

Davies, B. (1986). *Threatening Youth Towards A National Policy*. Milton Keynes, Open University Press.

Davies, E. T. (1965). *Religion in the Industrial Revolution in South Wales*. Cardiff, University of Wales Press.

Davies, G. (1973). *The Story of the Urdd 1922–1972*. Cwmni Urdd Gobaith Cymru, Aberystwyth

Davies, J. (1994). *A History of Wales*. Harmondsworth, Penguin Books.

Dent, H. C. (1969). *The Education System of England and Wales*. London, University of London Press.

Drakeford, M. (1997). *Youth Work Practice–Youth Work Training a Strategy for the Future*. Caerphilly, Wales Youth Agency.

Eager, W. McG. (1953). *Making Men (History of Boys Clubs and Related Movements in Great Britain)*. London, University of London Press.

Evans, W. M. (1965). *Young People in Society*. Oxford, Blackwell.

Evans, D. G. (1989). *A History of Wales 1815–1906*. Cardiff, University of Wales Press.

Evans, N. (1988). 'The Urbanization of Welsh Society' in *People and Protest: Wales 1815– 1880,* edited by Herbert, T. and Jones, G. E. Cardiff, University of Wales Press.

Evans, K. (1975). *The English Educational System*. London, University of London Press.

Evans, N. (1936). *Social Life in Mid-Century Anglesey*. Cardiff, University of Wales Press.

Fieldhouse, R. (1996). *A History of Modern British Adult Education*. Chippenham, NIACE.

Francis, H. (1976). The Origins of the South Wales Miners' Library, History Workshop, *A Journal of Socialist Historians*, (2), Autumn.

Jeffs, T. (1979). *Young People and the Youth Service*. London, Routledge and Kegan Paul.

Jenkins, H. and Smith, B. J. (1988). *Politics and Society in Wales (1840–1922)*. Cardiff, University of Wales Press.

Jones, G. E. (1997). *The Education of a Nation*. Cardiff, University of Wales Press.

Jones, I. G. (1988). *People and Protest: Wales 1815–1880,* edited by Herbert, T. and Jones G. E. Cardiff, University of Wales Press.

Jones, I. G. (1981). *Explorations and Explanations Essays in the Social History of Victorian Wales*. Llandysul, Gwasg Gomer.

Jones, I. G. (1992). *Mid Victorian Wales*. Cardiff, University of Wales Press.

Jones, G. P. and Pool A. J. (1971). *100 Years of Economic Development in Great Britain 1840– 1940*. London, Duckworth.

HMSO (1881). *Report of the Departmental Committee on Intermediate and Higher Education in Wales.* London, HMSO.

HMSO (1899). *Special Reports on Intermediate Education in Wales, and the Organisation of Education in Switzerland.* London, HMSO.

HMSO (1917). *Report of the Departmental Committee on Juvenile Education to Employment after the War.* London, HMSO.

HMSO (1982). *Experience and Participation (Report of the Review Group on the Youth Service in England).* London, HMSO.

Maclure, J. S. (1972). *Educational Documents England and Wales 1816 to the Present Day.* London, Methuen.

Morgan, K. O. (1981). *Rebirth of a Nation Wales 1880–1980.* Oxford, Clarendon Press.

Pate, W. J. (1972). *The History of the YMCA in Wales.* Cardiff, Welsh Council of YMCAs.

Rammell, T. W. (1850). *Report to the General Board of Health on a Preliminary Enquiry into the Sewerage, Drainage, and Supply of Water and the Sanitary Conditions of the Inhabitants of Merthyr Tydfil in the County of Glamorgan,* London.

Rooff, M. (1935). *Youth and Leisure: A survey of girls' organisations in England and Wales.* Edinburgh, Constable.

Rose, J. (1997). *Youth Work Practice – Youth Work Training, A Strategy for the Future.* Caerphilly, Wales Youth Agency.

Rose, J. (2000). *Signposts for the Youth Service.* Caerphilly, Wales Youth Agency.

Smith, M. (1988). *Developing Youth Work.* Milton Keynes, Open University Press.

Smith, D. (1999). *Wales a Question of History.* Cardiff, Seren/Poetry of Wales Press.

Watts, R. (1980). The Unitarian Contribution to the Development of Female Education 1790–1850, *History of Education* (9), (4).

Williams, D. (1950). *A History of Modern Wales.* London, Murray.

Williamson, H. (1996). *The Needs of Young People Aged 15–19 and the Youth Work Response.* Caerphilly, Wales Youth Agency.

Octavia Hill by John Singer Sargent. By courtesy of the National Portrait Gallery, London.

Octavia Hill

Chapter three

Street Play and Organised Space for Children and Young People in London 1860–1920

Keith Cranwell

'A city is more than a place in space: it is a drama in time.'
Patrick Geddes

In the late 19th and early 20th centuries social reformers and the Government were engaged in a debate about the need to regulate children's space and time out-of-school. This chapter is an attempt to revisit and recapture the spirit of this debate through an examination of the work of educationists and social reformers whose vision of play shaped the Playwork Movement in England and Wales.

During the 60 years under discussion there was a growth in children's play organisations and recreational clubs in London and elsewhere. In 1911 the National League for Physical Improvement carried out a national and international survey of the different types of out-of-school provision which listed information on play centres, uniformed groups and recreational clubs for children (Roper, 1911). Such information reinforced interest in provision for children's recreation and helped establish it as a central theme in educational and social policy. The child's environment in the city; play in the streets and the effects of insanitary dwellings on the health of the child all came under scrutiny as they were perceived as undermining the effects of schooling, impairing children's health, their moral development and parents' abilities to maintain a satisfactory level of care for their children. Harnessing children's play and recreation away from school was believed to ameliorate some of the effects of poverty, extend the influence of education in the community and provide respite to the family. The social reforms linked to children's play ranged from supporting schools in socialising the child, to improving the child's physical well-being through enhancing the quality of the play and recreational environment (Roper, 1911; Campbell, 1917).

Between 1860 and 1920 regulating children's activities out-of-school hours was a subject which exercised the interest of a large range of people including representatives of churches, missions, settlements, school governors, teachers, sports enthusiasts, housing reformers, environmentalists and members of open space charities. The fact that play and recreation was discussed by such a wide ranging body of social reformers stems in part from the different views that these groups had about how to address the problems posed by children and young people's street life. This chapter seeks to offer some insights into the idea that the street culture of the out-of-school child was a socially constructed phenomenon that needs to be understood as a combination of place, behaviour and culture.

Examining the difficulties in conceptualising these issues will help explain why such a diverse group of social reformers took up the provision of play and recreational space in the city as a matter of public policy. Assessing the ideas held by these social reformers about children's play illustrates the practical problems they faced in establishing the case for informal education through recreation. Looking at their work from the perspective of the play and recreational needs of children introduces another layer to the debate among school and community leaders regarding how best to meet the social welfare needs of the child. Investigating concern for the needs of the out-of-school child touches on the discussion of how childhood and play were understood in education, the relationship of the school to the community, and whether the state should intervene to legislate for facilities to meet children's recreational needs. The study of provision for out-of-school play in this period seeks to establish the claim that this work was integral to the advancement of social welfare and educational reforms for children.

The street economy

For economic reasons London acted as a magnet, drawing people from the country in search of work. In the late 19th century 'the growing proportion of the nation's children were urban dwellers, often, quite literally, children of the street' (Walvin, 1982, 18). The development of the railways and the need for new buildings such as schools and roads added to the housing problems. Overcrowding in housing was a major problem. There might be as many as eight people in a family sharing one room. In such conditions children and parents had to live part of their lives on the street. The widespread need for the mother to do homeworking such as taking in laundry, making matchboxes, removing fur from rabbit skins for the rag trade or making paper flowers, made the home a cluttered space where only a babe in arms was kept with the mother throughout the day. Children's play in the house might lead to accidents and the ruination of some of the woman's homework and therefore loss of wages. Having the child play outside the house was therefore often an economic necessity. The use of candles and coal fires were fire hazards which made some parents resort to locking children out of the home. Working-class children could be forced onto the street until well into the night. In summer, the dwelling might be so verminous that children, in an attempt to get a night's sleep, had their beds in the street or kept outside until late. The home was generally an unhealthy environment in which to raise and care for children.

Children also chose to be on the street to earn money. In the late 1880s legal restrictions were placed upon children's paid work. However, despite these constraints schoolchildren would be found running errands, babysitting or gaining the odd bit of employment in the street markets. Crude carts, made from old wood and pram wheels, were often not just playthings but served as transport when children needed to sell firewood or wheel younger brothers and sisters about while they were acting as carers. This unofficial economy of street employment reinforced the right of the child to be on the street. Out of necessity children played on the street and lived their childhood on it.

The geography of the street

In understanding the nature of children's play it is important to appreciate what the environment of the street was like in order to see how children used the space and the limitations placed on their use of the area. Prior to the turn of the century the street was often unpaved, being little more than an uncobbled gravel and dirt road. This enabled children to find stones and dig holes to play games of skill which required small objects or buttons to be thrown into a hole as part of the game called 'Ducks'. For a game such as 'Touchstone' a pile of stones was formed with a top stone that had to be dislodged without bringing down the rest of the pile. In 'Buck and Gobs' the stones were used instead of manufactured five stones. Cherries found in the markets provided stones to play a game like marbles called 'Cherry Oggs'. Date stones were the missiles in 'Date Hog' where the purpose was to knock over screws (Low, 1891).

This type of street play needed a degree of skill and dexterity to master the task and while it was in many ways quite limited it provided opportunities to develop new rules or to vary such things as distance for throwing or invent other forms of handicap. Norman Douglas in his book *London Street Games* (1916, 32) refers to the complicated rules that children invented for 'Date Hog' to determine the distance from which a throw should be made depending on the size of the screw that the players were trying to hit. These games required the participants to negotiate their own rules to suit the different skills of the players so as to make the game fairer.

The lack of any street planning controls meant that dwelling houses were situated in between factories, stables and various workshops which often created in-built deadends or backwaters which became ideal play areas for children. Living in close proximity to industries such as the docks or factories often gave children access to play materials such as old rope to hang from a lamp-post for a swing, straw to stuff a makeshift doll, paper to fashion a football or hoops taken from barrels. The deadend street enabled children to build 'grottoes' on the pavements. A grotto was a small piece of pavement sculpture made from shells, stones, buttons and any other material to create a magical cave which rested against a wall (Walker, 1989, 5). In this period there is also evidence (Acorn, 1911, 30) of children building miniature stages out of cardboard from which scenes and gags from the music hall were repeated or the 'penny gaffs' where children were charged to hear older children repeat the 'turns' they had seen the previous week (Bailey, 1978, 155).

The factory wall or back of a house might form the boundary of a court and was an ideal space for ball-games. The width of some of these roads was often not more that 30 feet but sometimes closer to 20 feet, which made vehicle passage through the area difficult. In general, except for deliveries, traffic avoided some of the poorer areas of London. For children the dangers from traffic were therefore relatively small. This lack of disruption from traffic encouraged games that could be played across the courts, giving space for skipping and a variety of running games. Since very few outsiders ever ventured into these deadend areas encroachment on children's territory by interlopers or other authorities, especially the police, would have been minimal (Steel, 1997, 6–10). The fact that these areas had back alleys provided different routes across the neighbourhood which meant that 'doing a runner' from the police was often a possibility when the children were playing football illegally or had rigged a rope from a house or lamp-post to knock off a policeman's hat (Roberts, 1975, 23).

The making of swings, cricket bats and carts all required cooperation with older children in the street and much of the play of this type demanded peer group acceptance and decision-making. The old fashioned gas street lamp acted as swing, cricket stumps or a home base for games. Ropes were strung from the top of a lamp-post to provide makeshift swings or games which involved twisting the rope around the post until the rope frayed and broke. T. C. Horsfall, a supporter of playgrounds in Manchester, viewed the existence of street lighting as training children to stay away from home and out-of-doors until very late at night (Interdepartmental Committee on Physical Deterioration, vol 3 xxii 1904, 84). Improvement to street safety, in his opinion, could only be helpful if accompanied by equal improvements to housing, wider streets and a larger supply of playgrounds and parks.

The street and the improvised nature of play and games was a collaborative feature of life. Given that older children were often carers to siblings (oral history evidence suggests it was not solely left to girls) the games played were not necessarily age segregated. Davin has drawn attention to the gender differences between girls' and boys' play which suggests girls were quite active in street play (1996, 63–84) albeit that their time was severely restricted since girls were expected to take a bigger share of the household chores. Equally parental pressure for girls to conform to the gender stereotype was often enforced by harsh parental discipline.

Play, in even the most unsavoury setting, provided a relatively safe environment in which children might invent quite rowdy and energetic games. The accidental areas created by the lack of planning controls was taken by observers to be a contributing factor leading to anti-social habits and behaviour. Values were attributed to young people's recreation by adults which made it necessary for them to either seek to discourage the play or punish children for making use of whatever materials were to hand. The walls of the factory at the end of the street provided the natural barrier for playing ball games which needed confined areas such as 'Wall Bouncing', 'Wallie' or 'Monday, Tuesday'. The freedom to play across the road using kerbs as natural boundaries suited games such as 'Queenie' which needed home bases. The length of the courts or streets were not too far to make it impossible to contain 'Tag' and prisoner-based games such as 'Tin Can Copper' with all the players knowing the exact boundary. This natural area with its known landmarks required no elaborate markings or pacing to establish pitches or perimeters.

The fact that the form of the games were determined by the children themselves required them to cooperate in their play and accept group standards and decisions (Roberts, 1975, 23). Games played on this basis could be adapted to suit the players with rules agreed and negotiated, whether by the custom of the previous day, the memory of an older child or even an adult who might remember some new development in the game. The natural networks, family relationships and the general streetlife which existed in these courts and streets applied informal supervision on children's activities. Although the lack of any adult controls and strong discipline might have been deplored by middle-class observers, the codes and standards of the area would have been readily understood. The intimacy of the street was preferred to being swallowed up by the anonymity of the city.

Play and imagination

The observers of child behaviour tended to see the negatives of street play rather than the inventiveness, use of imagination and the imitative qualities to children's play. For example, during the dock strike of 1889 children were observed making their own banners and holding mock rallies (Dixon, 1890, 358). Such play was seen as evidence of the increased influence of socialism. Similar imitative play around the time of the Boer War, however, was welcomed as true patriotism. Equally the lack of any communal facility other than the public house was viewed as encouraging poor moral development in children. A social observer cited the example of a group of small boys congregating outside the public house who would go into the pub for a 'drink' and come out the next minute wiping their mouth on their sleeve as though they had one. This was both an attempt by children to play imaginatively and a case of a poor moral example being set for them (Osborn, undated, 87–93). Similarly, dancing to the barrel organ outside the pub was another incident of children's street play that was supposed to undermine young morals. Young girls in groups parading along the street was sometimes observed as encouraging immoral behaviour among girls as the area around pubs were called 'promenades' and were known areas where men could be introduced to prostitutes. In 1914, as a war measure, police were empowered to arrest women found 'promenading' outside public houses (Middleton, 1970, 125–27).

Use of free time

The existence of street gangs went with street play. At its most extreme there were fights between streets or sometimes challenge races or football games. It was this more riotous behaviour which often attracted the attention of the local police. Similarly games that involved gambling whether for money or cigarette cards were part of street life. There were also many games of skill and chance which used items such as buttons, marbles, cherry stones or used tram tickets as their currency which created rivalries that were noisily played out daily and late into the evening. It was the behaviour of the children and the supposed triviality of the pursuits which so upset the mission house resident and, for example, created the demand for out-of-school provision to teach children to play at more rational recreation. The fact that the street could support such a range of 'anti-social' play activity was seen as undermining the attempts of the school to establish good conduct.

A collection of children's essays (Harvey, 1906) describing their Saturday in the Limehouse and Whitechapel areas of the East End indicates how much children's free time was dominated by work. In most cases the work paid for the boys' Saturday evening at the music hall or cinematograph. Of the 36 essays analysed only four boys played all day. For the rest play was fitted inbetween errands or work in the home. The sort of play recorded such as 'Tip Cat' and 'Release' were games which, although often repeated, were of relatively short duration. They represented the sort of play from which children could break off to do an errand and then return to later without a loss of continuity. Other more anti-social games like 'Knock Down Ginger' where children knock on doors and run away or 'Dusters' which involved waiting in hiding until someone with a pipe passed which the child attempted to knock out of the mouth of the smoker were recorded. It is possibly this type of play that settlement workers, who initiated the study of the child's Saturday, would have seen as evidence of the misspent time of children without a capacity to play. Harvey felt activities for children which treated them as individuals were much more likely to have a positive effect on play and behaviour. Those children who described organised trips to the Tower of London with a teacher or swimming in Victoria Park and team sports activities were closer to the appropriate play approved of by play centre and boys' club organisers.

Harvey also included essays by girls which showed their time was dominated by household chores and childcare. These activities Harvey found less interesting. The girl's Saturday evening, he disparagingly recorded, described their preparations for the following day Sunday when they would plait their hair and put on their Sunday best to walk in the park or go to church.

Organised play

Children and young people's organised play and recreation can be said to fall into three categories and each gave support to different types of children's play provision in the city:
- supervised playgrounds that were part of housing improvements as represented by the housing reforms of Octavia Hill;
- indoor structured play and recreation as exemplified by the Guild of Play; and
- planned playgrounds and parks designed to improve physical health, support team games and as diversionary activities to prevent offending behaviour.

Octavia Hill and supervised playgrounds as part of housing reform
The origins of supervised playgrounds in London can be traced back to the housing reform work of Octavia Hill. Such provision was integral to her notion of improving housing for the working class and formed part of her belief in the 'healing gift of space'. She was well aware of the effects of overcrowding both inside the dwellings she rented to her tenants and

the effects of the lack of space in the courts between the housing (Hill, 1970, 27–28). The close living quarters, she observed, brought out bad behaviour in her tenants, such as drinking and foul language. This behaviour was then displayed on the street undermining the improvement she was trying to secure by raising the quality of housing (Hill, 1970, 89–90).

The creation of communal space and places where tenants could pass some of their time with others, she felt, 'would be more powerful to calm the wild excesses' (op cit, 90) of behaviour she witnessed. In her 1866 development at Paradise Place, the idea of creating one large room for tenants to get 'together for all sorts of purposes' was planned and paid for by the profits from the rents (op cit, 28). In this room classes for boys and girls were held as well as at other times being a meeting place for married women and older girls. Through this work Hill contrived to develop a 'consciousness of corporate life' (op cit, 28). To improve the health of the children, Octavia Hill also arranged outings to Regents Park for rowing and day trips to the countryside around London were organised on a regular basis.

In 1867 Octavia Hill completed her first children's playground on the Freshwater Place housing development. This was not only for the use of her tenants' children but by those from the neighbouring courts. The playground was walled to enable the children to play safely at games of 'bat and ball, trap, swinging, skipping and singing'. The playground also boasted some swings and a see-saw which were very popular pieces of fixed equipment requiring almost constant supervision by volunteers for the sake of safety and fairness (Maurice,1913, 251). The playground was supervised by a paid worker, afterschool, Saturdays and during school holidays.

The children for whom the playground was provided, were described by Octavia Hill as 'habitually dirty, quarrelsome and violent . . . wholly ignorant of games and have hardly self-control enough to play at any which have an object or require effort'. As an example of this poor play Hill described a game she condemned as 'bad'. The game she derided consisted of singing 'Here comes my father all down the hill' and so on through various members of the family – until they reached their sweetheart for which the response changed from 'We won't get up for his ugly face' to 'We will get up for his pretty face' (Darley, 1990, 103–4). For Octavia Hill this repetitious and meaningless game held a bad moral purpose, despite its seemingly innocuous content. Clearly she looked upon some types of play as morally superior and suggested that these were games arranged with ordered companions, definite object and progressive skills which are more generally associated with cooperative and/or team games (Hill, 1970, 27). Octavia Hill's appreciation of the role of the playground suggested a strict adherence to the moral influence that appropriate play could impart.

The playground was not met by universal approval from young people. It was continually vandalised during building. Indeed the site appears to have been under siege from the children it was meant to benefit who 'did much harm by throwing the bricks about and breaking them'. The local children it seemed resented what they saw as an encroachment upon their territory and saw no reason to respect the rights of private property. Octavia Hill was herself threatened by 'a great dirty urchin' who told her 'I've been on the place oftener nor you, and I shan't move for you' (Hill, 1867, 446–8). An organised playground which set out to improve children's behaviour and limited opportunities for bad language and rowdy games was in direct conflict with the children who felt they already 'owned' the space. At one level this was a new and visible civic amenity but at another the restrictions on the time it could be used and the fact that there was a charge to use it was depriving children of a place to play.

By improving the courts Octavia Hill was also bringing an element of social control over the space insofar as the area was separated into communal and private areas. The division of the area in this way had the effect of changing how adults and children used the space. Prior to the playground being established, Octavia Hill described, in a derogatory manner, the habits of the people, indicating that women spent much of the day gossiping at their doors. The household chores, such as the washing of clothes were done to the rhythm of the individual with the clothes often hung out of the window to dry late into the day, something which Octavia Hill felt was unhygienic and unsightly (Darley, 1990, 90–91). But once the drying-ground/playground was established the job had to be completed before 4 o'clock when the area became a playground. Moreover since a drying area was now provided the tenant was no longer allowed to hang washing from the window necessitating a different style of organisation to household activity. An amenity to improve cleanliness therefore had the effect of changing the time management of the women on the estate.

Structured recreation

There were several types of play centre developed in the late 19th and early 20th century which can be drawn upon to evidence the ideas of the appeal of rational recreation namely the Children's Happy Evenings Association and the Mary Ward play centre. However, it is Grace Kimmins's work with young people at the Bermondsey Settlement through the Guild of Play which best illustrates the ideals of organised play as a form of social education.

In 1897, Sister Grace as she became known, organised the first Guild of Play (GOP) in the Bermondsey Settlement and at the end of the first year of operation had begun similar work in four board schools. By 1901, 12 branches existed in London and Scott Lidgett claimed the movement had spread to other parts of the country (*The Times*, 1901). In 1916, GOP branches were still in operation; Croydon alone had six. Guilds of Play were weekly two-hour events, membership was only for girls aged 8 to 14 and all members wore simple uniforms for Guild evenings. GOP was also the first play agency to provide handbooks of its work in the four volumes of *The Guild of Play Book of Festival, Dance, Songs and Games* published between 1904 and 1912 which illustrated its work and helped to promote its methods to a wider audience.

The ideas for GOP arose from Sister Grace's close observation and acquaintance with children in the community around the Bermondsey Settlement. She saw the London child's play as being instinctive, imaginative and inventive showing a keen sense of mimicry and an abundance of humour yet lacking self-control, which left their social development incomplete. Her close contact with children and the debates she attended on social issues at the monthly conferences for women workers (*Bermondsey Record*, 1896) informed her work and gave it a political dimension which is not apparent in other play pioneers of the period. In the *Bermondsey Record* she wrote about the importance of the Progressive Movement as awakening people to the need to improve the conditions of the working-class. In her work a concern for the social conditions of children was never far from the surface. She believed children's behavioural difficulties were the result of living conditions that gave them no chance 'to be good . . . [with] . . . all the youth and brightness crushed out of them by their lives of misery' (op cit). Social improvement, she held, would best be accomplished through social education based on organised play. Sister Grace recognised that play was an essential part of a social reform process to change children from within. The benign autocracy of the settlement worker and a play programme designed to bring out the qualities of self discipline would, she held, enable social improvements to naturally take root.

The GOP programme set out to rescue childhood for the child and the uniforms were meant to separate the child's everyday world from the play setting and open them to a world of the imagination and folklore. GOP chose to work exclusively with working-class girls as it was felt their play needs were not being met due to them having to undertake the burdens of household responsibilities (Kimmins,1906, 16–18). GOP was the first play body to view children's play as a right, seeing their role as improving the child's social conditions (op cit, *Bermondsey Record*). To this extent the GOP helper saw her function as being to supplement schoolwork and to cooperate with the teacher. Kimmin's ideas were Christian socialist in their origins and she felt strongly that 'the cause of children is the cause of every one' (Kimmins, 1907, xii). The value and role of play was seen as a real need for deprived children. The purpose of GOP was to give the child a place to experience real play that engaged the imagination and took the child outside of its lived experience or allowed it to spend time in 'ordinary pursuits – yet with a difference' (op cit, 1906).

GOP's work had a moral purpose to indirectly teach children a set of values. It was claimed that the uniforms and special frocks for the festival events had the effect of removing the 'attitudes of selfishness, rudeness and many indications of street independence' (op cit, 1906, 17). The combination of the programme and its props worked from the environment and the body of the child towards effecting changes in thinking and behaviour. GOP attempted to create a play environment, so unlike that of the street, that the child had to leave that world behind when entering it. Kimmins believed that the GOP environment would work first on the body through dressing up and then on the mind as the dress was associated with other acceptable positive behaviour. The combination of the music and words of folk ballads and the folk tales all combine to unconsciously direct the intellectual and aesthetic powers (op cit, 1906). The programme of songs, dances and games all sought to improve the child's speech and language. The nature of the games, which were circle-based, were used to denote a unity of purpose about the evenings as well as give a sense of equality to the members. Exclusion from the circle for misbehaviour was felt as a real punishment to the child and was used as an example of how self-awareness and discipline were achieved (*Birmingham Post*, 1905). The action and activities in the play setting of learning dances and devising the various tableaux required resourcefulness and initiative drawn from the children.

GOP hoped its methods enabled children to control their recreation and exercise free will through choice. Under these conditions the child's character and sense of self would thrive when exposed to opportunities for choice at GOP nights, given the right influences. The test of this was observed by Scott Lidgett (*The Times*, 1902) on the streets where quite regularly the children practised the dances and songs as part of their play with other children. The ideals of GOP thereby were passed to other children and the possibility of social improvement could be witnessed. GOP advocated play as a right but linked its expression to harnessing the child's imagination and developing self-control and discipline through play. The view that the play methods of GOP were essentially designed to condition and socially train girls into the right way of behaving and thus act as a civilising force for social improvement was always part of GOP work. This feature is best illustrated by the fact that Kimmins used to recruit 15 to 20 girls annually to work in service at her Chailly Home for Crippled Children and the training in social education was felt to turn out well-trained servants (Kimmins, 1912, 12).

Planned recreational space for children and young people

The Earl of Meath and his work with the Metropolitan Public Gardens Association is a little known part of the support he gave to creating provision for children and young people. The MPGA represented his advocacy for planned play provision in the city.

Meath also showed an awareness of the importance of appropriate provision near to housing and away from street traffic, believing that playgrounds had to be the retreats of children from 'the din and the uproar . . . the whirl and hurry, slavery and closeness' of the street. To reinforce the importance of protecting children Meath approved of the employment of an attendant to 'prevent tyranny and misconduct' and argued that children needed to be kept out of harm's way by having a space designated exclusively to meet their play needs as an alternative to 'the gutter and pavement' (MPGA, 1887, 37–38).

Meath also saw the importance of supervised open-air playgrounds as helping parents 'who would be able to send their children to them . . . between, before and after-school hours confident that they would be in safety and well looked after' (Meath, 1893, 269–270). Meath's major interest in advocating these playgrounds was to improve and promote the physique of city-bred children. This led him to concentrate a major part of his campaigning energies to reforming the use of playgrounds and the development of a physical education curriculum within the London School Board. Meath's view that physical and intellectual education should go hand-in-hand made him an early advocate of swimming and drill in schools; a supporter of provision for school meals and the country holiday schemes of Samuel Barnett and the Leicester Charity Organisation Society's 'boarding out' of children in summer.

It was Meath's wish that not only should play space be provided for school-age children but that the facilities ought to be available as options to juveniles who had left school, as a means of discouraging crime. Meath was particularly concerned that children were being punished for playing and that there was a 'cruelty of suppressing the playing of games, without supplying them any place where they might legitimately give vent to natural and healthy instinct' (Meath, 1890, 40). The opening of school grounds to ex-pupils, Meath considered, would act as a deterrent to a life of crime stating that 'prison statistics inform us that men rarely take to a life of crime after 21 years of age' (Meath, 1881, 80–89). Meath was aware that play areas for children had to be situated throughout the city, close to children's homes and to be properly supervised if they were to achieve the purpose of encouraging their physical health. In Meath's opinion, these should also provide a range of equipment appropriate to both sexes and meet the needs of a wide age range of children if they were to be successful (op cit, 1893, 270).

One of the measures of a playground's success, Meath felt, was to stop children being brought before the magistrate for committing a public nuisance offence by playing games in the street (op cit, 1890, 41). Meath also noted (op cit, 1893, 270) another effect of providing playgrounds was that they would be an attraction to truanting children and therefore help the school board attendance officer to return them to their schools. The playground, if properly regulated, Meath maintained, was a means to cut down road accidents; decrease the incidence of anti-social behaviour and deter children from crime; promote constructive play; and improve school attendance and health. Most of his evidence was anecdotal and based on a belief that supervised outdoor play would keep children occupied and away from moral harm. Such provision was also held to assist schools to maintain their influence on children. Meath's vision, while strongly-based on the tenets of 'muscular Christianity' (Mangan, 1970) showed that planning space for young people's play and recreation was a necessary part of the development of the city if the criminalising of children's street play was to be avoided.

Conclusion

Street play, despite the poverty of the child's circumstances, provided a variety of experiences that demonstrated that children and young people continually used play to form their identity and to control their environment. The mimicry, the rowdiness of the behaviour and the use of strong parodies of music hall songs, although frowned upon by the middle-class social commentator, showed that the play impulse was strong despite the harshness of life. The reformers of street play sought to improve the child's environment through campaigning and organising different types of provision. Although the ideas behind this indicated a strong moral purpose to reform the working-class child they did achieve much by way of highlighting the need for a space in the city. However, the fact that this was achieved without appreciating the meaning of play and richness of the young person's ability to independently meet their own needs was as much an issue then as it is today.

Bibliography
Primary source papers
Bermondsey Record (1895–1918)
Birmingham Post (1905)

The Times (1901–02)

Metropolitan Public Gardens Association Annual Reports (1887–1920)

Interdepartmental Committee on Physical Deterioration (1904) *Parliamentary Papers*, xxii

Secondary sources

Acorn, G. (1911). *One of a Multitude*. London, Heinemann.

Bailey, P. (1978). *Leisure and Class in Victorian England*. London, Routledge.

Campbell, J. M. (1917). *The Report on the Physical Welfare of Mothers and Children in England and Wales*. Dunfermline, Carnegie Trust.

Darley, G. (1990). *Octavia Hill: A life*. London, Constable.

Davin, A. (1996). *Growing up Poor*. London, Rivers Oram Press.

Dixon, E. (1890). A Whitechapel Street. *English Illustrated Magazine,* vol vii, 1889–90.

Douglas, N. (1916). *London Street Games*. London, St Catherine's Press.

Harvey, T. E. (1906). *A London Boy's Saturday*. Birmingham, St George's Press.

Hill, O. (1867). 'Poor Playgrounds', *All the Year Round*, May 4 1867.

Hill. O. (1970). *Homes of the London Poor*. London, Cass.

Kimmins, G. (1906). 'The Educational Value of Play', *Journal of Education* 1906.

Kimmins, G. (1907). *The Guild of Play Book of Festival and Song and Dance,* vol 1.

Kimmins, G. (1912). *The Guild of Play Book of Festival and Song and Dance,* vol 4.

Low, F. (1891). 'Street Games', *Strand Magazine*, 2 Nov 1891.

Maurice, C. E. (1913). *The Life of Octavia Hill*. London, Macmillan.

Mangan, J. (1987). *Manliness and Morality*. Manchester, Manchester University Press.

Meath, Earl of, (1881). 'Health and Physique of Our City Population', *Nineteenth Century,* vol 10, 1881, p80–89.

Meath, Earl of, (1893). Public Playgrounds for Children *Nineteenth Century*, vol 34, August, 1893.

Meath, Earl of, (1890). *Social Arrows*. London, Longmans.

Middleton, N. (1970). *When Families Fail*. London, Gollanz.

Osborn, E. B. (undated circa 1906). 'The Fairy CHEA' in R. H. Caine, (ed) *The Children's Hour Anthology*. London, Children's Happy Evenings Association, (ref: Guildhall Library).

Roberts, E. (1975). 'Learning and Living: Socialisation outside school', *Oral History,* vol 3, no 2, Autumn 1975.

Roper, R. E. (1911). *Organised Play at Home and Abroad*. London, National League for Physical Education and Improvement.

Steel, J. (ed), (1997). *The Streets of London. Booth Notebooks SE London*. London, Deptford Forum Publishers.

Walker, H. (1989). *Games Forgotten (or nearly so)*. London, Sewardstone.

Walvin, J. (1982). *A Child's World*. London, Penguin Books.

F. G. D'Aeth (top)

Chapter four

F. G. D'Aeth: A forgotten man 1875–1940

Margaret Simey and Cathy Hawkes

A more ordinary story about a more ordinary lad than that of Frederick George D'Aeth is hard to imagine. He was born in 1875, his father a clerk in the Bank of England, his mother an unidentifiable Elizabeth Gosling. The family was of Huguenot origin who had come to Suffolk in the previous century from Ath on the Franco-Belgian border. Frederick was evidently a jolly sort of boy, a good all rounder, intelligent and with a pleasing enthusiasm for the then current craze for cycling. All in all, he was typical of the emergent middle-class who are the stuff of the novels of H. G. Wells.

So the story runs on – his growing awareness of what was called 'the condition of the people', his disillusion with a career as a clergyman as an appropriate response, his subsequent search for some other means of reconciling the conflict between moral principle offers nothing to suggest that this was a man of outstanding originality of mind or nobility of purpose. He was indeed essentially ordinary, inescapably a product of his day and age. That being so, apart from its value as a minor contribution to social history, why bother to rouse interest in one who is to all intents and purposes, a forgotten man?

First the facts – on leaving his grammar school at the age of 14, he began his working life as an apprentice in business administration and book-keeping at the National Assurance Company. He had evidently already begun to plan a career in the church because, after pursuing his studies at home for some time, he attended classes at Kings College, which was then pioneering the provision of part-time further education. For lack of any information as to how this came about or who influenced his choice of a career, it seems reasonable to suppose that his inspiration came from his Huguenot heritage. The only clue lies in the fact that he was fascinated by his family's background and one of his hobbies was to visit cemeteries in Suffolk in search of gravestones bearing the family name.

Three years later he went to Oxford as a non-collegiate student, studying theology at St Stephen's House, one of the medieval halls for the training of clergy. Apart form the fact that he rowed for his college, nothing is known about this period in the story. Nevertheless, as a born participant, he cannot have failed to have been alerted to the storm of argument then taking place as to the nature and treatment of poverty. In Oxford this focused on the radical vicar Chevasse who was attracting to his services young undergraduates of every persuasion.

In 1899, armed with a BA, he was appointed as curate to an Anglo-Catholic church in Burnley, Lancashire. St Mathew's was one of six churches hurriedly built to cater for the rapidly growing population of what was at that time a boom town. There for the ensuing three years, he was able to observe at first-hand all that made up the way of life of a society of hardy people who lived under conditions of considerable hardship but who nevertheless constituted a vibrant community. After the sterility of life in the suburb of his upbringing, this came as nothing short of a revelation. It was on the basis of this experience that he developed his passionate commitment to the building of the community as an absolutely essential basis for a social policy. In an article for his college magazine, he attempted to put his enthusiasm into words. Burnley, he wrote:

> ... has a centre, it is a centre, with its town hall, its technical institute, its local management. The folk are Burnley folk; they live somewhere – in Burnley; they manage a place – Burnley. They have local concerts for the people of Burnley in their own town hall. They do their shopping in their own town. They live there, they work there, they meet together. Prominent local persons are known, recognised and greeted; there is no doubt about Burnley, as it lies surrounded by its fields and virtually shut in by rough hillsides. Anyone can see where it begins and where it ends. It is a place, a home, distinct, compact, self-contained, marked out, with its history, its traditions, its characteristics, its local life, its soul.

D'Aeth's next curacy was at St Margaret's in Leytonstone, to which he moved in 1902. Leytonstone was one of the huge areas of mass poverty in the East End of London, where the clergy were involved in relief work almost to the exclusion of all else. The wholesale squalor with which he was confronted there evidently profoundly shocked him. Poverty in Burnley was one thing but the total disintegration of the social structure of the community in Leytonstone was something he had never before even imagined. Leytonstone was, he wrote, no more than:

> ... a collection of streets and rows of houses, without cohesion, without name, without identity. We are no unit, no place. We are all schism uncircumcised and that is all, without local life, local tradition, local history; odd limbs without a body, stray facts without a soul.

Only faith in the teaching of the church could make it possible to continue with the unremitting drudgery of poor relief in such circumstances yet it was precisely the first-hand experience of social injustice which that involved that fatally challenged his commitment to his calling. At the same time, he cannot but have been deeply disturbed by the passionate campaigning on behalf of the poor by George Lansbury in the neighbouring Poplar. Honesty compelled him to acknowledge that:

> It is not fair that the poor are dull, but largely the conditions of life and labour under which they are compelled to live and which they are too ignorant to improve.

Deeply disillusioned as he was by the teaching of the established church, as to how best to deal with those who were regarded as poor unfortunates who had brought misery upon themselves by their own conduct, he found himself inevitably forced to question what part the church, and by implication, he himself should play.

> In the middle of twelve thousand lives such as these, exists – leaving unrecorded other religious

agencies – a church with its clergy – three or four men; three or four human lives with a scope of 12,000 to be influenced. What is the work the cleric or social worker finds ready for him?

Unable to resolve his own dilemma he soldiered on for another two years. Finally, in 1905, he abandoned his career as a clergyman. He never again referred to those years of doubt and indecision, and many of his future colleagues were not even aware he had once been a cleric.

How a failed curate came to be appointed as a lecturer in the highly innovative School of Social Work at Liverpool University remains a mystery. The fact that both he and his vicar resigned from their posts simultaneously cannot have failed to attract attention, not least that of Chevasse who was by now Bishop of Liverpool. Possibly he had had contact with Charles Booth, another of the Liverpool philanthropists, who was then engaged in his great survey of the *Life and Labour of the People of London*. So much is matter for speculation. There is no doubt that he was headhunted by the little group in Liverpool who were trying to establish a link between academic teaching and practical social work.

The precise proposal for a school of social work came form Edward Gonner, the immensely vigorous professor of economics at the university. The promotion of social work as a means of earning a living was only one of a whole range of projects designed by him to break away from academic tradition by relating teaching directly to employment. His plan became a practical proposition in 1902 when Elizabeth Macadam was appointed as warden of the Victoria Settlement for women. Macadam came to Liverpool from Southwark Women's Settlement where she had been employed as a youth worker and had taken part in negotiations for the training scheme which eventually developed into the London School of Economics. She lost no time. Stimulated by her Scottish drive, the demand for training expanded to such an extent as to be beyond the resources of the Victoria Settlement. Hence the creation of the School of Social Work in partnership with the university and D'Aeth's appointment as tutor there.

For D'Aeth, the opportunity offered by Liverpool must have come as a literal godsend. The unique combination of moral principle with social work practice exemplified by the proposed school provided a context within which he at last found peace of mind. No longer would he be required to exhort the public to fulfil its social responsibilities. Instead his job would be to devise ways and means of emancipating the poor from all the obstructions and harassment that prevented them from doing so themselves. The belief that they would be both willing and capable of grasping such an opportunity, which he had acquired in his Burnley days, gave him the courage to tackle all that this entailed.

On arriving in Liverpool D'Aeth promptly associated himself with a small group of Christian Union students who shared the belief that poverty was not an act of God but a disease of the industrial system, and who were struggling to establish a settlement for men in the south docks. Thanks to D'Aeth this came about a year later. Resisting the undoubted delights of life on the university campus, he himself became one of the first two residents, acting as honorary warden.

With only the shared use of a room in what had been a lunatic asylum before its

LIVERPOOL JOHN MOORES UNIVERSITY
LEARNING SERVICES

acquisition by the university, he was quick to realise that it was the well established Victoria Settlement that would provide the ideal vehicle for translating his brief into reality. The Women's Settlement provided the essential framework within which the interlock between the Settlement's regiment of potential students and the university course of training could become viable. Eleanor Rathbone, the city's first woman city councillor, was chair of both the Settlement and the embryo School of Social Work. Association with her constituted an unparalleled apprenticeship in the investigation of social problems and the preparation of reports, while through Macadam as their supervisor students would obtain a sound grounding in social work.

So far as the School of Social Work was concerned, D'Aeth saw his responsibility as being to act as the coordinator of the complicated negotiation involved in securing the recognition of sociology as an academic discipline and the establishment of a Diploma in Social Work as an approved professional qualification. This was no easy task in view of the widespread antagonism to the mere notion that charitable effort should be subjected to such an approach. No academic, he left the content of the courses to be determined by the teaching staff.

All that might have been assumed to be a solid enough assignment to keep him fully occupied for years to come but to D'Aeth's quick imagination, one thing invariably led to another; no sooner was one summit achieved than further heights were revealed. The second part of his brief was the promotion of the study of social problems as the basis for the making of social policy. This was hitherto unexplored territory the exploration of which tantalised and excited D'Aeth. Where to start?

Eyeing the wild confusion of the provision of relief by the charitable sector it seemed obvious to D'Aeth that the coordination of all the agencies involved, and especially of the voluntary bodies, was an absolute prerequisite for the preparation of a social policy. Opportunity to put this growing conviction into effect came with the recommendation of the Royal Commission on the Poor Laws in 1909 that every city should provide some machinery for the coordination of charitable effort.

D'Aeth moved with a speed that suggests news of the forthcoming recommendation had already been leaked to him, possibly through his contact with Hector Nunn, the founder of the Hampstead Council of Social Services and himself a member of the Commission. Within a matter of months, with a flourish of trumpets and a grand public meeting in the Town Hall, the Liverpool Council of Voluntary Aid came into being. Modestly installed as its director of reports was F. G. D'Aeth.

Using his appointment as a launching pad D'Aeth set about spreading the gospel of coordination with immense zest. To persuade the cohorts of the highly individualistic relief agencies to work together for the common good was a mammoth task but one which he set about with an enthusiasm which his contemporaries described as being 'well-nigh irresistible'. His combination of dogged persistence with a compelling vision of things as they might be, achieved remarkable results. His major asset was his sensitivity to what would now be called felt needs. No dogmatist, he never imposed his own preconceived ideas on other people but having identified a need on the basis of endless consultation he then proceeded to build on the contacts he thus made.

His life-long commitment to the boys' club movement is a typical example of his method. Soon after his arrival in Liverpool, he had been involved in the preparation of the evidence Eleanor Rathbone was about to submit to the Royal Commission on the harmful effects on boys of their employment as casual labourers on the docks. In the course of this, he was approached for help by a couple of small clubs who sought to set up a holiday camp. Lit up by his fertile imagination, this quickly developed into a full-blown campaign for the provision of clubs for boys to match that already available for girls. This was to culminate after 20 years of dogged persistence on his part in the launching of the National Association of Boys' Clubs in 1923.

The pattern was one that was to be repeated over and over again down the years. Though historically interesting, there is no need to describe in detail here the innumerable projects and pursuits upon which D'Aeth was subsequently engaged. The creation of the Personal Service Society in Liverpool and of the Citizens Advice Bureaux to which it gave birth, was only one of the many which could be quoted as illustrations. Perhaps the most notable was the establishment of the National Council of Voluntary Organisations which, it was generally agreed, might never have come about but for his skill and vision. By the end of the First World War in 1918, he had acquired a national reputation as a source of information and wisdom on all matters concerning welfare and the LVCA had become the flagship of the movement for social advance.

Happily married to Margaret Seville, the daughter of a cotton merchant, and with two sons and an established reputation, D'Aeth might well have rested on his laurels. Yet again, a peak had been scaled and what remained was the long heave of consolidating the lessons learned. For this, however, D'Aeth had little inclination. To him, the acceptance of the need for coordination by the voluntary agencies simply opened up a vista of all that might follow if the idea were to be applied right across the entire range of the management of the affairs of the community as a whole.

D'Aeth's starting point was the all too evident gap between those who managed the city's affairs and the people in general, consequent on the so-called intrusion of the state into what had always been assumed to be voluntary territory. Following what was by now his customary practice, he conducted a pilot survey of the situation at ground level. This demonstrated to him that the major obstacle to the involvement of the general public in local affairs was the quite literal lack of opportunities to do so. His first priority must therefore be to provide some means whereby individuals could contact those in authority. His years of work on behalf of the Guilds of Help, a relief agency for the organisation of voluntary workers, suggested to him that here was a useful growing point. In typical D'Aeth style, this rapidly mushroomed into a plan for city-wide civic centres. With the appointment of a full-time organiser several of these were set up, effectively serving as prototypes for what became community centres.

Meanwhile, demobilisation and the development of corporation housing estates, introduced an entirely new element into the situation. These in-comers were by no means the poor of charitable tradition but upstanding men and women of considerable experience, imbued with dreams of a land fit for heroes. Their demands were fuelled by the onset of the

Great Depression. Acutely aware of the fact that what they stood for was a challenge to the tradition of voluntary service, D'Aeth resolved to pull out of his national commitments in order to concentrate his attention on the situation on the home front. This proved more difficult than he had anticipated. He was, for example, deeply involved in organising a conference in Birmingham in 1924, convened by him to launch the National Association of Boys' Clubs. A group photograph shows him (modestly in the back row needless to say), as being as lively as any of the younger men present, as well he might be at that moment of achievement in his long campaign on behalf of the club movement.

Tragically, at that point, he fell victim to the epidemic of 'sleepy sickness' which devastated the post-war period and from then on, his life was one long struggle against creeping disability. On returning to work after a spell on sick leave, he attempted to integrate the groups from the brand new housing estates into the traditional framework of established community work in the city by setting up a joint community committee but the two groups proved to be incompatible. His imagination evidently seizing on the potential of this influx of a new breed of voluntary workers, he prepared a proposal for a project for clubs for unemployed men. This was presented in December 1931 at the last executive committee meeting attended by D'Aeth as its secretary.

As the weary years of his slow deterioration dragged past, he retreated into the evermore complete isolation of his suburban home, dependent on his wife whose loyalty is an unsung tale of heroism. The end came at last in February 1940. Courteous obituaries appeared in the local press but to the current generation he was a yesterday's man, his track record obliterated by the sands of time. The LCVA had not even a photograph of him to add to the collection on their board room walls. A sad and sombre ending to a life of such infectious vitality and commitment.

To end on that down beat note would be to betray the inspiration that was the heritage D'Aeth left us. True to his habitual practice of anonymity and overwhelmed by the horror of the physical decline he had to endure, he never attempted to write the justification of his life that would have corrected this sad impression. His brief history of LCVA's first 21 years published in 1931 was a bleak factual record. Fortuitously, this omission was made good on his behalf by his stalwart comrade-in-arms, Elizabeth Macadam. Even as he ended his formal connection with LCVA and slowly sank into obscurity she was engaged in writing a book which embodied the very reflections on his life's work such as might normally have been expected of a man on his retirement from active public life.

Macadam had left Liverpool for London in 1919. Since then she had been absorbed in the development of the Joint University Council for Social Studies, a truly D'Aethian enterprise aimed at the coordination of the efforts of all those involved in the training of social workers of any kind. She was, at the same time, an officer of the National Union of Societies for Equal Citizenship, a large non-party women's organisation with branches all over the country, most of which included among their activities the education of women voters. As a by-product of this campaign, she had come to appreciate the fact that though the propriety of academic study of social problems was winning recognition, too much attention was, in her opinion, being paid to the training of social workers in what was coming to be called casework. Supremely conscious of the complexities of the administration of the growing welfare services, it was evident to her that there was urgent need for attention to be paid to correcting this imbalance. Administration was a 'neglected and barren topic'. No-one else being prepared to make good this deficiency she determined to tackle it herself.

Whether Macadam contacted D'Aeth in writing the book is unclear. The intimacy of their 16 years of exceptionally close collaboration inevitable had ended when she left Liverpool, though their association must have continued in the course of his growing involvement in national developments. She was, however, emphatic that her sole credential for writing the book was her past experience as a social worker and a teacher of social workers in Liverpool when she worked with D'Aeth. What she had to say is so evidently an interpretation of their joint experiences that it is surely legitimate to regard it as a source of information about the thinking that had impelled their partnership. Over and over again, she uses phrases and expresses opinions that exactly echo D'Aeth's own reports. She had had time for reflection, which his creeping incapacity, and perhaps his inclination, had denied him, but there can be no doubt that she actually interpreted the conclusion to which they had come.

The New Philanthropy was published in 1934. Macadam chose as her subtitle 'A study in the relationship between the statutory and voluntary social services', characteristically going straight to the heart of the matter. Her starting point was the remarkable change in the relationship which had occurred during the first quarter of the century and which she believed had resulted in a system of administration 'quite unique to itself'. It was, she argued, the failure to give thought to the practicalities of putting this new system into operation that lay at the root of the muddle and confusion of the voluntary sector.

Doubts as to what role if any would be open to voluntary workers in the changed circumstances of the modern state were smartly dismissed. 'Private association is the safeguard of democracy', she stoutly affirmed. The blurb on the jacket of the book rather nervously disassociates the publisher from her trenchant declaration that 'to be effective, state action must recognise the value of personal contacts which the official machine cannot provide'. There was, she argued, 'an urgent need for the widest and most intelligent use of the privileges of modern democracy'. The public must be educated to be politerate, trained in cooperation and alerted to their social obligations as individuals.

Training for citizenship must be 'an integral part of the fabric of national education'. Society had need of a trained social conscience. Her final conclusion was both forthright and bold, quoting with approval a contribution by Lord Eustace Percy to a debate in the House of Lords on the distressed areas:

Voluntary effort has never been properly faced by Governments before. To secure cooperation between the Government and private effort, to mobilise private effort under general Government direction, requires a new technique of administration which has never been developed properly in this country.

(Hansard, 1932)

Macadam was quick to grasp that a 'new technique of administration' would depend on the existence of a new type of administrator, specifically trained for work in the social services and therefore quite different form the usual bureaucrat. The type of training required by entrants into this novel profession became for her a subject of life-long interest and it was indeed in order to pursue this line of thinking as applied to the welfare services in general that she had left Liverpool.

D'Aeth's interest, on the other hand, had always been focused on the problems of promoting the 'educated democracy', essential as the basis of any advance in social policy. To him that implied the existence of a strong and supportive social structure through membership of which ordinary individuals would be enabled to make their contribution. Such a framework was all too evidently lacking and it was to remedying this deficiency that D'Aeth was increasingly attracted.

The remarkable consistency with which he pursued this imminently practical objective is the clue to making sense of the free-ranging programme of activity on which he embarked. What might at first sight seem to be a welter of plans and projects, in fact added up into a calculated strategy aimed at the creation of a society within which active citizenship would be a viable proposition.

Seen in that light, all the bits and pieces of the jigsaw of D'Aeth's vast programme fall into place. Coordination is seen to be not mere obsession on the part of a man with a tidy mind, but takes pride of place as the essential foundation on which a strong social structure could be built. Given that, it was only logical that in erecting such a structure, steps must be taken to ensure that opportunities for the public to participate were built into it. That in turn raised the matter of how to motivate people to take up the opportunities thus made available, but D'Aeth firmly and steadfastly believed that altruism would grow from that on which it fed. No-one observed that, almost as a by-product, his endeavours added up to no less than demonstration of the theory and practice of community development, a notable achievement and one for which he richly deserves to be remembered. However, community development is now an established profession, its techniques widely adopted, its origins a subject for the social historian. What is universally overlooked is the fact that the outcome of the long saga of those years of learning-by-doing was something of much greater and more fundamental significance.

The gist of the argument that Macadam had so trenchantly voiced and that D'Aeth had put to the test of practical implementation, was that social advance is inextricably dependent on the existence of effective and efficient machinery for its management. The sting in the tail of this apparently innocuous statement was in the conclusion. No plans for reform or change could hope to succeed without the support of a system of administration specifically designed to meet the requirements of contemporary social circumstances. It was blatantly evident that this current practice failed to do so. There could be no evasion of the fact that a system based on the philanthropic patronage of past tradition would have to be replaced by a totally new approach.

With courage and imagination, D'Aeth reconnoitred on our behalf the unknown territory of life in the 21st century. Like a social orienteer, he surveyed the land through which he would have to journey and explored the potential of the options for progress. Not for him to argue the toss as to the ultimate destination. His role was simply to work out the practicalities of how that high ambition was to be achieved. Since the old ways of doing things was no longer relevant, what new system should take its place?

His message was crystal clear. Here in the recognition of the basic importance of what has come to be known as a social administration lay the clue to the resolution of the problem of how to bridge the gap between policy and practice. Subsequent events have diverted us from pursuing the way ahead as he indicated it. The failure to relate theory to reality has dogged our every endeavour to translate the dream of the welfare state into practice. There is, however, welcome evidence that the dominance of social policy by the value of the market place is giving way to a dawning appreciation of the fact that will entail the introduction of an entirely new system of administration. Never has D'Aeth's guidance been more directly relevant at the end of the century than it was at its beginning.

The story has come full circle. This chapter began with the question of why bother to resuscitate the memory of this forgotten man. The record of his achievement provides ample justification. If only we would have the humility to learn from his experience, to derive inspiration from his vision and to enter bravely into the heritage he left us.

Mrs Townsend, founder of the GFS

Chapter five

The Girls' Friendly Society and the Development of Rural Youth Work 1850–1900

Ray Fabes and Alison Skinner

Although most of the literature concerning the origins and development of youth work in the second half of the 19th century refers to work with boys and young men, there is evidence for a major focus on work with girls and young women in rural areas during the same period. This chapter discusses the various factors that influenced rural youth work with girls and young women and the motivations of its promoters.

The research was carried out in Lincolnshire. It concentrated on the parish of Spilsby and the activities of the Girls' Friendly Society (GFS) who established their first branch there in 1877. Three main sources of evidence have been used: the archives of Lincolnshire, of the GFS and research undertaken by the Spilsby Workers' Educational Association study group.

The wider context

Changes in the social life of 19th century rural Britain were marked by the growth of the nonconformist churches and the Temperance Movement which provided the conditions whereby women could become more active in social affairs. Heasman (1962) identifies the evangelical movement as being a key factor which, within the Anglican Church, validated women's involvement in the 'social gospel of good works'. Prochaska (1980, 1988) develops this theme, discussing mothers' meetings and the development of visiting societies. Vincinus (1985) analyses the wider impact of women gaining a 'licence' to become involved in a range of issues, organisations and causes which gave them an acceptable identity as well as a legitimate 'occupation'. Women became prime movers in Sunday schools (Laqueur, 1976), in singing groups linked to Temperance Society Bands, and in an array of Friendly Societies which provided opportunities for social and economic self help (see in particular Gosden, 1963, 1973; Morris, 1990). The organisation of the annual calendar of village life also fell mainly to women who used celebrations such as maypole dancing and harvest homes to encourage an unquestioning 'public observance of Victorian middle-class morality' (Newby, 1987, 96). Women were therefore often in a position to develop this voluntary activity specifically in relation to young people.

In examining the evidence for rural youth work in the period 1850–1900, major difficulties arise in establishing the motivation for adult engagement with young people and in identifying any recognisably educational content to such work. For instance, there is much evidence of young people meeting with itinerant preachers or Sunday school teachers informally on other days of the week to discuss issues of the day, but can this be deemed youth work? Sunday school outings in horse drawn wagons would not seem to be much different from trips out in today's terminology. Other leisure activities such as junior sports clubs, performance groups, bands, choirs and the like would fulfil some of the criteria for youth work, but key questions about the educative nature of some of these pastimes remain.

It is not clear from archival sources whether 'Juvenile Benefit Societies', which gave grants for anything from shoes to school materials have a modern equivalent, or whether they had young people on their decision making groups – one suspects not. Nevertheless much of what can be termed 'youth work in rural areas' between 1850–1900 has a direct equivalent today.

Citizenship education is represented by young people attending and participating in town and parish meetings, including a record of a young person actually recording decisions made (Gurnham, 1989). Those campaigning around issues of drink through their involvement in The Band of Hope have counterparts today and similarly Sunday night clubs for young people, sponsored by various religious groups, show continuity. Groups of young people meeting with concerned and interested adults on street corners, in market places and in the back rooms of public houses could be seen as examples of early detached work. Adults also conducted advocacy work with young women at hiring fairs, in the fishing industry and in the workhouse, getting actively involved in issues about young people's rights and campaigning about their working conditions (Money, 1897, 11; GFS Annual Report, 1880, 22).

What is much more difficult to ascertain than equivalence is whether these forms of youth work were a conscious attempt to engage with young peoples' interests, the natural development of socialist or nonconformist beliefs, well thought out programmes of social control, or random occurrences. Walvin (1982) offers some insight but certainly the work of the Girls' Friendly Society (GFS) with girls and young women – as examined next – developed what might be termed almost a formal youth work curriculum, long before similar thoughts were written down about the purposes of work with boys and young men in urban areas.

The work of the Girls' Friendly Society

The GFS was founded in 1875 and was the first Anglican organisation to be run entirely by lay women. A quarter of a century later it had 1,345 branches in England and Wales and was spreading overseas. At its peak in 1913 it had nearly 200,000 members and 40,000 'associates'. The latter were upper and middle-class 'friends' who shared a 'semi-maternal relationship' with 'working girl' members (Horn, 1991, 29). Although never intending to be a specifically rural organisation, its membership reflected the class divisions of rural Britain. Contrary to what one might expect, the GFS was neither envisaged as a 'friendly society', nor as a youth organisation. Its founder, Mrs Townsend had been moved by the distress of one of her 12-year-old maids who had been orphaned (a status she shared) and sought to find her a friend.

Money (1897) and Heath Stubbs (1926) record that the society was initially conceived in 1872 as an umbrella organisation for the many rescue societies that were being formed in Anglican parishes 'to save young women from falling'. It was initially envisaged that this organisation would link a number of young women's societies in a national network, thereby spreading the notion of friendship between women of different classes. A cynic might view the enthusiastic promotion of GFS activities by middle-class women as being simply their response to encouragement from the pulpit to become involved in the 'social gospel of good works'. Such enthusiasm certainly led to local rivalry and the records make clear that sometimes entire parish populations of young women were claimed as GFS members by enthusiastic branch organisers.

Percival first refers specifically to the GFS contribution to rural youth work when describing the organisation as 'the village girls' club movement' (1951, 86). However, the distinctive contribution of the GFS was always the personal friendship established between the lady associates and the young members. This aimed to counter the loneliness of young women entering domestic service in a strange place, to assist young women to find work and move easily between employers, and to be suitably entertained and educated in their out-of-work hours.

This relationship always had the capacity either to reinforce commonly held conventions, or to challenge some of the conditions in which young women had to live and work. As middle-class women grew more socially aware of the issues that affected the lives of young people from the poorest sections of society so they became more anxious about their dealings with them. For example, in relation to the recruitment of domestic servants, there is evidence to suggest that some increasingly began to worry that they might bring working-class habits (and diseases) into their 'respectable' homes which might influence (and infect) their own kin (Butler, 1871). Their social education responses were influenced, as Brew so pointedly observed, by this anxiety as well as being 'tinged with patronage and flavoured with a kind of piety' (1968, 88). The GFS certainly promoted notions of 'purity' and 'family values' reflecting the major features of late Victorian conservatism. The activities that took place at GFS meetings sought to instil in their participants habits of regularity, obedience, cleanliness, order, abstinence, Bible reading, thrift and domestic competence, all of which were rewarded in regular prize givings.

The Society, in its journals and records, showed no awareness of the contemporary movement to enfranchise women and the great political causes of the period seem largely to have been ignored or to have passed them by (Harrison, 1973, 130). In rural areas it would seem that the promoters of GFS were mainly concerned about their own households.

However, this was not the whole story. Associates not only organised local meetings, but also got involved in what might now be called 'advocacy' work on behalf of members. The GFS, nicknamed the Great Fuss Society, certainly annoyed some mistresses who exploited their female domestic servants, and who found that they had to account for their practices to GFS members who were closely vetting the treatment of servants. Not surprisingly the nature and extent of this advocacy work was a highly contentious issue within the Society for many years. As Percival records (1951, 86) this activity created a backlash when advertisements appeared with 'No GFS member need apply'.

GFS associates also became active on issues concerning the treatment of young women in workhouses, orphanages and factories in urban areas. In the Lincoln Diocese in 1878 there is a record of a grant of £10 being agreed 'towards defraying the salary of a paid worker employed to visit among the girls employed in warehouses'. There are also records of associates 'erecting special booths opposing the recruitment of servants through the hiring fairs' (Harrison, 1973, 125) and attempting to improve the working conditions of young women employed in the fishing industry in coastal areas. The GFS, like the Young Women's Christian Association, established hostels in towns and cities. The unique feature of this development was that it sought to offer some continuity of relationship, linking the rural club with the hostel whenever young female servants moved from place to place and job to job. According to Harrison, although some local causes were taken up by the GFS, 'the organisation was not consciously political, but its benevolence stemmed from the prevailing rural and philanthropic ideals of conduct . . . it never entirely shed its rural outlook' (1973, 118).

The authors located a few ex-members of the GFS who recounted their experiences as members. Most recalled a very controlling, patronising Society which rewarded them for their thrift and hard work, gave them glimpses of how ladies lived through their garden parties and teas, and brought them together for large church services. The one recollection common to all was the disgrace brought about by young women becoming pregnant and being expelled from the GFS:

> I remember the Lady of the Manor coming to tell the member off (even though we thought it was someone in her family who had made her pregnant) and saying 'Love is a beautiful thing and not to be played about with'.

(interview, Marston Moreteyne, Bedfordshire 1997)

Most found it hard to offer a critical appraisal of the organisation but some were straightforward in suggesting it was all part of maintaining the status quo and the power of the ladies. Others suggested that their GFS experiences were no different from other forms of youth work in rural areas. These views would seem to support Harrison's assertion that 'the GFS reflects the major features of late-Victorian conservatism; its timidity on social questions, its exploitation of deferential attitudes . . . its enthusiasm for empire, pageantry and monarchy' (1973, 131).

Spilsby

The earliest record relating to the small rural Lincolnshire parish of Spilsby is found in the *Town Book* which records the vestry meetings from 1720 to 1807 (Ancaster 3rd Deposit 3/23YA Lincolnshire Archives). This contains brief statements of decisions and occasionally of issues raised, including how to prevent noisy children from disturbing church services. Key entries in this period offer the earliest evidence of work with young people:

31st October 1784: That a spinning school be established . . .

26th July 1785: That the mistress do not spin on her own account . . . but employ her whole time in teaching and working for the said school . . .

14th February 1786: Hiring or fitting up a building, or a commodious room for the purpose of both a spinning and a Sunday school.

31st October 1786: That the mistress be also asked to work on Sundays to keep the children occupied and give them the benefits of a Sunday school.

22nd May 1787: All children until they are put out to places do diligently attend the spinning school at the stated hours.

There is no record of how the initiative of the spinning school developed and whether it had any connection with other ventures which sought to gain young people's interest or keep them occupied. The second set of entries are perhaps more important although the actual volume of the *Town Book* is now missing from the Lincolnshire Archive. Gurnham quotes from it:

In 1790 one G. Kelk was paid 6d. 'for keeping the boys from playing on a Sunday'. This was hardly likely to be a remuneration sufficient to cope with the problems on a long term basis and a few years later we find W. Humstance being paid 12s. 6d for his efforts during the previous 6 months 'to prevent Boys from Play on Sundays in Church Time'.
(1989, 6)

There may be a connection with an entry in the *Town Book* for 24th November 1792, 'that William Humstance be appointed watchman for the parish'.

At the end of 1796 there is, by modern standards, an extraordinary entry, 'that Miles Cash (be deemed) incapable of holding office as parish clerk as he is only 20'. Yet he would seem to have been actively engaged in this capacity for at least four years prior to this! Perhaps it was because young Miles had not reached the age of majority that he was prevented from attending. However, an archivist commented that it was probably because they could not pay him a salary.

The early references to Messrs. Kelk and Humstance would tend to suggest that an embryonic concept of youth work was flourishing in this small corner of rural Lincolnshire well before some of the other well-known instances of people being specifically employed to undertake such work in urban areas (e.g: YMCA in London in 1845). Notably even in Spilsby it was boys who were seen as the trouble makers and who required preventative work to curtail their anti-social behaviour.

Spilsby was one of the smaller parishes in Lincolnshire but as Gurnham recounts, 'in 1851 its population had risen steadily but unspectacularly in the previous 50 years, from a little over 900 inhabitants to a little less than 1400' (1984, 11). The population remained constant between 1850–1900 with high birth and death rates, while drainage and enclosure schemes changed much of the area into one that was both productive and profitable for farming. The prime sources of information about Spilsby come from Gurnham whose reports (1984, 1987, 1989) published by the Workers' Educational Association (WEA), are based on the work of a local history study group that met for almost a decade.

From the evidence of the 1851 Census, Gurnham suggests that the great majority of migrants were young unmarried adults. However, in terms of young people he adds 'that since 1801 the numbers leaving must have exceeded the numbers entering, and the emigrants like the immigrants, would be mainly young people, especially young men, unable to find work' (1984, 17).

Gurnham identified by far the largest occupational group in Spilsby (64 per cent) as domestic servants (1984, 16). This is of considerable significance for those girls and young women aged 15 to 25 who outnumbered young men by 2 to 1, who were often lodging with their employers. Only 31 out of 185 of them were born in the town. The young women coming to Spilsby from smaller villages 'brought with them the customs, superstitions, habits, ideas, culture, language of these villages – but the town (population 1,400) with its nucleus of highly educated, literate and politically aware doctors, solicitors and clergy, was quite a different place' (1984, 18). When examining the educational records alongside those relating to child and youth labour the study group raised a number of questions. Although 76 young people aged 10 to13 were listed as scholars in 1851, the group suggested that 'it would be interesting to know just how many attended regularly, or how many only attended on Sundays and what impact harvest, haymaking, potato planting and picking and other seasonal jobs had on attendance rolls' (1984, 31). The majority of scholars were male indicating that it was 'not thought necessary to teach girls to either write or to add up' (Gurnham, 1984, 54).

The WEA study group present a record of a parish that is full of civic activity in the second half of the 19th century with an impressively varied list of societies meeting at the Bull Inn. For a period the local branch of the GFS met there as well, although by the turn of the century its meeting place was The Shades (a Temperance Hotel), which was also the base of The Mutual Improvement Society.

The first record of the GFS branch comes from a news report of their second annual festival on 15 May 1879 (FL Vol.VI/35 p 165 July 1879, 65). A flavour of the festivities is given by the following extract:

A gathering of nearly 200 had been expected . . . a downpour led to the festival being postponed for a day . . . but the numbers were as follows: 122 members, 22 associates and two honorary associates . . . games filled up the interval (between the service) before tea tastefully set out on the lawn . . . games of all descriptions were resumed after tea and carried on with great spirit until after 7 o'clock . . . when Mrs C. T. Swan, the presiding associate spoke a few excellent words of counsel and advice.

Spilsby GFS branch records list names from 20 parishes and the range of activities include singing, country dancing, plays, needlework, lace making, cooking, dressmaking, hairdressing, sewing, flower arranging, rambles and flower gathering, making banners, parades, croquet on the lawn and 'how to answer advertisements'. Bible reading was encouraged and recreation rooms were open 'for free time at weekends'. Books from the Diocesan circulating library could be left in these rooms and young women helped and encouraged in their reading, to counter what was commonly regarded as 'poisonous literature', the product of the 'evils of the printing press'. Reports also refer to a 'stereoscope' show and other amusements. Accounts of the content of sermons and exhortations to members and associates alike suggest a flavour of the other messages the GFS sought to convey. Its strong temperance influence on members is revealed in the following which urged members 'to lead temperate lives, to give up intoxicating drinks, to get beer money rather than beer, not only on their own account, but as an example to others' (FL, 2/15 November 1877, 200). Another statement extolled the benefit and satisfaction of early rising (FL 4/34 June 1879, 143) and others were concerned about 'resisting temptations' and the need for 'purity'.

Opportunities were also provided for young men in the parish. Russell (1994) reports on the establishment of the Spilsby Reading Room for 'working men's literary recreation and daily information'. Young men and apprentices under the age of 18 were offered reduced fees to become members. Considering that this was just a year after the GFS was formed in Spilsby, it might seem as if there was sophisticated provision for the social education of young people by the late 1870s in this small mid-Lincolnshire parish.

Discussion

No record of clubs for young people could be found in Lincolnshire during this period. However, there was an enormous range of associations, organisations and initiatives seeking to develop socially educative activities. Some of them were obviously very controlling, but others were established to offer educational opportunities similar to those in urban areas, including Sunday schools, Juvenile Mechanics Institutes, libraries, reading rooms, Penny Readings, literary societies, young men's societies, Mutual Improvement Societies, formal youth organisations (uniformed brigades from the mid 1880s), sporting, and social clubs, and cultural associations to develop music, dance and drama.

Russell's history of adult education in North Lincolnshire 1830 to 1890 offers some tantalising references to night schools 'to counter young men's pranks' (1994, 11) and Juvenile Reading Societies to offer alternative activities as 'the only tuition they get is on the street' (op. cit, 62). Many of those to whom he is referring, were as young as 12 and the juvenile nights attracted '70 or more at the Spilsby readings in 1866' (op. cit, 114). This must have been a significant proportion of the young people.

The churches were at the forefront of many of the organisations. In Lincolnshire the nonconformists in particular were key players in the more socially educative ventures, along with the Temperance Societies who had a significant appeal for young people. The GFS had a particular place in this work from 1875. In the last quarter of the 19th century it developed a unique style of practice which has, to date, received little (if any) critical attention. It made a significant contribution to work with young people in rural areas, and although never claiming to be as influential as the Boys' and Girls' Brigades, did develop a style of practice that addressed many of the issues which its members encountered in rural Britain. It could be argued that if Spilsby is typical, rural youth work encompassed a higher proportion of those targeted than in urban areas.

Sadly we know little about whether the young valued these opportunities. There are some clues about GFS activities, but there are no first hand accounts or oral histories. From those available, it can be perceived (especially in the case of GFS) that the promoters sought to educate and widen the horizons of their members, but often in a very uncritical way. It would take considerably more detailed analysis than is possible here to ascertain what impact change in rural society at the time had on youth work. There are many parallels with current informal social education practice and clearly much can be learned from these examples of both positive and negative experiences that might inform policy and practice in rural youth work today.

Bibliography

Brew, J. Macallister (1968). *Youth and Youth Groups*. London, Faber and Faber.

Butler, J. (1871). 'Letters to my Countrywomen dwelling in the Farmsteads and Cottages of England', reprinted in S. Jeffreys (ed.) (1987) *The Sexuality Debates*. London, Routledge.

Gosden, P. H. J. H. (1963). *The Friendly Societies in England 1815–1875*. Manchester, Manchester University Press.

Gosden, P. H. J. H. (1973). *Self Help – Voluntary associations in nineteenth century Britain*. London, B. T. Batsford.

Gurnham, R. (1984). *Victorian Spilsby*. Spilsby, WEA.

Gurnham, R. (1987). *Edwardian Spilsby*. Spilsby, WEA.

Gurnham, R. (1989). *Georgian Spilsby*. Spilsby, WEA.

Harrison, B. (1973). 'For Church, Queen and Family: The Girls' Friendly Society 1874–1920', *Past and Present*, (61), pp 107–138.

Heasman, K. (1962). *Evangelicals in Action: An appraisal of their social work in the Victorian era*. London, Geoffrey Bles.

Heath-Stubbs, M. (1926). *Friendship's Highway: Being the history of the Girls' Friendly Society 1875–1925*. London, GFS.

Horn, P. (1991). *Ladies of the Manor: Wives and daughters in Country House Society 1830–1918*. Stroud (Glos.), Alan Sutton.

Laqueur, T. W. (1976). *Religion and Respectability: Sunday Schools and working class culture 1780–1850*. London, Yale University Press.

Money, A. L. (1897). *History of the Girls Friendly Society*. London, Gardner, Darton and Co.

Morris, R. J. (1990). 'Clubs, Societies and Associations' in F. M. L. Thompson, (ed) *The*

Cambridge Social History of Britain 1750–1950: Volume 3. Social Agencies and Institutions. Cambridge, Cambridge University Press.

Newby, H. (1987). *Country Life: A social history of rural England.* London, Weidenfield and Nicholson.

Percival, A. (1951). *Youth Will Be Led.* London, Collins.

Prochaska, Frank (1980). *Women and Philanthropy in Nineteenth Century England.* Oxford, Clarendon Press.

Prochaska, Frank (1988). *The Voluntary Impulse: Philanthropy in modern Britain.* London, Faber and Faber.

Russell, R. C. (1994). *Living and Learning in Lindsey, Lincolnshire 1850–1890.*

Vicinus, M. (1985). *Independent Women: Work and community for single women 1850–1920.* London, Virago.

Walvin, J. (1982). *A Child's World: A social history of English childhood 1800–1914.* Harmondsworth, Penguin.

Thomas Auld

Chapter six

Edwardian Boys and Labour in the East End of Sunderland: Welfare and work

Jean Spence

Welfare to Work policies have recently been presented as new, constructive and radical approaches to the problems of unemployment and poverty in modern Britain. Yet such policies have a long history in different guises and can clearly be discerned, for example, in the principles informing the operations of the Poor Law and in the activities of the Charity Organisation Society (COS) at the end of the 19th century (Rooff, 1972; Humphreys, 1995). Certainly the political philosophy which informs Welfare to Work is not new, and its history provides examples of contradiction, tension and conflict in practice. Using evidence gleaned from the records of a voluntary boys' club in Sunderland at the beginning of this century, this chapter highlights some concerns which have resonance in the current situation and which might provide a starting point for a more critical response to contemporary Welfare to Work policies than has hitherto been apparent.

The detailed minutes of the *The Sunderland Waifs Rescue Agency and Street Vendors' Club* suggest that its managers were pursuing an early prototype of Welfare to Work in a local and voluntary context. Obviously few direct comparisons can be drawn between the activities of a local boys' club in the years before the First World War and those of national Government nearly a century later. Nevertheless, the values, assumptions and objectives of the policy-makers suggest some striking continuities. In particular, in their focus upon positive arrangements and support for 'transition', their negative attitude towards 'welfare' and their presuppositions about the inherent benefits of skilled work, those involved in running the Waifs Rescue Agency and Street Vendors' Club articulated attitudes which would not be out of place within the discourses of New Labour (Player, 1999; Jeffs and Spence, 2000). At the same time, those working-class young people who were the object of the attention of the club's managers and workers frequently responded to the exercise of seeking work in ways which dealt primarily with their everyday reality and local knowledge of the labour market and this sometimes resulted in class-based tensions and conflicts which might not be unfamiliar to anyone who has undertaken youth work with young people in areas of high unemployment today. Examination of the responses of Edwardian boys to the work and welfare opportunities with which they were presented highlights some questions and problems which the Labour Government might do well to consider in the contemporary context.

The Sunderland Waifs Rescue Agency and Street Vendors' Club

The club whose intervention into the lives of the Sunderland poor demonstrates the longevity of the values and propositions enshrined in Welfare to Work, still exists as the Lambton Street Fellowship Centre. It was founded in 1901 by a local architect named Frank Caws and the story connected with its founding is a classic late-Victorian narrative of rescue with echoes of the Barnardos story (Wagner, 1979). It tells of Caws leaving his office one winter's night and finding a shoeless waif freezing on his doorstep. The boy had been selling matches. This prompted Caws to call together a number of wealthy and influential colleagues from the town who agreed to set up a club specifically for boys (Smith, 1951; *Sunderland Daily Echo*, 5/12/01). The purposes of the club are inferred in its title. It was to 'rescue' homeless waifs from the streets (Platt, 1972), and it was to respond to the problems of casual boy labour as exemplified by the prevalence of juvenile street vendors (Urwick, 1904; Bray, 1911; Stedman Jones, 1971).

From the very beginning, in the assumptions informing the constitution and management of the club, class difference and inequality was accepted as a given, although the working classes as such were not conceived as problematic by the founders. It was understood rather that those who were in need of intervention were boys from the families of the East End tenements and slums, from families which relied upon the irregular and poor wages of unskilled manual labour. In the East End of Sunderland, experience of unemployment was commonplace and poverty endemic (Tedder, 2000). In analysing the conditions of the unskilled poor at the end of the 19th century, Stedman Jones (1971) describes a similar population as 'outcast'. In contemporary language, there is little doubt that the children of the East End of Sunderland would have been defined as 'excluded', as an 'underclass'. The purpose of intervention in their lives was ultimately to work towards their 'inclusion' into the benefits and responsibilities of full adult citizenship (*Sunderland Daily Echo*, 5/12/01, 3). However, in the circumstances of Edwardian England, citizenship did not mean membership of a fluid, open, classless society. For those involved in the Lambton Street Club it meant rather encouraging the children of the poor towards full participation in respectable *working-class* life, towards accepting the conventions and rules of class relations and behaviour.

The records which detail the weekly proceedings of the management committee indicate that the key objectives of those involved in the Sunderland Waifs Rescue Agency and Street Vendors' Club were to provide an inviting alternative to the streets, and in the process of making contact, to offer paternalistic guidance. However, running alongside that agenda were other, less clearly expressed intentions. Human sympathy, charity and a concern for social justice were frequently tempered by the need to address popular and common worries among the middle classes about the relationship between welfare dependency and idleness, about problems of control posed by young people (especially boys) on the streets and about the responsibilities of families for children. Among the speeches at the opening of the club, the terms of reference which were to frame subsequent activity were clearly set out:

Coun. Summerbell said a great deal had been said about clubs of that kind taking upon themselves the feeding and clothing of the children of those people who had spent their money in drink, but they would be doing a grand work if even they succeeded in tracing the drunken parents who neglected and ill treated their children, and got them brought before the magistrates. It was their duty, however, if they desired to uplift the community morally and socially, to at least rescue the lads from drifting into a life of vice and crime by the institution of a club of that character.

Mr Perris said they would like to provide the lads with a comfortable home, to which they would come and be clothed and fed, and taught a good trade – to act as a sort of god-father towards them. But their present means were limited.

(*Sunderland Daily Echo*, 3/1/02, 3)

Up to the period of the First World War, the minute books are rich with references to family, welfare, reform, education and training which reveal some of the complexities and contradictions faced by the committee members in these matters. In their reliance upon the goodwill of the bourgeoisie of Sunderland in raising the necessary funding for the club and sponsoring its activities (e.g. *Sunderland Daily Echo*, 24/3/04, 3; Minutes, 14/8/02), it was important to take cognisance of prevailing views, and besides, these views often corresponded with those of powerful committee members. Goodwill from sponsors could only be sustained if 'outcomes' of the work could be assessed in acceptable terms. Yet at the same time, the committee members were concerned to intervene directly and do something practical to alleviate the individual suffering caused by the poverty of the families of the East End.

The two perspectives were not necessarily complementary. Resolution of tension was sought through what can be identified as a practical welfare to work approach within policy decisions. The idea of 'providing a comfortable home' assumed the discomfort of the family home, and was conditional upon the boys being prepared initially to obey club rules, but the possibilities of gaining access to clothing and feeding came to be linked directly with the willingness to be 'taught a good trade' and upon families conforming to standard measures of 'respectability'. These measures of respectability included conventional expectations of gender roles. It was considered as important that a mother should work to keep her home clean and in good order as it was that a father should be prepared to work and use his earnings for the benefit of his family (e.g. Minutes, 3/11/10). The club itself came to be understood by its sponsors as a means of aiding such efforts, as a supplementary instrument of transition between exclusion and inclusion, dependence and independence; it was a ladder which boys could use to climb out of the underclass, into the regularly employed and disciplined working class if they and their families were prepared to make the effort.

Welfare and the club

Policy which focuses upon the processes of transition from one state to another, implicitly assumes that the original state is undesirable and seeks to address what are claimed to be the causes of that condition. Intervention is often designed to break the cycle of reproduction and to subvert the socialisation process which brings about the undesired condition. The younger generation is a naturally identified target for inculcating new habits. In the case of the managers of the Lambton Street Club, the undesirable state of poverty was associated with irregular and unskilled work and that condition in turn was held to be related to non-conforming attitudes, values and behaviour consequent upon slum living. Like those who advocate welfare to work arrangements today, the key to breaking the cycle was thought to lie in the escape route of regular and preferably skilled employment. For those suffering the consequences of poverty and unemployment in their daily lives, constructive and practical interventions are generally welcomed. They bring the possibility of relief. Thus many of the boys of Sunderland's Edwardian East End responded positively to the possibility of belonging to a club which addressed their circumstances just as many long-term unemployed people today initially embraced the introduction of the New Deal (Jeffs and Spence, 2000).

However, this apparently harmonious foundation for building an infrastructure of transition is only so in the abstract. There is rarely an equal partnership between the providers and recipients of welfare. In reality there are inherent difficulties associated with definitions, priorities and with inequalities of power, right from the very inception of the policy. Living in conditions of poverty and unemployment is different from viewing those conditions from the outside and it is power relations between the providers and recipients which decide the priorities for transitional arrangements.

In the case of the Sunderland club, the perspective on poverty portrayed in the minute books is that of the managers, supporters and, to a lesser extent, that of the resident superintendent. The voice of the boys and their families is mostly silent, although occasionally it is possible to deduce from the text some of their concerns and perspectives. The view of the management committee was that there were two conditions of poverty. One was associated with misfortune and the accidents of life, such as widowhood or ill health (e.g. Minutes, 3/11/10; 4/12/03). The other was associated with unreasonable, undisciplined and 'unsanitary' behaviour and sometimes with idleness and drunkenness (e.g. Minutes, 23/10/02; 6/11/02). Overall, it was feared that whatever the source of the poverty, once a family found itself in that condition, its ability to care for and adequately socialise its children and young people became impaired. The poor family was considered to be deficient in the resources and skill required to prevent poverty being reproduced in the next generation. The strategy of the managers was to help make good those deficiencies, 'to act as a sort of god-father' while at the same time tailoring individual interventions according to the type of poverty encountered.

In a general sense, the club itself was understood to be a welfare benefit offering temporary shelter from the streets and from slum housing. Within that, the collective benefits of membership included opportunities for recreational activity, for occasional treats, such as trips, entertainments and food, and for self-improvement through association with the superintendent and managers, attendance at lectures and talks, and the use of the reading room. Although in theory these benefits were available to all those who fell within the targeted group, in practice, the rules of membership must undoubtedly have led to self-selection on the part of the boys. In some cases, breaking of rules led to exclusion from the club. The rules of membership were fairly general, but nevertheless, they were devised without reference to the boys themselves. At the very first meeting of the founders of the club, it was agreed that:

A placard to be put up in each room of the building. 'No smoking, swearing nor gambling allowed. If any member of the club is guilty of disorderly conduct he is liable to expulsion'.
(Minutes, 9/12/01)

Later, these rules were made more precise, including the injunction that the boys should be clean (soap and towel being provided in the yard for washing), that 'Gambling, smoking, swearing, spitting or dirty or disorderly conduct, are absolutely forbidden' and, as an addendum, that 'Boys who wish to get work or are in need of advice or help, should speak to the person in charge' (Minutes, 15/5/02).

The managers did use their power to enforce the rules with some discretion, but nevertheless they exerted their authority in relation to the behaviour of the members both inside and outside the club premises. Thus, for instance, in 1904, six boys were excluded for 'disorderly conduct' inside the club (Minutes, 2/6/04) and a further two for 'fighting and riot' outside the club (Minutes, 17/11/04). The minutes later record, without comment, that the six excluded in June were later arrested and imprisoned for gambling (Minutes, 30/6/04), thus silently affirming the wisdom of the decision to deny access to the undeserving.

Access to the general benefits of membership required no more than a willingness to observe the rules. However, in relation to particular benefits to individuals, access was much more diligently policed. All of the boys who used the club were poor. Most were also hungry and ill-clad. The role of the club was to provide help and support for poor lads, but only in the terms identified as appropriate by the committee, the members of which understood their task as a practical one of distributing limited resources in relation to need, and also as a moral one of prioritising those needs according to the attitude and behaviour of the intended recipients.

The men involved in running the agency were determined that their philanthropic efforts were not to be considered as dole for the poor. Their paternalism was significantly tempered by fears that their resources would be depleted by uncontrolled demand, that their goodwill might be exploited by the mercenary and that by misplaced generosity they might undermine the willingness of the poor to seek independence through work. They did not wish to offer handouts or ameliorate suffering by giving unconditional alms. They conceived their social duty to be that of distributing such charity only in exceptional circumstances when it could be proved that the need was unavoidable and genuine, for instance in the case of serious illness (Minutes, 7/1/09), or when it would be of value in enabling a member to participate more effectively in the labour market, for instance in purchasing from club funds the sixpenny birth certificates required by boys before they could take up offers of work (Minutes, 1/4/09).

In order to ensure that their good intentions were not abused, they worked with the

Charity Organisation Society and for a few years utilised the services of representatives of that organisation to investigate the circumstances of anyone who *asked* them for anything – in particular for help with clothing. In asking for material benefits, in expressing their needs in their own terms, individuals were immediately inviting inquiry into their personal situation. The COS had been created specifically to rationalise the charitable efforts of the Victorian middle classes (Bell, 1942; Rooff, 1972; Humphries, 1995). Its intentions were to ensure that such charity was fairly distributed, that fraudulent claims were not rewarded, and that benefits would be used to help the poor to help themselves. Crucially, charitable help was not to be used to encourage idleness or dependence. In order for the administrators of the COS to satisfy themselves that claims were genuine and that the poor in question were 'deserving' a system of visiting and interviewing those requesting help was devised.

Not surprisingly, most requests for material help were turned down on grounds which involved value judgements about the circumstances, behaviour and attitudes of the poor. In relation to the Sunderland Waifs Rescue Agency and Street Vendors' Club, the reports of investigators frequently suggested that either the parents of the boys in question were able bodied and weren't working – in which case members of the committee sought work for them – or that the family was not behaving appropriately – in which case other agencies such as the Society for the Prevention of Cruelty to Children might be brought in to further investigate.

> *Mrs Scott of 20 Hope Street (staying with her sister Mrs Gordon (or Hughes) there) waited on committee and applied for clothing for her son and nephew members of the Waifs club. After fully considering the matter and interviewing the two boys who seemed better clad than most members of the club, the committee could not see their way to give these two boys clothing at present. But on the advice of Mrs Seinfield who had visited 20 Hope Street and reported the miserable condition of things there, the committee decided to offer the husband of Mrs Hughes (and also the husband of Mrs Scott if he is physically fit to accept it) employment. Mr Nicol kindly undertook to obtain labouring employment for these men or one of them if the other proved unfit.*
> (Minutes, 23/4/02)

> *. . . a number of other members of the club applied for boots with the promise to pay so much a week for same. Mr Perris undertook to make enquiries as to Golledges father's circumstances.*
> (Minutes, 6/10/04)

> *. . . Mr Charlton reported that the result of Mr Coley's inquiry concerning the Golledge family was somewhat unfavourable as it appears that the father is regularly employed as a machinist by Messrs. McColl & Pollock, earning 27 shillings a week. The eldest son is also employed by Messrs. M & P and earns 25 shillings per week. Other members of the family also are well employed so that it appears that the two boy members of the club should not be in straightened circumstances or in want of boots. The application was therefore not entertained. Mr Cameron undertook to inquire through the Society for the Prevention of Cruelty to Children as to whether the parents could not be compelled to make better provision for these two boys.*
> (Minutes, 13th October 1904)

. . . Mr Caws was requested to obtain through Mr Cameron the Report of the S.P.C.C. agent as to the brothers Golledge . . .

. . . A lengthy report provided by Mr Cameron from Mr Stokes of the Society for the Prevention of Cruelty to Children dealing with the case of the Golledges which had been previously investigated by Mr Coley of the Charity Organisation Society through the mediumship of Mr Charlton, was read and considered.
(Minutes, 24/11/04)

Mr Caws reported that last Sunday night he had been informed that the Golledge boys desired to frequent the club (from which they had absented themselves since the investigation began) but their father had threatened to thrash them if they did.
(Minutes, 1/12/04)

In the extracts above, it is apparent that work, ability to work, and income from work were the key factors in the decision-making processes relating to the provision of clothing. In the case of Mrs Scott, even though the ill health of her husband was acknowledged, the answer was felt to lie in work rather than welfare. In the case of the Golledges, even though the application was only for boots *on credit,* it led to what must have been experienced as highly intrusive intervention from over-zealous investigators who assumed the moral authority to make judgments about how a family's income should be used.

It is possible to read between the lines of the text of the minutes some dissent between those members of the committee who were fully in favour of the authoritarian methods of the COS and those who wished to adopt a more liberal approach, making provision according to perceived need rather than in relation to questionable measures of respectability and industrious intention. Notably, Frank Caws, the founder of the club seemed less inclined to 'investigate' than other members particularly in relation to the distribution of clothing (e.g. Minutes, 6/11/02). It seems that it was only because of the personal eminence of Caws within the committee that his view was aired. The predominant feeling about welfare provision for individuals and families was authoritarian. Demonstrated willingness to work for the benefit of the family unit was the main measure of eligibility. When Mrs Scinfield, the voluntary and self-appointed COS investigator for the club left Sunderland, the resident superintendent, Mr Smith, picked up the visiting duties and although he carried these out much more informally, the pattern had been set. Subsequently, it was always assumed that free clothing, or clothing on credit, except in exceptional and accidental cases of need which would be identified by managing representatives of the club, would only be granted in association with the acceptance of employment.

The following extract is only one of a number of instances where such provision was discussed and debated in similar terms:

Mr Smith stated that Mrs Thorman had sent down some clothes for the boys. Reuben Baxter's case was discussed, Mr Smith stating that the boy was badly in need of a shirt, but confessing

at the same time that Baxter was a very unreliable lad and apparently would not stick at work when he got the opportunity. The committee refused to clothe Baxter.
(Minutes, 13/2/08)

No matter how poor or ragged, a boy who did not cooperate with the standards of behaviour associated with the compliant worker, was considered 'undeserving' of individual help. Willingness to conform rather than absolute need was the ultimate test of eligibility in the allocation of a welfare benefit.

Employment of boys

The question of 'boy labour' was an important social and political issue during the Edwardian era (Bray, 1911; Urwick, 1904). Reflecting the conventional gendered division of labour at the time (Montagu, 1904), it referred primarily to circumstances wherein boys from poor families left school as soon as possible in order to take unskilled, short term and casual work at rates of pay which were higher than those commanded in the skilled trades. Such boys were usually paid off as they approached maturity which entitled them to an adult wage. Families whose poverty was immediate, generating needs which could hardly be met day to day, were complicit in this process encouraging their sons to seek the highest wage. Because the labour supply was constantly swelled with new school leavers, employers could virtually do as they pleased. Often they employed boys for only a few weeks, finishing them if the work was slack or if the boys did not measure up to requirements.

A combination of necessity and the unreliability of the labour market compounded the problem for the poorest families whose children often began working well before they left school, as street vendors. In this, the most casual occupation of all, young people earned an irregular income on the streets without even the most basic control which would be imposed by an employer. For those who had been street traders, the transition to regular waged work was particularly difficult; the independence of the street did not easily translate into the discipline and rigours of waged labour. It was these young people who were the most unlikely to satisfy employers and who were therefore prone to lose any work they had on attaining adulthood. Adult unemployment and poverty were therefore blamed upon the habits learned under the conditions of boy labour, and street trading in particular was held responsible for ignorance, fecklessness, crime and prostitution among the urban poor (Urwick, 1904; Stedman Jones, 1971; Walkowitz, 1996; Davin, 1997).

The problem was one which clearly related to the conditions of the labour market, implicating employers as well as the employed. However, regulation of the labour market and of employment practices in general called for national legislation rather than local action. It required both political will and influence to intervene at this level. From the perspective of local activists and philanthropists who relied upon employers for their patronage and financial support, who indeed were sometimes themselves employers, it was never likely that this would be part of the agenda for change. Instead, they focused attention upon specific boys and their families. They were intent on changing the behaviour, attitudes and values which led to casual labour being accepted as the only option, providing alternatives where they could, and using welfare as a means of encouraging and supporting those who made efforts towards regular and respectable employment. Alongside this, they campaigned to regulate street trading, which did not implicate respectable employers (Minutes, 3/2/10 to 10/10/12). For the sponsors of the Sunderland Club, the main object was to secure the interest and compliance of their members in obtaining and retaining secure employment ideally via an apprenticeship (e.g. Minutes, 1/4/09).

Within this spirit of intervention, taking their lead from the example of the work of Barnardo's organisation and occasionally collaborating with Barnardo's (e.g. Minutes, 12/6/02; 9/10/02), the founders and managers of the Waifs Rescue Agency and Street Vendors' Club hoped that the regular employment of young people within the formal economy would begin to address the problems and issues associated with poverty of the East End of the town. They made it a priority of the club's work to seek positions within the local labour market for its members as they left school. The long-term strategy was to solicit the interest of employers in their endeavours while at the same time, through the activities, values and adult example practised in the club, training boys in the behaviour and attitudes appropriate to the respectable and respectful worker. The short-term strategy was to find suitable vacancies for boys as soon as possible after they left school, providing information, letters of introduction and material support in order to help the boys access the work.

From the very start of the Waifs Rescue Agency and Street Vendors' Club, a great deal of effort was expended in securing the cooperation of established local employers. The managers used their personal networks and influence; they circulated letters and used the opportunity presented by annual general meetings and fundraising events to publicise their work and to appeal for support from Sunderland firms.

SUNDERLAND WAIFS RESCUE AGENCY & STREET VENDORS' CLUB
15 Lambton Street,
April 1903

Dear Sirs,
The committee of the above agency are using their best endeavours to find employment for the boy street vendors who are at present growing up with no knowledge of or liking for, any regular work.

Feeling sure that such endeavours will commend themselves to you, the committee would feel greatly favoured if you would, at any time you are in need of boys of 14 years of age or upwards in your works, notify us at the above address, when we would at once endeavour to send you any likely boys whom we might have knowledge of.
Yours truly

(Copy of letter circulated to employers: appended to Minutes, 26/3/03)

Even though the club managers were acting as a sort of employment agency and taking some personal responsibility for the quality of the boys they sent, there was not exactly a rush of interest from employers to participate and offer openings. The same names emerge again and again. Some of these, particularly Councillor Summerbell who owned a printing business and Colonel Vaux, proprietor of the local brewery, had personal involvement in the club while Mr Charlton, an active management committee member involved in merchant shipping, procured a number of positions for boys on board his own vessels. As the coastal collieries began mining activities, they too took boys from Lambton Street.

In considering the nature of the employment offered, a number of issues emerge. Firstly, it is not clear how much of the work on offer really did fall outside the category of 'boy labour' as understood in the Edwardian period. Frequently boys were taken on by employers only to be dismissed after a very short period. In particular, there was a problem around joinery. On one level, joinery seemed an ideal trade through which to skill the boys and quite a few were fitted out with clothes, boots and occasionally tools in order to enable them to take up the offer of an apprenticeship. No doubt, many of these boys learned the trade. However, it emerged that boys were often paid off as they came towards the end of their apprenticeship when they would have been able to command a higher wage from the employer, and that there was an over-supply of joiners in Sunderland. Up to the First World War it seems that only one boy from the club, Thomas Doyle, managed to complete an apprenticeship in joinery.

> *J. Jackson 131 is to start at Young's as a joiner. Captain Foster advised the committee that these joinery works depended chiefly upon apprentices and that as soon as apprentices had served their time they were paid off. A discussion followed concerning this advice and the superintendent was consulted as to the desirability of sending more boys to these works. The final feeling of the meeting was that Doyle was doing well at Young's and that any boy could certainly learn the greater part of his trade there.*
> (Minutes, 21/10/09)

> *Jackson 131 has started at Young's Joinery works at 3/- per week and with reference to last week's discussion Mr Smith gave an excellent report of the work done in this shop.*
> (Minutes, 28/10/09)

> *Ernest Sinclair 135 and Martin Finn 190 are starting to work as joiners and undertakers at 4/- per week – with regard to this report Mr Charlton advised the committee as to a conversation he had had with Mr Ball of the labour bureau, when Mr Ball stated that several trades, especially joinery, are seriously overstocked in Sunderland districts. Mr Charlton suggested that Mr Smith might endeavour to procure employment for boys at trades which are not overcrowded.*
> (Minutes, 17/3/10)

> *Michael Quinn who is 15 years old was paid off from Young's joinery works, the manager*

stating that the lad was too small and ragged to be of any use. Mr Smith has, however, got Quinn started as an apprentice boiler maker at Clarks.
(Minutes, 23/9/10)

Thomas Doyle who is one of our oldest members has completed his apprenticeship at Young's joiner works and is now earning full money. The committee assisted Doyle by advancing the money for his tools, all of which has long since been repaid. Every credit is due to Doyle for the steady way in which he has served as an apprentice joiner for seven years.
(Minutes, 27/3/13)

Although the aim was to facilitate the transition to regular work through the opportunity to learn a skill, there was no guarantee that learning the skill of joinery would facilitate that. Moreover, during the period of working as apprentices, boys could be paid a very low rate of pay with no guarantee of ever graduating to the adult rate, unless they were exceptionally attentive and skilful as Thomas Doyle seems to have been. For the majority of the boys who pursued this option, there could have been very little difference between this situation and that of working in the unskilled sector, except that their wages might have been higher in unskilled work.

While the minute books of the club are particularly explicit about the problem of joinery, there is no indication that boys fared much better in other trades to which they were directed. The superintendent diligently reported the position of boys vis a vis their employment circumstances, and when there were reports of boys 'doing well' this was recorded in detail. Sometimes, a boy's name appears as 'doing well' at a particular trade only to reappear, weeks later, as engaged in completely different work, or as looking for work. It is perhaps significant that Thomas Doyle is the *only* reported case of a completed apprenticeship, although there are some indications that one other boy, Alma Hunt, who was sent to stables in Yorkshire to learn to become a jockey, was making good progress over an extended period of time (Minutes, 7/10/09; 21/4/10; 29/6/11; 1/2/12).

A second employment issue apparent in the minutes concerns the question of skill and training. The ideal of accessing the skilled trades unfortunately remained just that for most of the boys, an ideal:

[Coggins] was brought before the committee and said he had been obliged because of the drunkenness of the man he worked with to give up the slating job. He was sent to Mr Davison's at Southwick to take the place of Whitehead (65) who had left.
(Minutes, 28/8/02)

Mr Caws reported that Thomas Coggins (15), being paid only at the rate of 3/6 per week at the joiner work, his mother would not allow him to continue at that work though the boy himself would have liked to continue. So he had resumed his employment as a slater's help for which he was paid a much higher rate.
(Minutes, 4/9/02)

Mr Caws reported that Thomas Coggins (no 15) was gone to Candlish's Bottle Works after being fitted out with clothing.
(Minutes, 23/10/02)

It was reported that Tom Coggins (no 15) and Alfred Finkle (No 32) had left Seaham Bottle Works, their parents being unwilling for them to remain.
(Minutes 30/10/02)

Generally boys were found places in semi-skilled or unskilled work where formal apprenticeships did not exist, where training was minimal and wherein casualisation remained the order of the day for most youngsters. Sometimes the need to find work for particular boys was so urgent, that the question of finding a skilled trade was not even raised. Although a line was drawn to exclude any employment which was *in itself* casual or temporary and directly associated with boy labour, such as that of messenger boy, or which belonged to the category of street trading (e.g. Minutes, 21/5/08), there were occasions when even temporary employment was accepted:

Mr Caws reported that he had . . . fitted the boy [Coundon] out with clothing and boots and sent him to temporary employment with Mr R Bradford . . . Agent for the Hydraulic Scrap Power Company with whom he is to receive 5 shillings per week and 2/6 bonus at the end of four weeks.
(Minutes, 26/2/03)

Two weeks later:

Thomas Coundon explained to the committee that he had been sent away by Mr Bradford who did not require him longer.
(Minutes, 12/3/03)

As the first decade of the century slid towards economic recession, it became clear that finding any job for the boys associated with the club was considered preferable to the alternatives of unemployment or street vending. Not surprisingly, increasing use was made of the openings for boy labour in mining both in Sunderland itself and within the surrounding colliery villages of the Durham coalfield. Although the club sometimes received requests to send boys to particular pits, it is unlikely that this opened any particular opportunities for such work. In many cases, reporting in the minutes that boys had found work in a mine does not indicate anything other than that the boys were told jobs were available. Sometimes it is obvious that the boys found the jobs themselves. The main influence of the club in this respect was in the material support it could offer – i.e. in helping boys with boots, clothing and, where necessary, to find lodgings near their place of work.

The following eight boys have started work at New Seaham colliery at 8/- per week – W. Struthers 175, G. Pringle 154, J. Marchbanks 157, Walter Smith 61, Harry Finkle 50, David Kelly 25, Alfred McMann 85, T. McMann 86. Mr Smith went to Seaham Harbour

and arranged for lodgings. The lads are living all together in two houses, four in each house. Clothes have been provided for them at the following costs, Finkle 6/3, Kelly 9/-, Smith 3/9, Pringle 2/3, McMann 3/6 total £1–4–9. This amount will be paid out of the boys' earnings.
(Minutes, 23/12/09)

Between January 1908 and October 1914 over 50 boys are mentioned in the minutes as working in the pits. This is about 10 per cent of the total membership list between 1901 and 1914. The implications of this are that the club was having very little influence upon the employment prospects of many of the boys and that their situation was being determined almost entirely by the forces of supply and demand in the labour market. Indeed, the club was acting in this situation as an easy recruiting ground for the mines and in helping the boys with clothing and lodging was providing an indirect subsidy to the employers. The wages in the mines, compared to other possibilities was relatively high (averaging about 1s 8d per shift) and this more than any other factor probably persuaded the boys away from the alternative of street vending.

In a situation where poor relief was sought and provided only in the most extreme circumstances of destitution, and then only after considerable investigation and with much social stigma, it is unsurprising that the urban poor took a short-term view of opportunities to earn money (Stedman Jones, 1971). Wages were the primary concern. In many of the trades wages were often very low and frequently could not compete with the opportunities presented by unskilled work or street vending. Some of the boys refused to take the respectable and steady jobs offered through the auspices of the committee members simply because of this. Boys and their families could compare the possibility of earning 2/6 per week in the Co-operative store or 5/- per week as a slater, working under the direct supervision and control of foremen and managers, with the possibility of earning as much as 10/- per week selling newspapers without any interference from authority:

Mr Smith is . . . experiencing considerable trouble owing to the fact that apprentices' wages full time only amount to 3/1 per week, whereas the boys as street vendors, can make from 10/- to 15/- per week selling papers.
(Minutes, 1/4/09)

Young men and boys were seldom prepared either to make the sacrifice of the certainty of present gains for the uncertain possibility of a long-term regular wage or to sacrifice the personal independence which such a long-term investment implied.

Apprenticeships and training involved deferred gratification which could not be sustained by the family income, even if the boy himself was prepared to learn a trade. It was a luxury which families simply could not afford. The nature of the employment taken by boys, or their ability to stick to one particular job was not the main guiding principle for families. What was of concern was simply that the boys were earning their keep and contributing as much as possible to the family income:

The question of club members leaving their employment without giving the committee

satisfactory explanation was discussed – Mr Smith explained that he had great difficulty with these cases, and that as a rule the parents of the lads were chiefly to blame.
(Minutes, 10/8/11)

Sometimes to take regular employment implied work in both sectors for the boy concerned:
Robert Reekie 128 has been found employment at Vaux's Brewery as a Maltster at 7/- per week, he sells papers on Saturday mornings in order to help his home people. Reekie was formerly at Doxford's yard.
(Minutes, 7/10/09)

The main guiding principle of the club managers on the other hand, was not the wage but the principle of regular labour. They were concerned that the boys should view their jobs as a long-term situation wherein they might hope to 'do well' and through which they might attain a security of income and steadiness of habit which would enable them to gain access to 'respectable' working-class society. That success in changing attitudes was limited can be established from the absolute growth in newspaper selling at the outbreak of the First World War when the minutes report that boys could not be weaned away from this activity because the wages were so high (Minutes, 20/8/14; 3/9/14).

The different cultural perspectives regarding the definitions, meaning and purposes of work between East End families and the representatives of the club created tensions and conflicts which were indicative of class interests and differences. It is hard to imagine that boys and their parents were not informed about the conditions which they could expect within the labour market. On the basis of their own experience and the networks of communication in the community they would have been aware that conditions of work, whether within a trade or within the casual sector, were usually physically hard, frequently monotonous and boring, seldom rewarding and often dangerous. There are recorded instances of boys losing jobs found for them because they were not physically strong enough to undertake the work required. There are also cases of industrial injury and death recorded – two boys losing their lives aboard a ship owned by the management committee member, Mr Charlton, when it foundered in the Bay of Biscay (*Sunderland Daily Echo*, 28/12/11:3; Minutes, 18/1/12). The following case is indicative:
Martin Finn has left his employment owing to ill health. Mr Mann suggested that the boy should lie off for a week but Finn preferred to leave altogether as he did not feel strong enough for the work.
(Minutes, 15/2/12)

Martin Finn has started work at W. Thomas Summerbell's – printer at 4/6 per week.
(Minutes, 22/2/12)

Finn, owing to getting his hand hurt in a machine is laid off.
(Minutes, 7/3/12)

Martin Finn's (190) finger which was crushed at Messrs Summerbell's Printing works is quite useless and his mother is endeavouring to get compensation from Messrs Summerbell. Dr Illiff [honorary solicitor] has the matter in hand. The boy has been receiving 4/6 per week from his employers. Dr Bruce of the MonkWearmouth Hospital has reported that the finger may have to be amputated. Mr Routledge has offered to see Dr Bruce about the case.
(Minutes, 2/5/12)

Dr Illiff has agreed to accept £30 as lump sum compensation for Martin Finn's injury, the money to be paid into court until the lad is 21. Mr Smith has asked for £5.0.0 to be handed over for Finn's clothing and outfit, and Dr Illiff is endeavouring to arrange this.
(Minutes, 4/9/12)

Mr Charlton reported that the boy Finn had obtained employment at the Pit Prop Yard of Messrs Horsley but as he could not grasp the tools owing to his damaged finger he had to leave. Mr Charlton suggested that Finn might get engaged as a tram car conductor and he offered to make enquiries re same. Mr Lodwidge suggested that the boy might get employment in a time keeper's office.
  Mr Charlton also reported that another of our boys Richardson had started at W. Digby Nelsons slate yard and within 6 hours of starting had fallen 40 feet from a roof. He is now getting 5/- per week compensation and will probably by (sic) permanently crippled.
(Minutes, 24/10/12)

Both of the Finns are now working at Seaham Colliery and Mr Smith reports that he has had considerable trouble to get Martin Finn to work steadily since he recovered from his accident at Summerbell's.
(Minutes, 3/1/13)

For the majority of the poorest boys, work could have contained little of intrinsic value. Its worth lay primarily in its ability to provide the means of subsistence and where the worker was lucky, a little extra for leisure pursuits. Under these circumstances and in the face of the reality of the casualisation of employment, the response of some of the boys was to treat employment casually. They did not take the employment market too seriously except insofar as they needed the wages accruing from work. Outside periods of recession, when unemployment was a serious problem, they would seek work, gain work, lose work and change jobs in very short periods of time. They had no concept of a career and very little interest in present suffering for future gain. They would accept the benefits which the Lambton Street club offered in relation to accepting an employment opportunity, and just as easily would leave that situation for what might appear to their benefactors as a minor problem. This was nothing other than a rational response on the part of the boys to the conditions of the youth labour market and to their social and material circumstances. The work ethic advocated by the managers of the club simply did not seem to them appropriate to their situation (Stedman Jones, 1971). Training was not considered by most to be a serious option and education as experienced within school was perceived merely as a hindrance to the possibility of easing the poverty of the family sooner rather than later (Minutes, 22/2/06; Davin, 1997).

Conclusion

Finding places for young people within the labour market has seldom been solely about the benefits of work itself for the individual, or even about the requirement of the economy for skilled labour, although providers are keen to argue in these terms. There are inevitably other agendas concerned with social order, discipline and control which are associated particularly with negative assumptions about growing up in poor communities (Davies, 1986; Griffin, 1997). For the managers of the Sunderland Waifs Rescue Agency and Street Vendors' Club the practical help they wished to offer involved a public intervention in the lives of the poor which was validated by the argument that it was a means of addressing poverty through the instrument of work, diverting the younger generation away from the habits and values learned in the home and on the street.

The welfare interventions of those who managed and sponsored the club were motivated in the first instance by compassion and concern for the well-being of poor boys. In this context the economic recession of 1907 is instructive. As it hit the families of Sunderland's East End, the absolute absence of employment opportunities and the extent of the distress encountered led to a practical de-coupling of welfare and work in the club. For the duration of the recession, the management committee concentrated most of their energies upon the provision of food and clothing, opening a soup kitchen two nights a week and clothing boys in obvious need without reference to employment status or family attitudes.

Nevertheless, even at this time, the emotional response was constrained on the one hand by an awareness of the responsibilities involved in managing charitably donated funds and goods, and on the other hand by the political ideologies and sensibilities of the managers themselves in relation to the effects of charity upon the recipients. In their decision-making they were acutely aware of the public discourse of the period which considered uncontrolled charitable interventions to be both unethical and unhelpful to the poor. In order to maintain their public integrity and continue to benefit from subscriptions and fundraising activities, it was essential that the club be seen to be conforming to this dominant class biased view.

Decisions about the distribution of resources were unselfconsciously affected by the class power of the providers and without reference to the perspective of the recipients. However, when resources were distributed collectively, through the provision of the club, through treats and general benefits to the members, there was less tension or conflict than when individual need was at issue. It was through the allocation of individual help that class difference and tension became most acute.

Class differences were most obvious in relation to the question of work. It is clear from the minutes of the club that the managers used their power over the distribution of the resources of the club as a lever to encourage the boys into conforming with the attitudes and behaviour of a compliant labour force. Significantly, employers found it almost impossible to deliver the ideal which was sought in terms of regular, skilled work for the boys. However hard the club worked to encourage the boys to submit to work-based discipline, they had no control over the behaviour of employers and ultimately the attitude of the boys to work was shaped by their knowledge of the real situation rather than by what they were taught in the club. While the voices of the members of the club are absent from the minutes books, nevertheless, it is clear that not all the boys or their families were prepared to submit to the authority of either the club's managers or employers (who were sometimes the same people), and class based conflicts and misunderstandings were played out significantly around work and individual welfare issues between members and managers. It was here that some boys resisted efforts to control them, even in some cases at the expense of being denied badly needed clothing.

The story of the work of the Sunderland Waifs Rescue Agency and Street Vendors' Club suggests that linking welfare to work as a means of managing the behaviour of the recipients of welfare in relation to the needs of the employment market, has little chance of success when this is not matched by management of the behaviour and attitudes of employers. Those who depend upon welfare are not completely influenced in their attitudes and expectations by their material needs although they will often adjust short-term behaviour in the light of need. What is of as much significance is the reality of their relationships with the employment market and their understanding of what it can and cannot offer. Today some of the class-based issues apparent in the minutes of the Lambton Street boys' club are clearly still with us. Rather than ignore these issues, a more effective and just policy would attempt to address them and in doing so would de-couple welfare provision from moral exhortations and punitive strategies relating to 'willingness to work'.

Research for this paper was financed by the Leverhulme Trust.

Bibliography

Bell, E. Moberley (1942). *Octavia Hill*. London, Constable.

Bray, R. (1911). *Boy Labour and Apprenticeship*. London, Constable.

Davies, B. (1986). *Threatening Youth: Towards a national youth policy*. Milton Keynes, Open University Press.

Davin, A. (1997). *Growing Up Poor: Home, school and street in London 1870–1914*. London, Rivers Oram Press.

Griffin, C. (1997). 'Representatives of the Young', in Roche, J. and Tucker, S. (eds) *Youth in Society*. London, Sage.

Humphreys, R. (1995). *Sin, Organised Charity and the Poor Law in Victorian England*. London, St. Martin's Press.

Jeffs, T. and Spence, J. (2000). 'New Deal for Young People: Good deal or poor deal?' in *Youth and Policy*, No 66, Spring. Leicester, Youth Work Press.

Minutes Books of the Sunderland Waifs Rescue Agency and Street Vendors' Club, January 1902 to December 1913.

Montagu, L. (1904). 'The Girl in the Background' in Urwick, E. J. (ed) *Studies of Boy Life in Our Cities.* London, J. M. Dent.

Platt, A. M. (1972). *The Child Savers: The invention of delinquency.* London, University of Chicago Press.

Player, J. (1999). 'New Deal or Workfare Regime?' in *Youth and Policy,* No 64, Autumn. Leicester, Youth Work Press.

Rooff, M. (1972). *A Hundred Years of Family Welfare: A study of the Family Welfare Association (Formerly Charity Organisation Society) 1869–1969.* London, Michael Joseph.

Smith, J. (1951). *Fifty Years at Lambton Street.* Sunderland, Summerbell Printers.

Stedman Jones, G. (1971). *Outcast London.* Oxford, Oxford University Press.

Sunderland Daily Echo, 5/12/01; 3/01/02; 28/12/11, Sunderland.

Tedder, A. (2000). *Sunderland East End Revisited.* Sunderland, The People's Press.

Urwick, E. J. (1904). *Studies of Boy Life in Our Cities.* London, J. M. Dent.

Wagner, G. (1979). *Barnardo.* London, Weidenfield and Nicolson.

Walkowitz, J. R. (1996). *City of Dreadful Delight: Narratives of sexual danger in late Victorian London.* London, Virago.

Pearl Jephcott

Chapter seven

Gendering Young People – Work, Leisure and Girls' Clubs: The work of the National Organisation of Girls' Clubs and its successors 1911–1961

Annmarie Turnbull

This chapter arises from an exploration of the archives of the National Organisation of Girls' Clubs (NOGC) and its work with girls and young women[1]. The historiography of youth work to date is often either dogmatic or confused on the role of sex and gender in the work. In exploring the specific role of an organisation that initially espoused work only with girls, but gradually came to encourage and promote mixed youth work, a more complex picture of perceptions on gender and the requirements of the sexes emerges, and this suggests the need to reformulate some earlier assumptions about the gendered nature of work with young people. From my exploration of NOGC's records it appears that as the organisation developed over 50 years, it increasingly lost its radical and feminist focus, aligned itself with the status quo and became more limited in its interventions with regard to girls, and to gender roles in general. It changed from an organisation with a wide range of social concerns relating to working-class girls and women, to one with a narrower focus on vague notions of promoting girls' individual personality development, particularly as this related to their future roles as wives and mothers. In order to trace this development the chapter explores two themes: the organisation's contribution to girls' employment and to their leisure time.

Overview of NOGC

The 18 women who met in the offices of the Honor Club for Working Girls in Great Titchfield Street, London, on 1st February 1911, were convinced of the need for middle-class leisured women to work to improve the lot of their working, and this meant largely working-class, sisters. Their antecedents were threefold; the powerful traditions of Victorian religion-based female philanthropy; the more recent feminist and proto-feminist organisations which focused specifically on the education, work and welfare of women and girls; and to a lesser extent, the growing labour movement. There had been girls' clubs in existence, particularly in towns and cities, for many years and there was a flourishing girls' club movement in the USA (Murolo, 1997). But in Britain there was no coordinating body to drive the work forward. The women who met that day quickly established their objectives in meeting as the formation of a coordinating and facilitating organisation, rather than the founding of specific clubs to serve girls directly. It was to be 'a larger and a constructive organisation on behalf of girls' clubs' interests' and wanted to focus on 'developing and embracing industrial and social work under one head' (NOGC, Minute Book, 1/2/11). Thus from the outset it was aimed at working girls and it wished to embrace all aspects of their lives.

From an analysis of its records it is sometimes possible to pinpoint the precise moment when and the reasons why an organisation shifts its focus. Here it is not possible to outline in detail the vicissitudes of NOGC over time and its evolution into its present incarnation Youth Clubs UK. Instead what follows is three snapshots of periods in its history. These are the years from its inception to the end of World War 1; the 1930s, when it was called the National Council of Girls' Clubs; and the 1940s and 1950s when it had three reincarnations, first as the National Association of Girls' Clubs and Mixed Clubs (1944), then as the National Association of Mixed Clubs and Girls' Clubs (1953). It then became the National Association of Youth Clubs in 1961.

To 1918 – employment issues

The working girl was the organisation's focus and from the outset it concerned itself, both as a central body, and via the large numbers of girls' clubs affiliated to it, with a range of industrial and other employment issues. Its founders were convinced that women would play an increasing role in industrial and political life and that girls would need help to meet these new roles. The scope of its involvement was wide. It petitioned to obtain a one-hour dinnertime for all working girls and women. It sent deputations to the Prime Minister on the need for rest rooms for women working in exhibition halls like Earls Court and White City and for more women factory inspectors. It provided leaflets and speakers on the new National Insurance Act urging the involvement of girls and women, not only via contacts in the clubs, but by organising women to speak with working girls outside laundries in the early morning and at dining rooms in work dinner hours.

Its line on labour was, on the whole, progressive. It collected reported infringements of the Factory Act by employers from working girls and forwarded them to the Industrial Law Committee of the Women's Industrial Council for investigation. Via its journal, *Girls' Club News*, it urged girls to join the Anti-Sweating League. It advertised the merits of the Women's Co-operative Guild's campaigns for a minimum wage. However, reflecting the essentially moderate line (by contemporary feminist standards) of the executive members, and particularly of the two principal founders, Lily Montagu and Edith Glover, it was more equivocal on equal pay for women's war work (*NOGC Office Minute Book*, 28/10/15). Nevertheless it supported the women's suffrage campaign by working 'in close touch' with the London Society for Women's Suffrage. It also worked directly with the club members on employment issues, providing lecturers to individual clubs and conferences on topics such as industrial law, standards of wages and the Truck Act.

A major focus of the organisation's work was the employment and skills of the women club leaders. It acted as an employment agency both for volunteers and paid workers in the clubs and provided conferences for club workers with attendances of up to 80 women. In 1915 it negotiated and financed a training course at the London School of Economics for women leaders (*NOGC Minute Book*, 28/10/15).

Unemployment was regarded as an evil for girls and the *Annual Report* for 1913 notes one tale of the NOGC's pioneering of employment for girls:

> One girl called at the office to enquire for a French class to attend in the afternoon, because she was frequently alone in a flat from morning to midnight, and felt 'half mad with loneliness'. She was traced later under terribly sad conditions and re-instated as a worker owing to her chance enquiry at the office.

(Annual Report, 1913, 3)

The war, of course, temporarily ended unemployment for women and the *Annual Report* for 1918 explained:

> Since 1915 the NOGC has hardly heard of a girl out of work, in fact much has been done to encourage the girls to give up such work that was not of immediate value to the country, and enter into any and every department of labour for which their help was needed.

(Annual Report, 1918, 13)

To 1918 – leisure Issues

In the clubs a wide range of leisure activities were promoted. There was class teaching in remedial exercise, drill, morris dancing, artificial flower making, metal work, drama, singing, sewing, embroidery, wood carving, sculpture, painting, millinery and basket work. Besides industrial lectures, NOGC organised speakers on topics as diverse as foreign travel, recreation and religion, and food and indigestion. The wish to increase girls' knowledge of social issues was evident in the constant concern of the executive members, particularly Edith Glover, to promote newspaper or citizen classes on current affairs. In anticipation of the Representation of the People Act of 1917 and of partial female suffrage in 1919, there was a widespread interest within women's organisations in exploring the notion of sexed citizenship (Caine, 1997, 197). NOGC provided a syllabus for citizen classes and, on occasions, teachers for these classes (enlisting the aid of the LSE on one occasion). Rates and taxes, the Home Rule Bill, laws relating to shops and the contentious issue of purity were all discussed in the clubs. The account of a demonstration citizen class run for club leaders reveals both the range of issues the leaders were discussing in clubs and the ideological position on gender roles of one of its founders. Edith Glover was propounding social and economic relationships between the sexes founded on traditional sex role demarcations, but at the same time arguing for a more public role for women. This was a powerful current within the Victorian and Edwardian women's movement.

> *There was no set subject for discussion such as there is usually when more time can be devoted to the class, but each girl stated her opinions and difficulties on some special question which had excited her attention during the week, and the leader approved, criticised and explained. The subjects covered were women's suffrage, shop hours, the Insurance Act and boy cooks. For the last Mrs Glover was responsible; she had been greatly exercised that morning because the county council was teaching boys to cook and taking away from girls work which ought to remain peculiarly theirs. Mrs Hepburn said that the best cooks had been men, but Mrs Glover, standing up for her sex in her chosen role of class member, insisted that the council should not encourage such ideas and should train women to be really good cooks instead of helping the boys to compete against them.*

(*Girls' Club News*, February, 1913, 9)

In addition to classes, lectures and conferences for girls and workers, NOGC promoted a Guild of Health that, on request, supplied dressing cases, nail cleaners and toothbrushes to clubs. In the summer months outings, often hosted by London ladies, and rambles were organised. Between June and August 1918 it was reported that 1,551 girls and 67 of their leaders had attended Saturday afternoon rambles. Given a seaside bungalow by a benefactor, NOGC employed a superintendent there and in 1913, its first year, sent 592 girls on a week's holiday. They came from the clubs in groups of between 10 and 25 and were charged 7 shillings each.

Through connections with the Old Vic Theatre, a Shakespeare scheme was organised, with monthly socials at the theatre and Shakespeare societies in the clubs. The St Celia Singing competition and Festival for Working Girls was promoted annually. Although competition was a widespread activity in many of the clubs' leisure activities, it was, and was to remain, a contentious method of working in the clubs. Competition was chosen as the theme for the Club Leaders' Conference of 1912 and in the same year one contributor to *Girls' Club News* noted:

> *We have not been in for many competitions for we think more enjoyment is got out of a class where the exercises, songs, and other work are not set, leaving the girls to study what they care for most.*

(*Girls' Club News*, No 4, June 1912, 1)

So, there was a wide range of concerns encompassing employment and leisure as well as traditional women's home work.

To the 1930s

The 1920s saw many tensions in the organisation, which was both trying to involve itself in specific aspects of club work, and to address national girl (and women) related issues. This decade saw the resignation of the two founders, at least one of whom believed that the organisation had outlived its usefulness as a coordinating body for the girls' club movement and of Nelly Levy who from the first meeting had worked in the central office and had risen to become the general secretary in 1922. She had risen from earning £80 a year to become the general secretary in 1922, earning £300, but was then lured by Lily Montagu to work in her own club[2].

While some of the philanthropic upper-class women of the executive remained, the organisation's direction was increasingly influenced by a new type of worker – the well-educated, paid and sometimes trained girls' club leader or organiser. When, aged 27, Pearl Jephcott was appointed as organiser of one of the affiliated unions, the Birmingham Union of Girls' Clubs, she was a history graduate with experience as a club leader. She made an excellent contribution to the promotion and coordination of the city's girls work and was subsequently employed by NOGC, first as a regional organiser and later as publications officer (Turnbull, 2000).

The 1930s, then, might have seen the girls' club movement flourishing and indeed Rooff's survey of clubs in 1935 implies that it was (Rooff, 1935). Mass unemployment peaked at 22.5 per cent in 1932, but that it occurred only in some areas of the country alongside relative prosperity in others, meant that there were a wide variety of issues arising from girls' differentiated employment and unemployment experiences, across the nation and over the decade (Stevenson and Cook, 1994, 317)[3]. The post-war baby boom also meant there were many more adolescent girls (and boys) than previously. Numbers of school leavers burgeoned in 1933, 1934 and 1935. However, in comparison to the pre-war situation, the organisation's work in these years appeared too narrow in scope. Why? Full suffrage in 1928 had established women's constitutional equality with men, but by the end of the decade, as one historian of feminism has argued:

> *Although the number of women MPs grew, if very slowly and with constant setbacks, their feminist consciousness seems to have declined with its decline in the world outside. Eleanor Rathbone, perhaps the most important feminist in Parliament at that time, became absorbed in the family allowances campaign and in foreign affairs, and this illustrates, perhaps as well as anything, the prevailing mood of the time.*
> (Banks, 1981, 220–221)

Rathbone was a vice-president, but this symbolic involvement of a feminist in the organisation appears to be all that remained of the girls' club movement's earlier zeal in its work for girls and women, and of its links to organised feminism. It had lost its all-embracing character.

The 1930s – employment issues

Although by 1931, one in three employed girls under 18 worked in industry (Jephcott, 1943, 58) the organisation had moved from direct involvement in economic and workplace issues. Its employment department did continue to be involved in employment issues for club workers.

While from its founding, the organisation had claimed to be non-political, its early work was often explicitly political. Increasingly, lip service was paid to the idea of a broad politicising of girls with regard to their place in society, and the problems even this posed for the clubs were frequently seen to outweigh the possibilities. As one anonymous contributor to *Girls' Club Journal* (Girls' Clubs and Politics, *Girls' Club Journal*, 1927, 90)[4] bemoaned:

A club girl's life is a very full one, and when there is the opportunity of expressing herself in singing, drilling and acting, she has little time or inclination for politics.

An interesting journal article on The Club and Communism vividly illustrates the limits of the movement's political consciousness at this time.

The power to combat communism is, first and last and all the time, LOVE, and the body that loves and works among young people for the cause it believes in most, is the one that is going to be the dominant power in England. Therefore, if we really believe in a gospel of love, we must call all our forces against the doctrine of hate which meets the girls with such specious promises of prosperity.

(I. Piper, 'The Club and Communism', *Girls' Club Journal*, Vol. XIX, No 58, 1928, 11–12)

The organisation's first aim for 1929 was 'to unite local club unions and national societies which have for their primary object the spiritual, social, recreational, physical, educational and industrial advancement of working girls'. This shows how far employment-related issues had slipped in its priorities. There was still an awareness of work-related issues and inequities, but this was very limited. In 1930 concern was voiced regarding domestic servants spending their free time in station waiting rooms. In 1933 there was worry about girls, who to take advantage of cheap early rail fares into London, had to stand outside their still-closed workplaces for lengthy periods. But despite the fifth aim 'to undertake investigations and to arrange deputations to government departments and public bodies such as the local education authority, in connection with social or industrial amelioration, and to bring the club movement into closer touch with such bodies', there was no clear targeting of employers or government for action (certainly nothing appeared in annual reports or minute books). It was appreciated that economic conditions impacted upon social conditions and hence on the capabilities of the club movement, for example, in the Government's 'special areas', but little seems to have been made of the connection. In 1935 when Jephcott was working as an organiser in Durham, it was noted:

One great difficulty met with, particularly in Durham, in some of the isolated mining villages, but not common in the towns, is that of the apathy of the young people and their inability to sustain the first enthusiasm. Perhaps the following quotation from one of our organisers will go a long way towards explaining this:

> *The main difficulties with which we have to contend are dirt, continual dirt, bad premises and illness. Many of the girls look and seem undernourished and are constantly having minor illnesses. When you visit an absent member you constantly find one of the family ill in bed in the living room of the house.*

(Annual Report, 1935/1936, 18–19)

But it does not seem that the forthright campaigning, the lobbying and pressure group politics that had characterised the past were ever employed. Noting and reporting seemed to be the order of the day. The internal concerns of the club movement for the lack of discipline of the girls and the problem of attracting 'the outsider' who avoided the club altogether, were the paramount concerns. There seems some irony in the National Council of Girls' Club's symbol – a signpost and the legend 'To a Fuller Life for Greater Service.'

There are no signs on the post. Which way was a girl to go and who and what was she to serve?

The 1930s – leisure issues

In 1930 it was still assumed within the organisation that girl school leavers and young women would enter employment. That year's *Annual Report* noted:

> *Because of trade depression and unemployment girls' clubs are more needed than at any previous period in the history of the movement . . . Unemployed girls need their clubs more than others so that they may keep themselves spiritually, mentally and physically fit and be able to return to work at the earliest opportunity.*

(Annual Report, 1930, 7)

But by 1932 the organisation had started to concern itself primarily and overwhelmingly with leisure, whether enforced or freely chosen:

> *The clubs . . . make a special effort to allow the unemployed girls to take part in the normal activities of the clubs so that they may not feel that the fact of being out of work in any way separates them from their fellows.*

(*Annual Report*, 1932, 6)

Ironically the wish to avoid stigmatising the unemployed girl may have moved the organisation and the movement further towards a conception of women that was increasingly leisure and home focused. The growing impact of psychology on education and welfare was also moving it to an emphasis on individualism. The use of leisure was 'an opportunity for the development of her personality' (ibid).

A general trend towards a concern with the physical affected much of Europe in the inter-war period. Cycling, rambling, camping, physical fitness, sports and youth hostelling flourished (Stevenson and Cook, 1994, 35).

Undoubtedly spurred by the grants offered under the 1937 Physical Training and Recreation Act, physical training and physical health appear to have been the main issue of concern for the council during the decade. From 1934 the council's new symbol showed the way.

In 1930 two physical training organisers were appointed. In 1931 the council was promoting camping holidays and by 1934 it was employing physical training organisers to work both across the nation and specifically for the Lancashire Keep-fit Movement (with funding from the Pilgrim Trusts). Of the 19,437 letters and circulars the council claimed were sent out that year, 45 per cent (8,708) concerned physical training.

The organisers were well aware of the potential pitfalls of physical activities in girls' clubs and discussed these at length in their reports. Among concerns were issues as diverse as the use of rallies, displays and festivals as opposed to competitions and tests – the former were growing in popularity; the use of music, 'the real value of a physical training class is very much lessened if music is used' we hear, and 'the tendency towards tap and chorus dancing . . . which can be very vulgar' (*Annual Report*, 1933/1934, 22). The term 'drill' was not recommended while a 'keep-fit' or 'slimming' class was, 'although the actual work taken may be the same' (*Annual Report*, 1935, 21).

The other two priorities of the movement at this time were hobbies and the ubiquitous, but perhaps increased, emphasis on crafts – that is mothercraft, needlecraft and housecraft. An article by Alison Dobbs, the organising secretary of the council implored:

> There is one thing which we ought to make sure of, namely, that every single member in a club learns to do at least one thing well. This may be a hobby or a really useful craft.

(The Development of Club Work, *Girl's Club Journal*, Vol. XXV, No 76, 1934, 2)

The 1940s and 1950s – employment and leisure

The war brought a renewed impetus to youth work. Circular 1486, *The Youth Service After the War* spoke forcefully, if vaguely, of the 'serious menace to youth' war conditions brought. The solution was the 'the better use of leisure, on which the welfare of youth largely depends'. While the 'unduly long hours, often on work of a dull and arduous nature' were acknowledged, they were not to be a focus of youth work; instead 'constructive outlets for their leisure hours and for voluntary national service' were to be promoted (Board of Education, 1943).

The organisation's Executive War Time Committee responded to the call for service by taxing Pearl Jephcott and her colleagues with the development of Service Cadet Companies for 14 to 16-year-olds and 16 to 20-year-olds. Unlike the male pre-service units these did not have the support of Government war departments, but rose on demand from various organisations for girls including girls' clubs[5].

The companies involved the girl cadets in weekly voluntary service and weekly training in a predictable range of subjects – first aid, fire fighting, wartime cooking, household repairs, child welfare and secretarial work. A 17-year-old Wolverhampton Cadet reported:

> *We choose as our training nursing . . . or swimming and we are sending helpers to the Eye Infirmary . . . and the Boys' Club Canteen and are running our own allotment. We feel we are really doing our bit, we all agree it's great fun.*
> (*Annual Report*, 1941/1942, 3)

There was a great deal of wartime activity in the clubs including 'a noticeable increase in serious activities' (ibid, 6) and many new clubs were opened including war workers clubs. Mixed clubs saw a marked growth: 'Clubs for girls only are out of date,' said the *Lancashire Organiser* in 1941 (ibid, 5). Nevertheless the *Annual Reports* suggest that, by the war's end, NOGC was uncertain of its aims. The 1946 report notes: 'This is indeed one of the most difficult times to be young – and it is hard to know how to assess the situation at the moment' (*Annual Report*, 1945/1946, 25).

Speculating on the future, one wartime report had suggested that more emphasis on 'the girls' special provision of domestic work' and on marriage and future family would be 'particularly necessary in view of the need for larger families during (the) next three decades if the birth rate is to be maintained' (*Annual Report*, 1941/1942, 9). With the post-war trend to earlier marriage and motherhood this pro-natalist line was adopted in girls' club work, albeit usually implicitly (Tinkler, 1994).

The world of employment became invisible. In 1948 an article discussing where NAGC and MC's work went on is unintentionally ironic in its depiction of the industrial world. The work took place 'in factories like March Youth Club in Cambridge, which meets in a disused factory and garden which were borrowed by the committee and cleaned and decorated by them' (*Annual Report*, 1947/1948, 10).

Two years later the organisation's new aims show significant changes: there is a final severing of links to women and girls' employment and an equal commitment to boys and girls. The distinctive focus on the special needs of girls was lost:

> *The aim of the Association shall be to help girls and boys through leisure time activities so to develop their physical mental and spiritual capacities that they may grow to full maturity as individuals and members of society.*
> (*Annual Report*, 1948/1949, Foreword)

From 1952 the Association's education adviser, Josephine Macalister Brew (see chapter 13), made links with industry in developing courses for working girls which were run at the Association's holiday homes. But while the early girls' club workers had been explicitly concerned with the present, with bettering current conditions for women at work and providing improvement and enjoyment outside, her focus was on girls' future responsibilities as wives and mothers.

Of the first Girls in Industry courses it was reported:

> *With few exceptions these girls look forward eagerly to marriage and children, and we feel strongly that if they can have one week in which they are encouraged to think seriously of the*

importance of their lives as women, and the duty they have to equip themselves to be the good wives and mothers they all desire to become, we shall be contributing something to the future well-being of society.
(*Annual Report*, 1952/1953, 10)

The courses' mix of current affairs, speech, deportment and grooming all aimed, as one employer explained, to raise the self-confidence of the girls, thereby 'enhancing their value as employees' (*Annual Report*, 1963/1964, 12). By contrast when equivalent courses were started for boys the aims were to encourage endeavour and instil characteristics of leadership. Financed by the King George's Jubilee Trust and later by the Nuffield Foundation the courses ran throughout the decade and into the 1960s. Sandra Wood, a secretary, described her course in wholly positive terms:

Then there were lessons on deportment which culminated in our being individually assessed as we walked down the broad oak stairs, attempted to sit down gracefully and made a smiling exit from the room. In conjunction with these efforts to make us more graceful were some talks on good grooming and the art of make-up.

She ended her account,

We had been mixing with girls who had completely different interests and backgrounds from our own and had learned to accept their ideas and realise that our views weren't the only ones that counted. New interests were stimulated, new friends made, and many of us learned that people are interested to hear what we have to say and so gained self-confidence. If we were able to take just one of these things into our everyday working lives, I know that our week at Avon Tyrrell was a week very well spent.
(*Annual Report*, 1963/1964, 13)

In 1950, along with astronomy and filmmaking, charm school had been classed as an 'out-of-the-ordinary' activity in the clubs, yet only four years later the lead article in *Club Leaders' Notes* advocated the club charm school as:

A most popular activity for adolescent girls . . . culminating in a grand final competition at the close of the course to find 'the most charming girl in the Club'.
(Katherine Lewis, 'The Club Charm School', *Club Leaders' Notes*, Vol 3, No 4, 1954, 1)

In this period the organisation that had started with a wide focus on the needs of females and a commitment to bringing them together in groups, increasingly came to find girls in girls' clubs a problem. This was a strong perception, reported often (Macalister Brew, 1943; Jephcott, 1943; Ette, 1949). The 1949 *Annual Report* noted:

It is possible to detect certain situations in clubs which present problems which, so far, have found no solution. One of them undoubtedly is that of activities for girls. This occurs both in the good clubs for girls and in the good mixed club. At this age the girl does not easily arrive at the self-discipline required for self-education; nor can she always see that an individual contribution of some sort of discipline is required for the production of community fun. In other words she

can be hard to work with and harder to play with. She doesn't want to join tonight. Why not? Oh, well, she just doesn't. An hour later, perfectly sweetly, she will want to join in but it may be too late. The instructor is already packing his tools, or the discussion group is ready to give place to dancing. What patience is here required . . . and with a similar problem too: for girl members' attendance is not as reliable as that of boys. But in this, as the leader knows, the girl herself is rarely at fault. Any emergency at home, be it the arrival of auntie or the arrival of a baby, calls for making use of the girls in the household. This is quite a natural state of affairs but it sometimes plays havoc with the club arrangements. On certain evenings a stranger to the club might well go in and see a host of boys actively engaged in one thing or another and a seeming absence of all activity among the girls.
(*Annual Report*, 1949/1950, 22–23)

On reading this, one is tempted to ask were the clubs for the girls, or the girls for the clubs? Certainly by the mid 50s Pearl Jephcott, who had left the organisation in 1945, was clear that girls and clubs were no longer compatible. Her research showed that girls found little to attract them in clubs, whether single-sex or mixed. She found 50s girls were absorbed in experimenting with their own appearance 'and this they could best do at home, aided perhaps by one or two onlookers' (Jephcott, 1954, 114). The mixed clubs themselves were often responsible for the alienation of young women, she argued:

When a mixed unit had to cut down its programme it was the girls' activities which were jettisoned. The girls were alleged to be more difficult to understand that (sic) the boys, less ready to take part in group activities and altogether less clubable. Moreover, to move to more urgent matters, the police had much less trouble with the girls; so that even the claim that your organisations stave off delinquency weakened the cause of the weaker sex.
(ibid, 116)

Females were abandoning the clubs, not only as members but also as leaders. There was always a shortage of leaders, male and female, but by the 50s less than 30 per cent were women. Of 1,506 leaders only 451 were women (*Annual Report*, 1950/1951, 8).

Conclusion

The cover of the *Annual Report* for 1962–63 shows four club members 'helping to build a club for a new town'. The photograph depicts two girls in aprons watching two boys at work on the building. It is an image of female passivity. A pioneer of girls' clubs, Emmeline Pethick Lawrence, recalled in her memoirs the sad state of many women's lives at the end of the 19th century and her conviction to change this through the club movement. 'We could only vow that we would put such a spirit into their daughters that they would never submit to being so brow-beaten' (Pethwick Lawrence, 1938, p78). At the beginning of the 20th century Lily Montagu had written a warning to girls' club workers:

They are inclined to ignore the industrial life, they like to forget the grim truth that if girls

work for less than a living wage in a vitiated atmosphere, they are not likely to become the strong, self-controlled women whom we desire the clubs to train.
(Unwick, 1904, 249–50)

But by the 1960s the National Association of Mixed Clubs and Girls Clubs had lost touch with women's work worlds. Its conceptions of the possibilities of gender were limited and limiting for females. It had appointed its first male chair, John Wolfenden, and an organisation, which in 1911 had argued for a statutory one-hour dinner break for all women workers, had become one in which female club leaders were instructed on 'how to make a good cup of tea' (*Club Leaders' Notes*, Vol 2, No 2, 1952). Less than 15 per cent of the Association's affiliated clubs were girls' clubs: the girls' club movement had died[6].

Footnotes

[1] My thanks to the staff of Youth Clubs UK for the hospitality they gave me while I was working with their archives.

[2] For further information on the work of Montagu and Levy, see Spence 1998.

[3] The authors broadly assess the experiences of young people in the period. See also their discussion of youth unemployment p 70–71.

[4] The Christian-based organ of another overseeing organisation, the Federation of Working Girls' Clubs, *Girls' Club Journal* was being published in cooperation with the National Council of Girls' Clubs by 1933.

[5] For an interesting discussion of sex differences here and the repercussions of this, see Ette, 1949, p30–34.

[6] Of 2,584 affiliated clubs only 364 were girls' clubs in 1959.

Bibliography

Banks, O. (1981). *Faces of Feminism: A study of feminism as social movement*. New York, St Martin's Press.

Board of Education (1943). *Circular 1486. The Youth Service After the War. A report of the Youth Advisory Committee*, HMSO.

Booton, F. (1985). *Studies in Social Education, Vol 1 1860–1890*. Hove, Sussex, Benfield Press.

Bunt S. (1975). *Jewish Youth Work in Britain: Past, present and future*. London, Bedford Square Press, National Council of Social Service.

Bunt, S. and Gargrave, R. (1980). *The Politics of Youth Clubs*. Leicester, National Youth Bureau.

Caine, B. (1997). *English Feminism, 1780–1980*. Oxford, Oxford University Press.

Carpenter, V. and Young, K. (1986). *Coming in From the Margins; Youth work with girls and young women*. Leicester, National Association of Youth Clubs.

Club Leaders' Notes (1952, 1954).

Ette, G. (1949). *For Youth Only*. London, Faber and Faber.

Girls' Club News (1912, 1913).

Girls' Club Journal (1927, 1928, 1934).

Jephcott, P. (1943). *Clubs for Girls*. London, Faber and Faber.

Jephcott, P. (1954). *Some Young People*. London, George Allen and Unwin.

Macalister Brew, J. (1943). *Clubs and Club Making.* Bickling, Kent, University of London Press.

Milson, F. (1970). *Youth Work in the 1970s.* London, Routledge and Kegan Paul.

Montagu, L. (1904). 'The Girl in the Background' in Urwick, E. J.(ed) *Studies of Boy Life in Our Cities.* London, J. M. Dent.

Murolo, P. (1997). *The Common Ground of Womanhood; Class, gender and working girls' clubs, 1884–1928.* Urbana and Chicago, University of Illinois Press.

NOGC, *Annual Reports, Minute Books* (1/2/11 to 30/12/64).

Pethwick Lawrence, E. (1938). *My Part in a Changing World.* London, Gollancz.

Rooff, M. (1935). *Youth and Leisure: A survey of girls' organisations in England and Wales.* Edinburgh, T. and A. Constable.

Spence, J. (1998). 'Lily Montagu. A Short Biography' in *Youth and Policy, No 60, pp 73–84.*

Stevenson, J. and Cook, C. (1994). *Britain in the Depression: Society and politics, 1929–1939.* London, Longman.

Tinkler, P. (1994). 'An All-Round Education: The Board of Education's policy for the leisure-time training of girls, 1939–1950' in *History of Education,* Vol 23, No 4, pp 385–403.

Turnbull, A. (2000). 'Giving Girls a Voice: Pearl Jephcott's work for young people' in *Youth and Policy*, No 66, pp 88–100.

Frank Caws, club founder

Chapter eight

The Impact of the First World War on the Development of Youth Work: The case of the Sunderland Waifs Rescue Agency and Street Vendors' Club

Jean Spence

> *Who does not feel that since August 1914 England has in many ways broken with her past and entered an entirely new epoch in her history, marked by transformations of every kind, so that when the day of peace arrives, be it soon or late, we shall be confronted at home by an altogether altered situation.*
> (W. H. Dawson, (1917), quoted in Marwick (1965), 135)

Despite the fundamental changes wrought in British society by the First World War, there is little in the existing historical literature which indicates the nature and extent of its impact upon the direction and development of youth work. When it is discussed, the war is held responsible mainly for lost opportunities in the development of youth work on the national stage. In particular, the creation of the Juvenile Organisations Committees in 1916 and Fisher's Education Act of 1918 are noted as policy moments which contained potential lost through an absence of political will and financial support during the 1920s and 30s (Eager, 1953, 396; Macalister Brew, 1957, 122; Jeffs, 1979, 11–12; Davies, 1999, 15). Yet the records of the Lambton Street Fellowship Centre in Sunderland, recorded in the minutes of the management committee meetings, suggest that the impact of the war was not simply one of loss. It radically diverted the course of the work in the club, significantly redefining boundaries, methods and content.

Some of the changes were obviously common throughout the country. For example, describing the effects of war on the Shaftesbury Club in Birkenhead, Dawes, talks about the loss of life, the militarisation of organised youth work, the opening up of the club premises for community use and the change of name from The Shaftesbury Club for Street Boys and Working Lads to the Shaftesbury Boys' Club in 1916 (1975, 103–5). All these features are apparent in Sunderland between 1914 and 1939 and can be noted from a straightforward reading of the records.

However, a deeper interrogation of the historical evidence, which includes reading the silences and gaps in the minutes and a comparison between the pre-war and post-war situations, suggest more complex changes. Organisationally the balance of power shifted between middle-class providers and working-class recipients and also between the voluntary middle-class management committee and the worker in charge of the day-to-day running of the club. This shift was reflected in practice in a move away from social case work in favour of the distinctive features of collective welfare and recreation which is associated with modern youth work and the process of clarification continued throughout the 1920s and 30s. The impetus for change came not from policy, but from the day-to-day necessities of maintaining the club and the negotiated interests of those involved within a particular organisational and social framework. The model of youth club work which evolved in this situation set the scene for the manner in which statutory youth work evolved after 1939.

The immediate impact of the war

Like everywhere else, the outbreak of the war seemed to catch those associated with the Lambton Street Club almost unawares, even though there had been threats and rumours gathering for some time (Pankhurst, 1987). The club had been closed for three weeks during the superintendent's holiday and the Scouts' camp and when they returned on 6th August war had been declared the previous day. Although somewhat brief, the minutes of the management committee meeting that evening proceed as though nothing had happened, with discussion about the rates, attendance figures and the summer camp. However, in the penultimate paragraph, after a report that 20 Scouts had learned to swim during the summer, we read:

> He (the Scoutmaster) suggested that the Scouts would probably be called upon to render their services in connection with the war, and the committee agreed that the boys should be allowed to serve should the occasion offer.

(Minutes, 6/8/14)

Two weeks later, the second item of the meeting, under the heading 'The War: Our first contribution', reads:

> Mr Smith stated that 25 of our boy scouts are serving as despatch bearers and messengers in connection with the troops stationed here. Also that 15 of the institute members are serving as territorials.

Later in the same meeting:

> Mr Smith reports that the boys are very busy selling newspapers and that some of them make as much as 6/- and 7/- per week.

(Minutes, 20/8/14)

In these three minutes the scene is set for much of what was to follow. Firstly, the Scouts became increasingly important within the life of the club, a change of emphasis characteristic of the national growth in uniformed organisations consequent upon the war. This was to deeply affect club life afterwards. Secondly, increasing numbers of older (institute) members and ex-members joined the forces, many of them to become casualties of the conflict. This earned them a level of social respect never previously experienced and changed the terms of their own relationships and the relationships of their families with the club and its sponsors. Thirdly, although the central purpose of the club since its inception had been to address the problem of casual boy labour, to encourage boys to attend school regularly and to take jobs which would train them for a trade, the labour market conditions of the war totally undermined this approach. During the war there was a *de facto* lowering of the school leaving age in order to enable boys to replace those joining the forces. Tawney (1924) estimates that 800,000 young people were prematurely pushed out of school and into work. As the war progressed, it therefore became increasingly difficult for the management committee to have any practical influence at all either upon school attendance or upon the work which the boys undertook.

The Scouts

The Waifs Rescue Agency and Street Vendors' club had seen the development of one of the first scouting troops in Britain. An influential business in the town at the beginning of the century (which closed in 1999), was the Vaux brewery. Major Vaux had soldiered with Baden Powell in the Boer War and played host to him when he arrived in Sunderland to speak about Scouting in the local YMCA in January 1908. Vaux was clearly excited by Baden Powell's ideas and within days he had visited the Lambton Street Club with a suggestion for developing the 'Scouting scheme' as he understood it. The start of Scouting in Sunderland is recorded in some detail in the minutes (20/2/08; 27/2/08; 19/3/08; 26/3/08).

However, after an initial flurry of excitement and interest during which time the Vaux Own Scouts were established, they ceased to occupy any major part of the discussions of the management committee and apart from noting for example that they had enjoyed a camp in the Grindon grounds of the Vaux estate, or had attended a parade the existence of the Scouts went virtually without comment. They were incidental to the main philanthropic work of the club. Vaux, on the other hand, expanded his interest out from the Scouts and made intermittent forays into the general work of the club. He became a key, if somewhat volatile provider of 'treats' and 'entertainments' for all the boys.

A photograph of the Vaux Own Scouts in the archives of the club dated 1913, shows a group of almost casually dressed boys and young men lounging in relaxed poses. Then in May 1914 the minutes note that the Scouts had not been making very good progress, that the Scoutmaster had resigned and that it was 'extremely desirable to reorganise the Scouts'(14/5/14). In response to this discussion, a Scout's committee, operating as a sub-committee was formed with its own members and its own finance. The timing of this reorganisation of the Vaux Own Scouts was fortuitous, providing a basis for continuing youth work during and immediately after the war in a manner which reflected the mood of the country and which demonstrated the allegiance of those involved in the club to the dominant values of the moment. This was, perhaps, a not insignificant issue in view of the fact that the club's superintendent was to gain exemption from military service for most of the war and the secretary for the whole of the war. Another photograph of the Scouts dated 1915, shows Major Vaux in the centre in full military dress. The Scouts themselves are in uniform and standing to attention in military order. Meanwhile the minutes noted the participation of the Scouts in 'recruiting demonstrations' (17/9/14), the centrality of 'military drill, physical drill and gymnastics' in their programme (15/10/14), and their efforts to raise funds for the 7th DLI Prisoner of War Fund (17/6/15). In July 1915, it was reported to the management committee that:

> Major Cuthbert Vaux has presented our Scouts with a big drum.

and that:

> A new troop of Scouts is being formed up out of the raw material, and that these boys are being trained up by Mr R.C. Gowdy . . .
> (Minutes, 1/7/15)

As the war progressed, the Scouts moved to the centre of the agenda of the main management committee meetings and to the forefront of the practical work:

> One hundred and twenty street vendors were entertained to tea at Roker on Saturday afternoon. The boys marched down to the North Sands led by the bugle band of Vaux's Own Scouts.
> (Sunderland Daily Echo, 25/9/16)

In particular, Douglas Caws, the secretary whose exemption from active military service was probably due to his personal responsibilities as sole provider for a widowed mother and four unmarried sisters, directed his voluntary energies primarily towards Scouting. After Jim Smith, the superintendent joined the forces in 1917, Caws took personal responsibility for keeping the club open and, perhaps partly as an expression of his own frustrated military ambitions, concentrated almost exclusively upon Scouting. By February 1918, Caws was expressing ideas that the general work should be more disciplined and involve organising the boys into military style troops:

> Mr Caws . . . advised the committee that in his opinion the nature of the work had completely changed since the inception of the agency. The boys matured very rapidly and required careful attention, and what was really wanted to create a really great work was to have one good man over a section of 25 boys. As the institution has ample accommodation four or five troops of boys could be controlled in this way, if after the war men could be induced to take up the work wholeheartedly.
> (Minutes, 18/2/18)

By May 1918, the 'old premises were closed for the summer, as there was no need to use them as a shelter', and the only activity was that of the Scouts meeting twice each week. For a while after the war the activities of the club, its organisation and its methodology seriously followed the ideas advocated by Caws so that by February 1919 the local newspaper was reporting on the work of the Vaux Own Scouts as though they were the primary work of the institution explaining that:

> The officers of the . . . well known troop of Scouts are at present discussing a new programme, which will permit of three troops being run in connection with the Sunderland Waifs Rescue Agency instead of one . . . It is the object of the committee and staff to do all in their power to help the boys of the working classes, and more especially those of the poorest homes. Through the medium of good physical and mental training, and through many bright hours spent in the club rooms amongst their friends and pals, the lads grow up to a splendid manhood of self-reliance and physical fitness.
> (Sunderland Daily Echo, 19/2/19)

This was different from the objectives expressed by one of the speakers at the club's formal opening in 1902:

> Mr Perris said they would like to provide the lads with a comfortable home, to which they could come and be clothed and fed, and taught a good trade – to act as a sort of godfather towards them.
> (Sunderland Daily Echo, 3/1/02)

The new regime maintained the welfare theme, but the emphasis had changed. What had become much more important as a consequence of the war and the related emphasis upon Scouting was that training and association had moved to the centre of the agenda with the anticipated outcomes of masculine independence and physical fitness. Paternalism had disappeared from the discourse. This was indicative of a new phase in the history of youth work.

Joining up

In the context of the origins and methods of Scouting, it is not surprising that the Scouts were the most active of the members in supporting the war effort, nor that the first of the adults to leave their Lambton Street commitments for military service were those associated with the Scouts. Major Vaux and Scoutmaster Parker left Sunderland during the very earliest months of the war. However, what is most noteworthy is the number of the club's non-Scouting members who volunteered. Just prior to the war, the club, which had always concerned itself primarily with children up to the age of 14, had opened an institute to cater for older members. By September 1914 the superintendent was reporting that:

> Forty-one of our institute members have enlisted in the army, while eleven are serving as territorials in the 7th Durham Battalion. This is a splendid record for our agency, and the committee feel proud to think the institute members have come forward and offered to serve, so

readily and so willingly. It was agreed that the secretary should write letters from time to time to all who are in the army, conveying the committee's good wishes.
(Minutes, 3/9/14)

By the end of October, the first death had been noted. In November it was decided to halt letter writing because of difficulties with addresses. By 10th December, 84 members had enlisted. Those who chose to volunteer received unconditional encouragement from the management committee, as did those who were later drafted into service. However, as the war progressed, and as management meetings became less regular, there is less detail about individuals joining up and mention of casualties ceases completely after August 1916.

There are no records indicating how many of those associated with the Lambton Street club ultimately participated in the war, nor of those who became casualties. This reflects the situation noted by R. D. Blumenfeld, the editor of the *Daily Express*:

One would have thought, before the war began, that the single report of the killing or disablement of any friend or acquaintance would be terribly disconcerting. So it was at the beginning. The first eight or ten casualties had as much publicity as all the rest put together. People discussed deaths of young second lieutenants with bated breath. Gradually the familiarity of the thing became apparent. You receive the news of the death of your friends as a matter of fact.
(Quoted in Marwick, 1965, 41)

It may be that the silence surrounding the level of death and injury suffered by those in the fighting was due to growing familiarity; it may be that the numbers were overwhelming. In addition, the Defence Of The Realm Acts (Pankhurst, 1987, 36) might have encouraged self-censorship, curbing the desire to even discuss, never mind commit to writing, what was known about the level of carnage from everyday information. Whatever the cause, the absence of attention to the fate of individual young men associated with the Lambton Street club is symptomatic of a general move away from the casework approach to individual boys and their families which took place during the war and contrasts sharply with the details discussed before 1914. The experience of mass death and injury, the sacrifice of the individual for the collective welfare massively destabilised the liberal individualism of the pre-war years. Never again were the names and details about the circumstances of individual members to be recorded regularly in the minutes of the Sunderland Boys' Club.

It has been possible, by cross referencing names from the pre-war minutes books with death notices in the *Sunderland Echo*, with the Roll of Honour from the Parish Church in the East End of Sunderland and with the commemorative information recorded on the website of the Commonwealth War Graves Commission to positively identify 22 deaths (http://yard.ccta.gov.uk/register). Another 60 names correspond but require further research to confirm their identity. From the 360 names available (representing about 50 per cent of the membership between 1902 and 1914), including boys too young for active service, it is possible to suggest that the impact on the Sunderland club would have been broadly similar to that in the Shaftesbury Boys' club and it is likely that between 5 per cent and 10 per cent of those young men known to the club lost their lives in the conflict, to say nothing of the incidence of terrible injury or the loss of fathers and brothers.

Whatever the real reason for the response of the club's members to the call of war, and there is little doubt that poverty and appalling working conditions were among the push factors, the managers believed from the outset that this demonstrated the success of their efforts to create responsible and respectable citizens of their members. The number of members and ex-members volunteering for active service must have seemed the ultimate proof of the achievement of that 'Christian manliness' so admired among the pre-war middle classes. Vaux (now Lieut Col) made the link between these virtues and the demands of the war explicit when he wrote to the club in 1915:

Dear Caws,

Before I go, I must write you a few lines. No work done in Sunderland beats the Waifs and Strays Home. I have seen so much of the improvement of lads, and the wonderful list you have of old lads, prove it is what we want to lift the poor little lads up, without putting them under compulsory control. It is no doubt the finest way to make a good man, and we will need them. I enclose a cheque to help you with your good work. Kind regards to the committee, Smith and all the lads.

> *Yours very sincerely*
> *(Sgnd) E. Vaux*

(Quoted in the Minutes, 22/4/15)

The pride of the club in relation to those who served lay partly in the contrast between the way in which the young men presented and behaved as members of the forces and their previous condition:

Doyle and Trotter, two of the oldest club members who have recently been called up and joined the army, looked in to say goodbye to the committee, as they have received their last leave and expect to be drafted to France or elsewhere shortly.

Both men looked very smart and fit, and one could hardly credit the fact that a few years ago, comparatively speaking, they were two of the poorest lads in the Club[1].

(Minutes, 1/6/16)

However, these very changes of condition, this very pride in the new status of the young men concerned, began to shift the terms of the relationship between the club's providers and those whom its work targeted. After the war, it would no longer be possible to patronise or to offer 'charity' in the same conditional terms to the families of those young men who had seen active military service and proved their worth as patriotic citizens. No longer would it be acceptable for voluntary middle-class philanthropists to visit the homes of the poor as 'investigators'. No longer would it be creditable to suggest that poor people were not deserving of support because 'they were not industrious' as had been wrongly suggested (Minutes, 23/9/10) in the case of the family of one boy who died in France in 1915[2], or that poverty was caused by ignorance and the want of discipline required to learn a trade.

Indeed, the circumstances created by the war completely undermined the philosophy

LIVERPOOL JOHN MOORES UNIVERSITY
LEARNING SERVICES

around which the Lambton Street Boys' Club had developed and flourished. The idea that the deprivations and depravations of the poor were a consequence of casual and unskilled labour and the failure of families to support their sons in learning a trade could hardly be sustained in the face, not only of the discipline and blood sacrifice of unskilled men who fought as private soldiers, but also in relation to the demands of the war economy for juvenile labour and the rise in status and wages accorded the boy labourer.

Boy labour

The name of the Lambton Street organisation Sunderland Waifs Rescue Agency and Street Vendors' Club betrayed its roots not only in the 'rescue' movement of the beginning of the century (Platt, 1969) but also its concern for the dangers of street vending for children. Throughout the Edwardian period, immediately preceding the war, the managers of Lambton Street not only attempted to woo their members away from street trading but also campaigned relentlessly for control and legislation of this activity (e.g. Minutes, 9/3/08). In doing so, they confined their attention to boys of school age and conceived their work as a supplement to the influence of school and often as a counterbalance to the influence of the family (Smith, 1952, 2). Their target group was specifically the boys of the lower working classes, children of casual labourers. Their aim as far as each boy was concerned was to provide a refuge wherein he could develop the self-respect, self-discipline and clean and orderly habits which would fit him mentally and physically for respectable work. Their ideal was to establish each individual boy in a trade. The material support offered by the club, particularly in terms of medical help and clothing was intended primarily in support of this ideal.

After the outbreak of war, although the principles remained, all previous practical considerations within the club relating to the 'problem of boy labour' were overwhelmed by the new realities as young people eagerly took up opportunities for employment and were offered wages hitherto unimagined, as the demands of the war economy began to take absolute precedence over theory and principle and as representatives of the state began themselves to undermine the legal restrictions upon young people's work (Marwick, 1965, 117). By September 1914, the minutes are recording that:

Joblins Foundry wants two boys. Mr Smith states that it is difficult to get the boys off the streets at present as they are making such good money selling newspapers.
(Minutes, 3/9/14)

and the following month:

Mr Smith again advised the committee that the boys refused to start work at trades while they can make as much as 10/- a week selling newspapers.
(Minutes, 22/10/14)

As if by way of compensation, in November 1914, Smith told the committee that despite the good money to be made from newspaper selling, those boys who were in work already when the war began were 'mostly sticking' to their positions (5/11/14) while two boys had taken jobs as apprentice moulders at 5/- per week. Nevertheless, the *Sunderland Echo*, reporting the treat of 'tea at Roker', noted that:

After tea there were various races, after which the lads marched back to the town in time to sell
the evening papers.
(*Sunderland Daily Echo*, 25/9/16)

The powerlessness of the club to intervene in street vending had clearly been accommodated in its timetable!

By the following year, Smith was reporting that 'there is a big demand for boy labour' but that 'all our boys are working' (Minutes, 29/5/15) and at the end of 1916 it was reported that 'Carrick's wanted a milk boy and were prepared to pay 15/- a week' (Minutes, 7/12/16). This compared with wages recorded between 2/6 and 6/- before the war.

During its course, the war brought massive profits to industrial capitalists (Cole and Postgate, 1968, 515) and for some members of the working classes, particularly young people and adult women, the opportunity to earn a regular wage definitely offered improved levels of prosperity. However, this was not the experience of all, nor was it apparent at the outset. The disruptions endured by the enlistment of breadwinners and the failure of the War Office to pay wages appropriately and when due meant that some families faced destitution, particularly in the early months (Pankhurst, 1987, 24–25; Marwick, 1965, 117) while the rises in the cost of living to a large extent offset gains made from increased wages. Although there is no allusion to these specific issues in the Lambton Street minutes, it is clear that the club's welfare work continued at least until the middle of the war. Throughout the war the numbers of boys attending the club showed no sign of diminishing. Although Smith was able to report 'better conditions in the homes' in 1915 (Minutes, 21/10/15), nevertheless, appeals for clothes and financial help continued (*Sunderland Daily Echo*, 6/12/14) and Douglas Caws and some of his friends still found it necessary to offer financial support for the provision of porridge suppers in the club during the winter of 1915 (Minutes, 18/11/15). As late as 1916 Caws was asking other members of the committee for help 'to secure some cast off boots and stockings' for the Scouts (Minutes, 1/6/16).

What is significant is that although the work *seemed* to carry on 'as normal' after the outbreak of the war, the terms of reference under which it was pursued shifted. Members of the committee continued to believe that reform was necessary to control street trading. Early in 1919 they protested against the inclusion of a special clause in the Education Act allowing 'the employment of boys before and after school hours' (Minutes, 30/1/19) and agreed to write to the education committee asking that:

The present provision should be adhered to with due consideration for the health of boys being
impaired and overtaxed, by hurrying to school cold and hungry after working undue hours.
(Minutes, 6/2/19)

Similarly they continued to discuss the control of street trading and Superintendent Smith strongly argued that the club should be responsible for registration of street vendors for the whole of Sunderland (Minutes, 6/2/19). However, although the pre-war agenda was continued at this general level, it no longer had a practical corollary of intervening directly in the lives of the boys and their families.

In the context of high levels of military participation and a labour market greedy for boy labour, little effort was made to divert boys from street vending, while the support for poor families offered by the club was now undertaken outside the terms of the Welfare to Work philosophy which prevailed before 1914. Moreover, the contribution of the club to the lives of poor boys previously explained as a private boon for individuals and their families based on private philanthropy, actually had more caché in the new situation if it was presented as a contribution to the collective needs of the nation. By providing unconditional support for the sons of families whose fathers were at war and whose mothers were perhaps struggling to work in the war industries at the same time as attempting to maintain family cohesion, the workers and managers could be seen to be making their own contribution to the maintenance of stability on the home front.

State support for club work

That the continuing work of the club was officially recognised as having some impact in the East End of Sunderland can be ascertained by the fact that when Superintendant Smith received his call-up papers in May 1916, the management committee, with the help of their honorary solicitor, were able to argue that his work was both necessary and of a specialist nature and his appeal was allowed. As a result of winning this appeal, although there was continuing dispute with the military over the decision, he was able to stay out of the forces until September 1917, when despite the committee being prepared to appeal again on his behalf, he decided as an individual to resist the draft no longer.

Although the concrete terms of the appeal are not made clear in the minutes, the fact that it was granted at all should be seen in the context of the national concern for the welfare and control of juveniles in the circumstances of war. Jeffs (1979, 11) has argued that there is no evidence to support the widely held view that there was a massive increase in juvenile delinquency during the war although other writers seem to accept the official view (Macalister Brew, 1957, 120; Marwick, 1965, 118–19). Whatever the reality of delinquency, the disruption to family and institutional controls occasioned by the war certainly led to a relaxation of the restrictions on the behaviour of young people. The Report of the Board of Education for 1916–17 identified children in the 11 to 13 age group as particularly likely to be delinquent. This was precisely the age group in which the Lambton Street Club specialised and was seen to be most effective. Meanwhile the final report of the 1917 Departmental Committee on Juvenile Education eloquently described official concerns:

> *Parental control, so far as it formally existed, has been relaxed, largely through the absence of families from their homes. Wages have been exceptionally high, and although this has led to an*

improved standard of living, it has also in ill-regulated households induced habits of foolish and mischievous extravagance. Even the ordinary discipline of the workshop has in varying degrees given way; while the withdrawal of influences making for the social improvement of boys and girls has in many districts been followed by noticeable deterioration in behaviour and morality. Gambling has increased. Excessive hours of strenuous labour have overtaxed the powers of young people; while many have taken advantage of the extraordinary demand for juvenile labour to change even more rapidly than usual from one blind alley occupation to another. (Cmnd 8512; cited in Marwick, 1965, 119)

Charles Russell who was to chair the Home Office Committee charged with considering the role of juvenile organisations committees as part of a response to delinquency, had visited the Lambton Street Club in 1907. In his book, *Clubs for Working Boys*, co-authored with Lillian Rigby in 1908, he had commended the work of the Sunderland club as dealing effectively with the children of those social groups which could not be reached by those boys' clubs which were designed for the older age group and the 'respectable' working classes (Russell and Rigby, 1908, 24). No doubt as part of their efforts to keep Jim Smith out of the forces and keep their club open, the committee would have been able to refer to this evidence as well as making reference to the activity of the Scouts and to the numbers of older members and ex-members serving with the troops.

There is very little evidence that the Lambton Street club had ever been centrally concerned with delinquency as such, although members of the management committee had campaigned for juvenile courts and had intervened with the police and magistrates on behalf of particular boys (e.g. Minutes, 8/11/06; 11/4/07; 9/1/08). The significance of the official concern about juvenile delinquency and the link with Charles Russell is probably not so much the development of the juvenile organisations committees themselves but rather the manner in which the terms of reference of the debate about delinquency won official recognition for the *preventative* nature of club work. Despite the fact that punative measures were more vigorously pursued during the war as a response to criminal activity among young people, the principles enshrined in the 1908 Children Act (the Children's Charter) which were still being developed at the outbreak of the war in terms of 'regulation within rather than removal from the community' (Clarke, 1985, 241; 251) were not suddenly abandoned. Indeed, the appointment of Russell as chair of the main juvenile organisation committee implies a continuing, if secondary, liberal agenda.

Having Smith's presence in Lambton Street for an extra 18 months, was of inestimable importance in enabling the club to survive until the end of the war. After he joined up, the agency limped along for the remaining months. That it remained open for the whole of the war was partly thanks to the efforts of his wife whose contribution is acknowledged in the minutes of 1918, as well as of Caws who worked as a volunteer during Smith's absence. However, the records of this period are few and portray a secretary who was stretched to his limits by the demands on his time and patience.

Balance of power

Before the war, the management committee of the club normally met every Thursday evening for two hours. In October 1915, it was agreed to change this to once a fortnight. However, after Superintendent Smith joined the forces in 1917 it clearly became impossible to maintain this regularity. During 1918 only five meetings were held. The most immediately obvious impact of the war, in terms of the records, was this disruption to the regular proceedings of the management committee.

The effect of this rupture was two fold. First, it is clear that Superintendent Smith, who attended management committee meetings as a servant of the committee had actually become the key to its organisation. This is not apparent from the content of the minutes and was probably not apparent from his presence in the meetings. Certainly the tone of the minutes up to 1918 suggests that he was fully aware of his place in the hierarchy of power. It is his absence which reveals his importance, both in the text of the minute books and, undoubtedly, in the reality of the everyday life of the club. Smith's real influence and power was based upon his experiential, everyday knowledge of the affairs of the organisation and his ability to mediate between the class-biased interests of his employers and the interests of the club's members, but that power was concealed by the formal relations of class and employment until the committee began to consider how it might manage without him. In reporting the view of the military that a substitute might be appointed in order to facilitate Smith's call up the minutes record:

It was pointed out by the chairman and again by the secretary at a subsequent interview with Lieut Thompson that the experience obtained to carry on such work successfully was considerable, and that in other words the work is quite of a specialist nature.
(Minute, 8/3/17)

In the very act of imagining the club without Smith, and arguing the case for his exemption, members of the committee began the process of articulating his importance and identifying the skills required to undertake his work.

Second, the actual absence of Smith and the irregularity of ensuing meetings meant that the management committee lost the means whereby they could make decisions about both the cases of individual boys and the detail of the manner in which the club should be run. Only Caws managed as an individual to retain any real power in matters of practice, and this was based upon his own involvement as a voluntary youth worker rather than his role as secretary.

After the war the management committee made an effort to meet monthly, but this could not be sustained. Some of the older members of the committtee died or retired and it proved increasingly difficult to find new members who had the time or inclination to take on roles of responsibility. The committee experienced problems in recruiting both a chair and a secretary. The generation of middle-class men who emerged from the war were simply not as keen as their predecessors to engage in philanthropic activity in a manner which involved them in personal responsibility for the poorer members of the community. Had they done so, they would no doubt have found their power to intervene directly diminished or at least received with less gratitude.

Thus, the management committee after the war adopted a different style and met less regularly. The scale of the change can be weighed by the size of the minute books. Four hard-backed quarto sized minute books cover the period January 1902–October 1914. A fifth book, of similar size, serves the whole period November 1914–May 1929. The style changed from one of intimate involvement to one of broad functional decision making. Concerns about boys and their families were left almost entirely in the hands of the superintendent who no longer reported on these matters except in impersonal terms. Instead, the committee concerned itself with general finance, major issues relating to the building and key events in the life of the club such as funding, Christmas festivities, summer outings and concerts. This in turn reinforced the power and influence of the superintendent in the interpretation of policy and the creation of the club's programmes of activity and methods of proceeding. Relations between worker and management committee during the 1920s evolved much more into what we would recognise as the relationship between them within a youth club setting today. Although Jim Smith never lowered his deferential stance within the committee meetings themselves throughout the 50 years of his career in the club, he became much more confident and his own views about the work begin to find expression in the minutes whereas previously they had been wholly absent. As early as 1919 he was asserting his ideas:

> Mr Smith explained the details and difficulties of dealing with the raw material. Many of these
> lads come to, and go from, the club when they like and how they like. Constant
> superintendence was necessary, and in his opinion they could be only dealt with by giving them
> generally plenty of Swedish Drill and general games.
> (Minutes, 13/11/19)

The evidence suggests that during the 1920s Smith was given almost a free hand to mould the club's programmes and methods. He did so in a manner which stressed the centrality of organised activities as a means of developing self control, discipline and 'character' among the boys. In this way he eventually created a club much closer to the standard boys' club for the respectable working classes (Russell and Rigby, 1908) and one whose appeal moved away from the poorer boys of the East End of Sunderland. The new methods and the popularity of Scouting as the predominant model of youth work meant that the Lambton Street Club became instead a town-wide facility whose local community and family welfare functions were virtually defunct.

The withdrawal of the management committee members from the daily life of the organisation reflected changes which were taking place in other voluntary organisations throughout the country (e.g. Montagu, 1943; Eager, 1953). Into the vacated space was stepping the 'professional' youth worker. The practical acknowledgment of the skill and importance of the worker was clearly significant as an expression of the changes in class relations. The new professional was usually only informally trained. Jim Smith himself was a joiner by trade. There is no doubt that his working-class credentials made him immediately recognisable and accessible to the boys and their families: he could be seen to represent them so much more than could the management committee and part of his power lay in his ability to mediate between the two groups. The expansion of Smith's institutional power reflected a general increase in the power of the respectable working classes – albeit a small one. However, it also represented a consolidation of the significance of masculinity within the values, activities and aspirations of the club.

The symbolic representation of the shift towards masculinity was facilitated by Scouting and its enthusiastic promotion of boxing. Gymnastics, drill, football and cricket had always been part of the programme in Lambton Street, but boxing had never been allowed by the management committee. Yet in January 1920 the purchase of boxing gloves took place without a murmur of dissent and by April of that year the Scouts were involved in a boxing jamboree. Since that time, boxing has been a major activity of the club, a central plank of its training programme and a lucrative source of fundraising. Recently the club has been making local headlines on account of training its first female boxer (*Sunderland Echo*, 2/10/98, 11; 15/10/98, 21; 16/10/98, 27). This is portrayed as a triumph of equal opportunities, but in many ways signifies the absolute supremacy of masculine values within the club. The diminution of middle-class male power during the war was accompanied by an almost total loss of middle-class female influence which current equal opportunities policies have been powerless to dislodge despite the mixing of the club membership and the appointment of female staff during the 1980s.

Gender relations

Although there was never any question of the club having been created for boys and boys only, the question of gender intruded time and again into the proceedings before the First World War. It emerged at a very early stage in the debates around appointing a male manager/superintendent to replace the female working-class caretaker, Mrs Winter, who, it is implied in the minutes, was becoming too influential in the day-to-day running of the club (Minutes, 26/11/03). Working-class female influence was formally eliminated with the replacement of Mrs Winter in 1904 by Jim Smith who was originally a part-time worker engaged primarily in organising drill and sporting activities among the boys (Minutes, 12/11/03; 20/10/04). The minutes record discussions in relation to clothing schemes and sweated labour later in the decade, which demonstrate concern for the condition of working-class women in the abstract, but after the removal of Mrs Winter from both her home and her job, there was never again any position accorded to working-class women in the life of the club as a boys' club, except as cleaner.

In contrast, a large number of middle-class women, mainly friends and relations of the key sponsors, were present at the inaugural meeting of the organisation where they were positively encouraged to help both as volunteers on special occasions and more particularly, as supporters through a ladies' committee. The minutes detail occasions when women turned up to help with Christmas parties, when they participated in outings and entertainments and when they volunteered their services to organise particular activities – notably those associated with arts and drama.

Some of these volunteers participated in the ladies' committee, the function of which was mainly fundraising. That was an important role which included raising the public profile of the club through the organisation of events such as dances, crafts fairs, bazaars and theatrical productions. Such fundraising did not, of course, lead to decision-making power and when the ladies' committee decided on one occasion that the funds they had raised should be targetted on purchasing clothes for the boys, the committee disagreed and emphasised that all income must be paid into the general fund for the committee to disburse (Minutes, 3/12/08; 10/12/08; 17/12/08). In addition, there existed a loose network of individual female supporters who made donations, collected secondhand clothes, arranged fundraising activities in their own time or organised events such as tea parties in their own homes for groups of boys.

Occasionally, a particularly influential woman found her way onto the management committee, as with a Mrs Seinfield who represented the Charity Organisation Society and at the outset volunteered as a lady visitor. Her influence was very important in setting the tone for the early casework. Her reports upon the conditions which she found in the families she visited and her recommendations for action were seldom questioned, even though the outcomes were not always in keeping with the more generous intentions of some of the male committee members. Mrs Seinfield seems to have been the arbiter of what constituted ethical behaviour in relation to the distribution of 'charity' to individuals. Social work based upon investigative visiting was experienced as an essentially middle-class female activity, and the men never presumed to question her expertise in these matters. Yet when she left for Sheffield in 1904, she was never replaced. Her 'visiting' duties were absorbed within the superintendent's work. Visiting by Jim Smith appears to have been pursued as part of the general process of befriending rather than as investigative activity. Although he was required to comment in the management meetings on individual cases most of the outcomes of his visits were recorded in generalised statements about the 'conditions of the homes'(Minutes, 21/10/15) and he never made detailed reports in the manner adopted by Mrs Seinfield. The impression in the minutes is that Jim Smith was never comfortable with casework and it was his approach which was to prevail in the post-war period. After the war when he was forced to work at another job during the day to supplement his wages in the club, which was enduring financial difficulties, he concentrated all his attention upon internal club activities and programmes and simply allowed visiting to peter out. By that time, there was no ladies' committee and no women at all with any influence upon the club's affairs.

Although there was an effort to re-establish the ladies' committee after the war, by 1920 references to the idea had disappeared and the whole female network seems to have declined to the point of disappearance. Only when the Rotarians became involved during the 1920s did female support re-emerge and that was mediated by the Rotary organisation. There were clearly both push and pull factors in the decline of female influence after the war. The main push factor was possibly the increased masculinity of the club itself which was reinforced by a new commitment to the institute comprising young men, as opposed to the work with children. This commitment was to be affirmed during the 1930s when the club joined the National Association of Boys' Clubs. Alongside this the loss of commitment to family and local community welfare work and the withdrawal from active participation of middle-class men in practice implied the exclusion of both the interests of the women and the mechanism for their participation. The pull factors no doubt included a significant decrease in the leisure time of middle-class women after the war (Marwick, 1965, 303) and an opening up of opportunities for either professional welfare work or for participation in specifically female voluntary organisations.

The decline in the influence of middle-class women involved not only a loss of a significant, if intermittent fundraising source, and an activities input which represented female interests – particularly in the field of drama and entertainment, but it also represented the final separation of youth work in Lambton Street from social work. And the youth work which remained was to pursue an uncompromisingly masculine agenda throughout the remainder of the century.

Network

At the beginning of the war the ladies' committee had ceased to function. That committee had been only one part of a network of organisational support into which the club was integrated before the war and its collapse was symptomatic of the decline in the whole voluntary network of institutional relations which had cushioned pre-war youth work.

Prior to the war, cooperating organisations which could be relied upon to share the same or similar values and principles in philanthropic work with the poor included the Charity Organisation Society (COS), the Waifs Rescue Agency in Newcastle, the Swan Homes in Sunderland, Barnardos and the NSPCC. This voluntary network was supplemented by contacts with the statutory authorities – the police, councillors and Poor Law Guardians in particular and underpinned by a subscription-based relationship with a series of employers who used the club almost as a personal labour exchange.

The changed direction of the work consequent upon the war undermined the importance of this network of relationships. By 1918, there are no longer any references in the minutes to the COS, the NSPCC, Barnardos or similar 'social service' agencies. In one respect this indicated a contraction in the work of the club, and a greater emphasis on the need to re-establish itself 'on a sure footing' as an individual agency after the insecurities of the war. Such a process was undoubtedly also taking place within other organisations. However, it also marked the club's accommodation to the needs and interests of boys and young men as young people rather than as the sons of poor families. Hitherto the work was to be developed within a network of supporting agencies which were specifically concerned with the needs of youth qua youth.

The organisation began its association with the Rotary Club in 1922. As the representative of the established trades and professions in the town this became its main source of local sponsorship (Minutes, 5/10/22). The practical connection, in which members of Rotary undertook voluntary work in the club proceeded, not surprisingly, via Scouting:

> The committee discussed a proposed scheme for cooperation and assistance on the part of the Rotary Club, and it was agreed that the Rotarians should be invited to form a group of 12 senior lads, and to call same the Rotary Sea Rovers, and to appoint a leader for same and to do all in their power to help and improve the chances and condition of these lads, finding them work if necessary through the influence of the Rotary Club.

(Minutes, 17/1/24)

Although sponsorship by the Rotary Club did not entirely displace the personal connections with individual firms, it removed the individual patronage implied in the subscription based relationship and signified something of the more general move towards collective rather than individually based arrangements in institutional life.

After the war, the national Scouting organisation provided the main external network which facilitated the activities of the club and not only the Scouts but the general members benefited from this. So, for instance, appeals for funds or for clothing were made for the club in general, through advertising the success of the Scouts and the headquarters of the Scouts were used as a location for general fundraising meetings for the club (Minutes, 4/12/24). Scouts themselves participated in national, regional and local events which were often partly funded from the Scouting organisation with the remainder coming from the Lambton Street funds. Meanwhile, the activities pursued within Scouting were used as the foundation for the development of other work and mixed events between Scouts and others were organised (Minutes, 7/6/23). The Scouting organisation thus acted as a bridge as the Waifs Rescue Agency and Street Vendors' Club worked to establish its new identity after the war.

From 1926 until 1931 the minutes record association with the Juvenile Organisations' Committee (25/2/26) mainly through participation in festivals of youth and boxing tournaments but during the late 1920s most of its attention was focused introspectively upon raising funds for the new building opened in 1931. The transformation from social welfare agency to boys' youth club, with all that that implied, was virtually completed by February 1936 when two proposals were put forward at the management committee meeting. The first was that the committee should consider changing the title of the agency and the second was to invite Captain Radcliff to 'come down and talk to the committee on the work of National Boys' Clubs' (Minutes, 20/2/36). After some discussion, the name was changed to Lambton Street Boys' Fellowship Centre in June of that year with the following justification:

> (a) The boys coming to the institution, though of the working class, are of a higher social standard than was the case 30 years ago, and the description 'Waifs rescue' no longer truly applies, for, because of changes in the law, and State help, there are now no street traders under 16 years old, and there is not the same degree of destitution as formerly.
>
> (b) In the case of boys in the Scout section, many parents object to the term 'Waif' and the same dislike is not unknown amongst the boys themselves.

(Report of the Subcommittee on Change of Name, 30/4/36)

The affiliation to the NABC was not to be so easy as it implied a formal recognition of the change of policy away from work with junior boys and a development of the work with adolescents. Spurred on by a visit from Duke of Gloucester, as a representative of the NABC (Minutes, 30/7/36) and from Basil Henriques, who spoke at the AGM (17/10/36) the committee embarked on a series of special meetings and discussions, and in September 1937 (Minutes, 23/9/37) it agreed to change its terms of reference and affiliate to the NABC. This affiliation, which remains important to the club today, began the process of a move away from the domination of the Scouts and at the same time completed the process of change set in motion by the First World War. The network had changed completely from a loose association of charitable welfare agencies to one of a more clearly identified association of specific youth agencies.

Conclusion

The transformation of the Lambton Street Club from a child welfare agency to a modern youth club was accomplished in the wake of the social and economic upheavals set in motion by the First World War. The key features of this change included an adjustment of class and gender relations which impacted upon the definition of what was established as statutory youth work after the Second World War and which continues to have implications for the work today.

In particular, the conception of youth work as an activity separated from the community and social relations in which it takes place; as something responding to the particular masculine connotations of the behaviour of working-class young people; and as something which proceeds through the medium of programmes or curricula based upon physical activities, are aspects of the work which remain embedded in contemporary practice.

Of course the details of the processes of adjustment and change which took place within the Lambton Street Club were peculiar to itself and its own conditions and history; it would therefore be unwise to make sweeping generalisations from this particular story. Nevertheless, the tale surely provides some pointers for understanding the peculiarities of the history of youth work and for a re-evaluation of the significance of the First World War as a key moment in that history.

Research for this paper was financed by the Leverhulme Trust.

Footnotes
[1] Doyle was to die in France in May 1918 while Trotter was to be badly wounded '*immediately he got into the front line*' in August 1916.
[2] I am indebted to Mrs Brigid Brewster for information about her uncle, Michael Quinn, who fought in the war under the name of Michael Conlin.

Bibliography

Clarke, J. (1985). 'Managing the Delinquent: The Children' 1913–30' in Langan, M. and Schwarz, B. (eds.). *Crises* Hutchinson.

Cole, G. D. H. and Postgate, R. (1968). *The Common People: 1*

Commonwealth War Graves Commission: *http://yard.ccta.got*

Davies, B. (1999). *From Voluntaryism to Welfare State: A history Volume 1, 1939–1979*. Leicester, Youth Work Press.

Dawes, F. (1975). *A Cry From The Streets: The Boys' Club Move...... in Britain from the 1850s to the present day.* Hove, Wayland Publishers.

Eager, W. McG. (1953). *Making Men: Being a history of boys' clubs and related movements in Great Britain.* London, University of London Press.

Jeffs, A. J. (1979). *Young People and the Youth Service.* London, Routledge and Kegan Paul.

Macalister Brew, J. (1957). *Youth and Youth Groups.* London, Faber and Faber.

Marwick, A. (1965). *The Deluge: British society and the First World War.* London, Macmillan.

Minutes of the Lambton Street Fellowship Centre, 1902–1938.

Montagu, L.H. (1943). *My Club and I: The story of the West Central Jewish Club.* London, Herbert Joseph.

Pankhurst, E. S. (1987). *The Home Front: A mirror to life in England during the First World War.* London, The Cresset Library.

Platt, A. M. (1969). *The Child Savers: The invention of delinquency.* Chicago, University of Chicago Press.

Russell, C. E. B. and Rigby, E. (1908). *Working Lads Clubs.* London, Macmillan.

Tawney, R. H. (1924). *Secondary Education for All.* London, Allen and Unwin.

Smith, J. (1952). *Fifty Years at Lambton Street.* Sunderland, Summerbell Printers.

Sunderland Daily Echo, 1902–1937.

Urwick, E. J. (1904). *Studies of Boy Life in Our Cities.* London, J. M. Dent.

Sunderland Daily Echo, 1902–1937 and *Minutes of Lambton Street Fellowship Centre*, 1902–1938.

Lady Baden-Powell

Chapter nine

'The worst girl has at least 5 per cent good in her': The work of the Girl Guides and the YWCA with 'difficult' girls during the inter-war period

Carolyn Oldfield

'At this moment in history, there can hardly be a more important group of people than those who are in close touch with working girls in their clubs.'
(*YWCA Bulletin*, May 1921, 2)

This statement reflects both the widely held view that the First World War and its aftermath had brought about radical change in social behaviour and the role of women, and the way in which youth organisations positioned their work with girls as central to both individual and national welfare.

This chapter will explore the ways in which the Young Women's Christian Association and the Girl Guides consciously set out to meet the needs of the 'modern girl'. It will look specifically at their work with those considered to be 'difficult' or vulnerable because of their behaviour or circumstances, a perception usually associated with their sexual activity. Unlike some other organisations – for example, the Girl's Friendly Society which did not abandon its ruling that girl members should be 'chaste' until the 1930s, despite the issue first having been raised in the 1890s – girls who became pregnant were until then forced to leave the society – both undertook specific work in this area. In addition to its hostels for young women living away from their families, the YWCA made specific provision for unmarried mothers and for young women who found themselves in 'moral difficulties', while the Guides ran companies in a range of rescue and reform institutions.

Contemporary commentators believed that the war had brought about major changes – both positive and negative – in the status of women. The war was perceived to have increased women's economic and social independence, while the granting of the franchise in 1918 to women over 30 offered all women a new role as potential or actual citizens. Young women, in particular, were believed to hold a central role in post-war reconstruction. According to one influential account: 'The Great War . . . freed the Englishwoman' (Graves and Hodge, 1985, 39). However, there was also a widespread perception that the behaviour of women and girls had been negatively affected by wartime conditions. Female sexual behaviour was represented as having deteriorated during and immediately after the war, as young women were believed to have succumbed to 'khaki fever' (Woollacott, 1994). The changing role of young women and what was seen as their increasing independence was widely discussed in the press. New awareness of the incidence of venereal diseases and the immediate post-war rise in illegitimate births provided a trigger for increased public discussion about sex, while eugenic concerns about the falling birth-rate and the quality of the population resulted in a new emphasis on motherhood. These concerns had existed before the war, but were now intensified (Weeks, 1989; Lewis, 1980).

Both the YWCA and the Guides were internationalist, interdenominational Christian organisations. The YWCA was founded in 1877 to provide 'institutes for respectable young women to rest in, seek advice, and enjoy "genial gatherings of various kinds" ' (quoted Beaumont, 1996, 22). During the First World War its attempts to reach girls 'swayed by excitement or beset with temptation' led some members to criticise its 'downward drift' and new 'worldly methods'. In particular these members objected to clubs and hostels allowing smoking, dancing, card-playing and theatre-going (*The Referendum Movement*, 1918–1920). Following a referendum in which the protestors were defeated, they left to form the Christian Alliance of Women and Girls (CAWG) (YWCA, 1918–20; YWCA Review 1920–21, 2). The significance of this split was highlighted at the Association's 1921 conference, when the Bishop of Norwich contrasted its willingness to adopt new approaches to 'touch the needs of a new age' with the CAWG's desire to 'stand firm and still on the old and tried paths' (*YWCA Bulletin*, 1921, 2).

The Guide movement was formally established in 1910. The Guides' own history of the movement admits that Baden-Powell 'had not been particularly keen on the idea of Scouting for girls' (Kerr, 1932, 34). However, girls had formed their own scout companies where their 'zeal at times outran their discretion' (*Annual Report*, 1920, 11), and he therefore set out to develop a modified form of Scouting which would direct girls' enthusiasm into 'channels which would benefit both the girls themselves and their country' (Kerr, 1932, 35). Guiding, in his vision, would counter national decadence, in which young women – and young men – were 'learning to lead aimless, profitless lives'. He explicitly ascribed this decadence to the inadequacies of women as mothers, and identified the need to educate young women to fulfil their roles as the mothers and moral mentors of the future. Guiding would serve to enhance, rather than undermine, girls' femininity; while opponents of Guiding feared that it would turn girls into tomboys. These accusations were dismissed by Baden-Powell and Kerr (*Annual Report*, 1920, 31; Kerr, 1932, 37).

Despite their differing origins, both organisations endorsed the view that war had brought about permanent change, and that new ways of working with girls were needed. On the negative side, Baden-Powell's concern with girls' behaviour was endorsed in the Guides' immediate post-war annual reports, which located the need for Guiding as rooted in the rise in juvenile delinquency and sexual immorality among older girls (*Annual Reports*, 1918–21). Less censoriously, the YWCA refused to endorse 'the often expressed view that immorality is markedly worse now than in pre-war times', but agreed that the 'general independence of the very young in these days does constitute a danger' (*Annual Report*, 1923, 3).

Both organisations also saw the aftermath of war as offering girls new responsibilities and opportunities. A 1921 report from the Guides declared that 'the girl of today is of a very different calibre to the girl of ten years or even five years ago. The war has made tremendous changes, but no greater change has been effected than in the status of women' (Committee for the Extension of Guide Training, 1921, 33). The YWCA believed that 'the whole language of today is Reconstruction – a new age, new possibilities for women' (Kinnard, 1920). It claimed that public opinion did not understand the problems facing girls in the post-war world, describing the modern girl as 'a gallant figure who carried a double responsibility, industrial and domestic' (*Annual Report*, 1922, 1–2).

While both organisations positioned themselves within the ideology of domesticity, they recognised that some girls would not in fact marry because of the post-war gender balance, and promoted girls' wider roles as future citizens. Neither organisation identified itself as feminist, yet feminist views were aired in the publications of both. Former suffragist Maude Royden contrasted the expectations placed on modern girls – to be 'clever and efficient and public-spirited' – with that of our foremothers, who were expected to be 'unselfish and gentle and devoted' (Royden, 1924, 20). The YWCA's vice-president, also a suffragist, argued that every girl should 'seek to fit herself for independence', since marriage was out of the question for so many (Picton-Turbervill, 1922).

Both organisations aimed to reach all young women, regardless of class. The conceptualisation of adolescence as a critical time of life characterised by turmoil, stress and uncertainty, during which future adult development would be determined, meant that all girls were defined as vulnerable and in need of protection. Both the Guides and the YWCA subscribed to and popularised this concept, and their publications contained frequent discussions of adolescence and adolescent psychology (e.g. Crichton-Miller, 1926; Matthias, 1928). This understanding of adolescence had originated at the turn of the century, particularly through the work of G. Stanley Hall, but it was widely accepted and developed following the First World War (Griffin, 1993).

Both organisations also universalised the experience of girlhood. Despite their acknowledgment of the changed lives and expectations of young women, they propounded an essentialist representation which united girls across boundaries of class, race and time. Writing in 1920, the British president of the YWCA argued that:

> Girls' lives are very different now from what they were then, so much more free and independent, and their occupations are so much more varied. Yet I do believe girls' hearts and needs and longings are just the same all over the world and in all times.
> (*Our Own Gazette*, November 1920, 4)

Nearly 20 years later, readers of the YWCA's annual report were assured that the apparently sophisticated working girl of 14 to 18 shared with her middle-class counterpart the 'eagerness and perplexity of immature minds in need of guidance' (*Annual Report*,

1938–39, 2). Delegates to a YWCA training conference heard that the 'country girl was not so very unlike the girl in the city' (*YWCA Bulletin* 1922, 3). At times, this insistence on the common experience of girlhood takes on a note of desperation. Discussing the Rangers movement (the branch of Guiding for over-16s) an anonymous writer pleads that despite 'the modern girl's selfishness, pleasure seeking and frivolity, the sacrificial instinct is surely there' (*Ranger Problems and Possibilities*, 1924, 341).

However, this universalisation of the experience of girlhood was accompanied by the belief that some girls faced additional risks because of their social and economic circumstances. During the 1920s and 1930s girls' sexuality was the subject of scrutiny and regulation by a range of professional groupings including medicine, social welfare and education. Sexual activity outside marriage was defined as the main indicator of delinquency among girls, and sexually active girls categorised according to their perceived levels of vulnerability or culpability (Burt, 1926; 1927).

Working-class girls were perceived to be most at risk of irregular sexual activity. The National Birth Rate Commission's investigation into the moral education and protection of young people highlights the main lines of concern (National Birth Rate Commission, 1923). Significantly, this report considered both the moral education (including sex education) of young people, and society's responsibility to protect the adolescent. Working-class girls who left school at 14 were depicted as endangered by the premature removal of educational and parental forms of supervision and their precocious exposure to adult life, including the potentially corrupting influence of friends and other workers, novels and magazines and increasingly, the cinema. Cities were seen as particular sites of danger. Although discussion of the causes of prostitution – which, for at least the 10 years following the war, was reconceptualised to include girls engaging in casual sex as well as the professional prostitute – tended to downplay the direct role of poverty. Commentators often stressed the importance of girls' love of 'luxuries' as a causative factor (Burt, 1926). Unemployment, insecure jobs and some conditions of employment – the monotony of factory work, the isolation of domestic service – as well as specific occupations such as acting or waitressing, were all believed to encourage girls to seek a 'good time'. However, attention increasingly focused on leisure time – including enforced leisure through unemployment. As the Commission's report put it, 'the hours of leisure are the hours of danger' (National Birth Rate Commission, 1923, 20).

While holding that their provision was suitable for all girls, both the Guides and the YWCA claimed work with working-class girls as a priority. Baden-Powell identified the 'girls of the factories and of the alleys of our great cities, who . . . get no kind of restraining influence' (Baden-Powell and Baden-Powell, 1912, vi) as most in need of Guiding. Guiding was seen to widen the horizons of factory girls – bringing romance and new vistas to the 'child of the slums' (Roch, 1918, 153) – and to improve their performance both as employees and daughters. The 1921 *Annual Report*, for instance, included quotes from a factory forewoman on the helpfulness and self-reliance of Guides, and a mother praising her daughter's behaviour after attending Guide camp (*Annual Report*, 1921, 18–19). Similarly, the YWCA's reports highlight the movement's success in reaching 'the very roughest type of girl,' and its provision for specific groups such as 'herring girls' in Wales and hostels for 'theatrical girls' (*Annual Report*, 1921, 13; *Blue Triangle Gazette*, 1930, 8–9; *YWCA Bulletin*, July 1928, 2).

Much of the YWCA's work focused on providing hostels for working girls, who were believed to need protection because of their isolation from their families. Its London hostels had first opened in 1878 to provide accommodation for the 'respectable working girl or young woman' under 25, employed in workrooms, shops and offices. They offered practical assistance to young women on low incomes, charging them on a sliding scale according to wages, and tiding over residents who lost their jobs or were put on short time. In any one year they provided accommodation for between 700 and 1,000-plus young women (*Homes for Working Girls in London: These fifty years, 1878–1928*).

Reports of the London hostels' work between 1916 and 1937 appear to be written by one woman. Adopting a discursive style and fulsomely Christian tone, they offer a narrative of sexual danger. Young women are repeatedly portrayed as surrounded by the temptations of the city – commercialised amusements and casual relationships – to which low or irregular pay and loneliness make them vulnerable. London is described as a 'whirlpool of . . . seductive and alluring sin', as a 'great pleasure machine' and as 'a vortex' which fascinates and engulfs young women (*Annual Report*, 1922, 17; 1928, 28; *Homes for Working Girls in London: These fifty years, 1878–1928*, 10). It is notable that in contrast to commentators elsewhere, who stress the improvement in London streets and the diminution of prostitution, these reports claim that 'sin has not been banished from the streets' (*Annual Report*, 1934, 6).

To counter these attractions the hostels offered protection within 'home-like freedom' with no unnecessary rules (*Annual Report*, 1920, 16; 1931, 8–9), in a strongly Christian environment which mimicked a (middle-class) home which provided the girls with 'motherly care' (*Annual Report*, 1924, 17). The reports represent the girls as welcoming this approach – each girl 'knows it is "up to her" to live happily in the family circle' (*Annual Report*, 1931, 9). Yet some girls rejected this 'family circle' – apparently finding some rules irksome rather than necessary. At various times the reports highlight problems of theft; smoking and playing cards; residents described as religious or political 'cranks' exerting a dangerous influence on younger girls; pressure (resisted) for later closing hours or latchkeys; residents' 'selfishness and inconsiderateness'; even attacks on superintendents leading to residents' incarceration in asylums (*Annual Report*, 1918, 33; 1919, 30; 31, 1922, 18; 1935, 11; 1923, 11). There are indications that residents accepted the religious rituals of the homes with at best resignation; the 1930 report admits that if homes were administered according to residents' views 'we could omit practically all religious observances', yet goes on to say – with no apparent sense of contradiction – that most girls 'voluntarily support' weekly Bible-talks, Sunday religious classes and the daily prayer (*Annual Report*, 1930, 21, 23).

The reports stress that most girls resist the temptations of the city; the average modern girl 'is just splendid in her bravery and fortitude as she faces up to her personal and peculiar problems' (*Annual Report*, 1934, 17). Yet – far more than other YWCA literature – they also offer repeated criticism of modern girls as rebellious, too independent, and obsessed with pleasure and 'having a good time' (e.g. *Annual Report*, 1919, 13; 1936, 9). Similar ambivalence is revealed about the culpability of girls engaged in sexual irregularities. On one hand, they are portrayed as victims of loneliness, poverty and the overwhelming lure of the city, who succumb to temptation without understanding that 'the cost in life and character is beyond computation' (*Annual Report*, 1923, 7; 1932, 6). On the other, considerable opprobrium is reserved for those who wilfully court danger by rejecting the protection of the YWCA in favour of lodgings. These girls are described as having an exaggerated sense of 'their need of "liberty" (so called!) – or rather licence, to do just what they want'(*Annual Report*, 1932, 8). Such a choice is portrayed as always leading to 'disaster', even pathologised as resulting in 'a disease that could be designated one-room-itis', and potentially leading in turn to other disorders (*Annual Report*, 1933, 21). The challenge they posed to the hostels' regime is expressed in the confrontational description of one girl who went astray because she 'took a room rather than submit' (*Annual Report*, 1924, 21–22).

The young women who choose to live in lodgings rather than in the London hostels seem to be excluded from the rhetoric of moral reform and reclamation offered elsewhere by the association. Their desire for independence and pleasure is represented as leading to irretrievable disaster. This is in sharp contrast to the language used to describe the YWCA's rescue work with girls. The YWCA had opened four hostels during the war for girls described as being in dangerous surroundings or morally wounded (*A Review*, August 1914 to January 1920, 11). Two of these continued during the 1920s: a maternity home for unmarried girls, and an open-access hostel for any girl in difficulties (*Annual Report*, 1920–2, 4). By 1932, when the hostel for unmarried mothers was closed (on the grounds that adequate provision was made by other agencies), it had catered for between 400 and 500 lone mothers:

> *The influence of the two matrons . . . has been the means of helping hundreds of these girls back to the path of purity and self-control from which they had temporarily strayed, and their friendship and after-care have in many cases, succeeded in restoring to those who were disappointed and disillusioned the faith which they had lost.*
> (*YWCA Bulletin*, April 1931, 3)

This account highlights the importance of relationships between girls and workers. The increasing influence of psychology during the inter-war years offered both the YWCA and Guides a new scientific discourse to underpin the value of these relationships, and to enable them to develop a programme appropriate to individual needs. Training for leaders in both organisations increasingly included discussion of psychology and its application to adolescent girls. YWCA workers who had attended a training conference found that 'psychology became a tool in the hands of the worker, which would unlock the door to a way of approach to the individual girl with whom each had to deal (*YWCA Bulletin*, March 1924, 2).

This increased focus on issues of individual identity and development was located within a discourse of citizenship which sought to develop girls' own moral agency. Introducing a survey of girls' organisations in the mid-1930s, Madeline Rooff contrasted the older approach to youth work – offering an alternative to the streets – with a more positive, modern approach which aimed to cultivate members' 'independence of spirit which will fit them to take their place as citizens of the community' (Rooff, 1935, 3). While Baden-Powell located the need for Guiding in concerns about national wellbeing, its programme addressed the problem at the level of individual character development. The Guiding programme meant that girls learnt of their own volition, rather than having 'knowledge impressed upon them from outside' (Girl Guides Association, 1918, 11). The YWCA offered a similar approach to developing the responsible moral being. Writing towards the end of the 1930s, Margaret Bondfield MP stressed that 'our programme should aim at teaching girls to live – to live courageously, with a steadfast adherence to principle' (1936, 198).

The principles of voluntarism and internalisation of moral values were seen as particularly important when working with girls who were considered difficult or dangerous. The Guides had operated companies in girls' industrial schools, reformatories and rescue homes since the war years. The auxiliary branch, headed by Mrs Crichton Miller, was set up in 1924 to bring a new focus to this institutional work, and to ensure that 'the special problems and difficulties of this side of Guiding' could receive more attention. These difficulties were defined as 'the limited time, the complications of institution life and regulations, and above all the often abnormal human material with which they worked'. While she admitted that this work was 'difficult and in many ways unattractive' with limited tangible results and many disappointments, she stressed that it was of great and lasting national significance (*Annual Report*, 1924, 35–37).

Guiding in institutions drew upon a continuum of behaviour between 'normal' girls and those who had 'gone wrong'. Baden-Powell declared that:

the worst girl has at least 5 per cent of good in her somewhere. The work of the Guider is to find it. The first step is to treat the girl as a normal and responsible individual instead of as merely one of a tainted herd.

(Committee for the Extension of Guide Training, 1921, 4)

Despite the compulsory or quasi-compulsory nature of girls' detention in these homes, it was emphasised that girls' involvement in Guiding remained voluntary. It was argued that, although external discipline might have a temporary effect on a girl who had 'gone wrong', no lasting good would be accomplished until 'she herself has seen something better, and voluntarily sets out to attain it' (Committee for the Extension of Guide Training, 1921, 10). Leaders stressed that even the most difficult girls responded well to Guide methods – one guider claimed with apparent satisfaction that her company was made up of all the girls whom 'the matron thinks are mentally or psychologically unbalanced' (*The Guider*, February 1935, 69).

The extension of Guiding (and Scouting) into these institutions was supported by the children's branch (the section of the Home Office responsible for reform schools). However, it seems that those in charge of institutions did not always share this view. The movement was introduced to Aylesbury Borstal (the country's only girls' Borstal) in 1919 but later withdrawn; one reason given was that the Guide leader lacked experience 'in the ways and villainies of the type with whom she is dealing' (Forsythe, 1990, 54–55). While this may mean that she was unable to cope with their behaviour, it could also indicate her refusal to categorise the Borstal girls as totally different from 'normal' girls. Institutions also appeared to expect Guiding to solve all their discipline problems; one district captain reported that in one home, all reprimands to the girls who had joined a new Guide company ended with 'and you a Guide too'. Not surprisingly, other girls were put off joining the Guides (Committee for the Extension of Guide Training, 1921, 30).

By the late 1930s, however, Mrs Crichton Miller claimed that the obstructive matron had virtually disappeared, replaced by the 'ever-increasing number of the friendly, co-operative matrons' (*Annual Report*, 1937, 34). As part of this cooperation, Guides in institutions were increasingly brought into contact with other Guides. By the 1930s institutional companies were encouraged to take part in local and regional activities so that they felt part of the movement as a whole. The 1930 *Annual Report*, for instance, drew particular attention to the large proportion who were welcomed to district and county rallies, sports or competitions (*Annual Report*, 1930, 63). Guides who completed their term in institutions were encouraged to transfer to ordinary companies, to help support them against succumbing to 'the down-dragging influence of old temptations' (*Annual Report*, 1935, 75). Many girls also appear to have maintained contact with their former institution's Guider.

While the work of the auxiliary branch remained small-scale throughout the 1920s and 1930s, growing from 12 to 40 companies 10 years later (*Annual Reports*, 1924, 35; 1934, 65) – those involved sought to maximise its impact. In particular, Mrs Crichton Miller drew on its experience to offer a critique of mainstream guiding. Discussing 'the difficult girl' – by which she meant young women who were sexually active – she argued that girls in penitentiaries were not a 'type apart, a purely abnormal product' but were excitable and troublesome girls, who 'with half a chance and a little intelligent treatment would have been steered safely past the danger point'. However, she claimed that Guiding was failing these girls – many companies were simply too dull to offer 'a wholesome alternative to a restless older girl' (Crichton Miller, 1924). Guiding would only work if it was sufficiently challenging and responsive to individual needs. She argued that:

> A dull Guide company run by an unenlightened Guider feeds the auxiliary branch; a 'live wire' captain with open eyes and some understanding of elementary psychology will do much to prevent the disasters which our branch exists to help in retrieving.
> (*Annual Report*, 1933, 72)

Her critique was supported by an internal review examining the reasons for the decline in Guide numbers in the 1930s, which concluded that although the aims and ideals of Guiding remained valid, much practice was unadventurous, inward-looking, and dependent on learning by rote rather than exploring ideas and values (Committee on the Drop In Numbers in the Girl Guides, 1937).

Guiding's attempts to reach difficult girls are illustrated by a series of case-studies published in *The Guider* during 1934–35. The problems discussed include an uncontrollable 15-year-old girl, a 17-year-old in service who steals from her (sympathetic) employer, and the admission of an unmarried mother into a company (*The Guider*, November 1934,

422–23; May 1935, 204; November 1935, 457). Although mainly hypothetical, these case studies were said to reflect the reality of Guiding, showing 'that the movement is not a collection of prigs, but can appeal to the lively youngster who has great potentialities for good or evil'(*The Guider*, August 1935, 350).

Most responses to these dilemmas stressed the importance of individual psychology, and the need for a 'constructive and compensating' approach, neither condoning or condemning (*The Guider*, June 1935, 245). So, suggestions for dealing with the girl who stole included ensuring that she had enough money to meet reasonable needs and helping her understand the reasons for her theft. The problem related to the unmarried mother was not whether the captain should agree to the young woman's social worker's request to admit her – 'Of course I agreed' – but whether the other Guides (middle-class high school girls) should be told about her circumstances, and whether their parents would object (*The Guider*, November 1935, 457). Most responses argued that the other Guides should be told and would respond well. Several endorsed the view expressed by Mrs Crichton Miller that if parents removed their daughters 'in order that they may not be contaminated I think it is better we should lose them than have to turn out the girl with the baby' (*The Guider*, December 1935, 502). This approach is in marked contrast to the frequently expressed belief that 'innocent' girls needed to be protected from those who were seen as precociously sexually experienced (see, for instance, the Departmental Committee on Sexual Offences Against Young Persons, 1925, 78).

Arguing that Guiding should stand not only for 'the cure but the *prevention* of social evils' Mrs Crichton Miller identified a clear role for sex education in this work – both for Guiders and Guides alike. As early as 1924 she argued that Guiders needed to be able to 'discuss frankly and unemotionally with their older girls the many questions involved in the relationship between boys and girls and men and women'(Crichton Miller, 1924). At headquarters level the association recognised this need, and in 1928 published a booklet to help Guiders and Rangers deal with members' questions about sex without embarrassment (Girl Guides Association, 1928, 5). Mrs Crichton Miller, however, appears to have believed that more needed to be done, continuing to claim that Guiders in ordinary companies needed help to develop a 'better understanding of the many underlying sex problems' facing girls (*Annual Report*, 1933, 72).

Similarly, members of the YWCA sought to gain more organisational support for sex education; delegates at a 1928 conference agreed that the association had not given enough thought to education in moral hygiene, and urged its education committee to consider the matter further (*YWCA Bulletin*, August 1928, 6). The YWCA also made use of the propaganda produced by the British Social Hygiene Council, the main official source of sex education material during the 1920s and 1930s. Following a film presentation at a YWCA Pioneer Conference participants reported 'a deeper understanding of the whole content of sex and the part it plays in the world, both spiritually and physically' (*YWCA Bulletin*, February 1932, 2). By 1936 the BSHC had prepared a course of three lectures on social hygiene for the YWCA's organiser of work in distressed areas, which included a clear explanation of the physiology of human reproduction (BSHC, 1936). In the late 1930s, a

YWCA committee looking at physical education incorporated discussion of both health education and sex education within this (YWCA, 1937–39).

Both organisations were actively addressing the issue of sex within a discourse which increasingly posited heterosexual sex within marriage as a source of future fulfilment for both women and men providing it was not jeopardised by premature experimentation (see, for instance, Griffith, 1935) – but also in the context of expectations that many girls would not in fact marry. An article on the dangers of books which aroused sexual thoughts or feelings in the YWCA's magazine for young women acknowledged the importance of sex in life, and reassured its readers that it was perfectly natural to think about sex. It then went on to discuss how girls should deal with their sex instincts should they not marry, recommending the redirection of sexual urges into service or creative activities. Two alternative approaches – indulging in 'immoral practices' or denying all sexual urges, were both dismissed as damaging (*Book Worm*, 1929, 5).

In general, approaches to sex education during the inter-war period reveal an increasing emphasis on developing positive motivations for sexual restraint in both young men and women, as part of an overall approach to creating self-managing citizens. Youth workers were exposed to these arguments that young people needed more than diversion or messages of danger. Writing in the YWCA's journal in 1934, a woman doctor discusses how youth workers should respond to girls contemplating sexual experimentation:

> *Give her positive ideals, not negative reasons against it. Above all, don't sound unsympathetic. We must re-think our own approach to these questions so that we may give good and sound reasons, not just conventional ones. In fact, what the world is needing very badly just now is a new presentation of a sound moral code of sexual relationships.*
> (Lowenfeld, 1934)

The Guides and the YWCA were actively engaged in managing heterosexual development by providing opportunities for young women to meet and develop relationships with young men in a supervised environment. As early as 1920, a speaker at the YWCA's biennial conference argued that the association should provide opportunities for girls to meet and get to know men '*under proper management and good organisation*' (Swainston, 1920, 20). By the mid-1930s most YWCA town centre clubs were open to girls and their boyfriends on Sundays, and the organisation was experimenting with a holiday hostel for girls and their boyfriends (Rooff, 1935, 11–12). In 1936, the association believed that 'segregation of the sexes is a thing of the past' in many areas of life (*Annual Report*, 1936, 6–7). Reports from the Guides stressed joint ventures between Rangers and Rovers (the Scouts' movement for young men over 17); its 1929 report calls attention to initiatives, many arranged by the members themselves, which help remove 'awkward self-consciousness and restore a healthy attitude of mind which takes the opposite sex for granted' (*Annual Report*, 1929, 60).

While some historians (Humphries, 1988; Gillis, 1985) have argued that strict segregation of the sexes continued to be the norm during the inter-war period, it is evident that despite their single-sex status, both the Guides and YWCA saw it as within their remit to promote heterosexual development. Through sex education and supervised heterosexual contact they aimed to ensure that young women developed the right kind of attitudes and relationships, rather than being exposed to the uncontrolled atmosphere of the streets and the unregulated sexual information available through peers and in workplaces.

These organisations' attempts to regulate young women's behaviour, particularly in the arena of sexuality, during the inter-war period were, of course, nothing new. Janet Batsleer has discussed the continuities between 19th century concerns and current practices, highlighting the existence of a 'consistent agenda of seeing girls as "at risk", in need of protection and training in becoming a woman' (Batsleer, 1996, 16). What was new, however, was the development of a discourse which problematised girls' unregulated sexual activity not just because of the dangers of pregnancy, disease and social isolation but because such activity would jeopardise their future sexual fulfilment. Within this, sex education was allocated a vital role, as earlier equations of ignorance with innocence gave way to formulations which stressed the importance of knowledge as a basis for moral choice (Bland, 1992). The popularisation of the concept of adolescence as a formative period of life and the increasing reliance on the insights of psychology created a new focus on issues of individual identity. This was reinforced by the stress on women as citizens and the greater independence and opportunities (actual or perceived) available to young women. Sex education therefore formed part of the project of creating responsible citizens – including those girls who had already transgressed acceptable behaviour – whose actions and values were determined not by protection or segregation imposed by external agencies, but from the exercise of individual moral choice. As the records of the YWCA's hostels indicate, provision formulated in terms of the protection of girls by others did continue in the inter-war period, but increasingly both the YWCA and the Guides represented themselves as endeavouring to lead girls to a positive basis for behaviour based on their own moral agency and self-regulation.

Bibliography

Batsleer, J. (1996). *Working with Girls and Young Women in Community Settings*. Aldershot, Gower.

Beaumont, C. (1996). *Women and Citizenship: A study of non-feminist women's societies and the women's movement in England, 1928–1950*. PhD thesis, University of Warwick.

Bland, L. (1992). 'Guardians of the Race or Vampires upon the Nation's Health: Female sexuality and its regulation in early twentieth-century Britain' in *The Changing Experience of Women*, E. Whitelegg, (ed). London, Basil Blackwell.

Bondfield, M. (1936). 'A Challenge to the Freeborn, notes of an address', in *Blue Triangle Gazette*, Vol 54, No 12, p 197–98.

'Book Worm' (1929). 'On Reading' in *'Our Own Gazette,* 1929, Vol 47, No 5, pp 4–5. British Social Hygiene Council (1936), minutes of the Social Hygiene Committee, 12 May.

Burt, C. (1926). 'The Causes of Sex-Delinquency in Girls' in *Health and Empire*, December, pp 251–71.

Burt, C. (1927). *The Sub-Normal School-Child: Volume one, the young delinquent*. London, University of London Press. (2nd edition.)

Committee for the Extension of Guide Training to Mentally, Morally and Physically Defective Girls (1921). *Girl Guide Companies in Institutions*. London, Girl Guides Association, 1921.

Committee on the Drop in Numbers on the Girl Guides (1937). *Report*. London, Girl Guides Association.

Crichton Miller, H. (1926). 'The Adolescent Girl and the Guide Movement' in *Annual Report*. London, Girl Guides Association.

Crichton Miller, Mrs (1924). 'The Difficult Girl', in *Girl Guides Gazette,* October, p 275.

Crichton Miller, Mrs (1933). 'Auxiliary Guides', in *Annual Report*. London, Girl Guides Association, pp 70–73.

Departmental Committee on Sexual Offences Against Young Persons (1925). *Report* [Cmd 2561]. HMSO, London.

Forsythe, W. J. (1990). *Penal Discipline, Reformatory Projects and the English Prison Commission 1895–1939*. Exeter, University of Exeter Press, 1990.

Gillis, J. R. (1985). *For Better for Worse: British marriages, 1600 to the present*. Oxford, Oxford University Press.

Girl Guides Association (1918–1939). *Annual Reports*. London, Girl Guides Association.

Girl Guides Association (1918–27). *Girl Guides' Gazette*. London, Girl Guides Association.

Girl Guides Association (1928–39). *The Guider*. London, Girl Guides Association.

Girl Guides Association (1918). *Girl Guiding*. London, Girl Guides Association.

Girl Guides Association (1928). *The Transmission of Life* (1928). London, Girl Guides Association.

Graves, R. and Hodge, A. (1995). *The Long Weekend: A social history of Great Britain 1918–1939*. London, Abacus (First published 1940).

Griffith, E. F. (1935). *Modern Marriage*. London, Victor Gollancz.

Home Office (1923). *Report on the Work of the Children's Branch*. London, HMSO.

Humphries, S. (1988). *A Secret World of Sex: Forbidden Fruit: The British Experience 1900–1950*. London, Sidgwick and Jackson.

Kerr, R., (1932). *The Story of the Girl Guides*. London, The Girl Guides Association.

Kinnard, E. (1920). 'To the Girl of To-morrow', in *Our Own Gazette,* June 1920, p 15.

Lewis, J. (1980). *The Politics of Motherhood. Child and maternal welfare in England, 1900–1939*. London, Croom Helm.

Lowenfeld, M. (1934). 'Notes on Living in the Modern World', in *YWCA Bulletin* Vol 12, No 9, p 7.

Matthias, Miss (1928). 'The Characteristics and Claims of Youth' in *YWCA Bulletin,* Vol VIII, No 9, p 2.

Ministry of Health (1920). *First Annual Report 1919–20*. London, HMSO.

Ministry of Health (1921). *Second Annual Report 1920–21*. London, HMSO.

National Birth Rate Commission (1923). *Youth and the Race: The development and education of young citizens for worthy parenthood*. London, Kegan Paul, Trench, Trubner.

Picton-Turbervill, E. (1922). 'Should Girls Remain at Home?' in *Our Own Gazette,* Vol 40, No 3, p 5.

Picton-Turbervill, E. (1926). 'A Great Adventure: The story of the moral care hostels', in *Our Own Gazette,* Vol 44, No 6, p 17.

Porter, R. and Hall, L. (1995). *The Facts of Life: The creation of sexual knowledge in Britain, 1650–1950.* London, Yale University Press.

'Ranger Problems and Possibilities' (1924). In *Girl Guides' Gazette,* December, p 341–42.

Robertson, C. G. (1925). 'Why I believe in the Girl Guides', in *Annual Report,* p 23–26.

Roch, F. (1918). 'Romance', in *Girl Guides' Gazette,* November, pp 152–55.

Rooff, M. (1935). *Youth and Leisure: A survey of girls' organisations in England and Wales.* Edinburgh, T. and A. Constable.

Royden, M. (1924). 'The Good Turn', in *Annual Report.* London, The Girl Guides Association, pp 19–20.

Swainston, Z. (1920). 'How an Association like the YWCA can meet the needs of the average girl', in *Our Own Gazette,* Vol 38, No 9, pp 20–21.

Weeks, J. (1989). *Sex, Politics and Society: The regulation of sexuality since 1800.* London, Longman.

Woollacott, A. (1994). 'Khaki Fever and its Control: Gender, class, age and sexual morality on the British homefront in the First World War', in *Journal of Contemporary History,* Vol 29, pp 325–47.

Young Women's Christian Association (1918–39). *Annual Reports.* London, YWCA.

Young Women's Christian Association, *The Blue Triangle Gazette* 1928–33.

Young Women's Christian Association, *The Blue Triangle Gazette,* 1934–38.

Young Women's Christian Association (undated 1919?). *Fathers and Mothers of Happy Girls.* London, YWCA, leaflet.

Young Women's Christian Association (1937–39). *Health and Physical Education Minute Book,* November 1937-June 1939, YWCA.

Young Women's Christian Association (1918–38). *Homes for Working Girls in London Annual Reports.* London, YWCA.

Young Women's Christian Association (1918–20). The Referendum Movement 1918–1920, unpublished papers, YWCA.

Young Women's Christian Association (1920–27). *Our Own Gazette.* London, YWCA.

Young Women's Christian Association (1914–1920). *A Review August 1914 to January 1920.* London, YWCA.

Young Women's Christian Association (1921–1934). *YWCA Bulletin.* London, YWCA.

The Reverend Canon Dr E. G. Pace

Chapter ten

Durham House Settlement: Its history and place in the settlement movement

Ian McGimpsey

In 1883 Toynbee Hall opened its doors. Calling itself a university settlement, it was headed by its warden, Canon Samuel Augustus Barnett. The first of its kind, Toynbee proved to be the beginning of one of the most widespread and significant social reform movements of the last two hundred years. Just under half a century later Durham House Settlement began its life under the wardenship of Eric S. Barber. Many may know of Toynbee Hall, but it is likely that few recall the Durham House Settlement. While the history of Toynbee Hall and a number of other settlements have been well recorded, the histories, life, particular struggles and achievements of a hundred or more other settlements remain undocumented. To understand Durham House Settlement, it is important to first look at the ideas and heritage from which it emerged.

Born in Bristol Samuel Barnett had a relatively undistinguished early life. After gaining a degree in history and law at Wadham College, Oxford he joined the established church in 1870. Barnett came under the wing of a progressive clergyman, William Henry Fremantle who believed that the church, in the face of increasing pressure to be disestablished, should square up to its responsibilities to become 'much more than it is now the Church of the People…[otherwise] its power of doing good will be lost through the cessation of its hold on the respect of the people' (Fremantle quoted Kadish, 1986, 56). Equally influential on both Barnett and his future wife, Henrietta Roland, was Octavia Hill. Working closely with the Christian Socialists, Hill came to meet and be greatly affected by John Ruskin (Carson, 1990, 3–4). Ruskin also supported her work financially enabling her to improve properties for rent to the poor (Anthony, 1983, 184). She enforced prompt payment of rents and in return the profits were used for the improvement of the building, the organisation of activities and community provision such as playgroups. She employed middle-class people to become friends, rent collectors and moral leaders to the poor. She hoped thereby to teach the poor responsibility, give them some pride and sense of community, and to re-connect rich and poor through personal contact (ibid, 4; Briggs and Macartney, 1984, 36). It was while working for Hill that Henrietta Roland and Samuel Barnett first met.

After working with Hill and Fremantle, Samuel Barnett was offered the living at the age of 28 of St Jude's in Whitechapel, London. Bishop Jackson, who had arranged the living, described the area as the 'worst in my diocese' (Pimlott, 1935, 15), with an unenviable reputation for criminality, violence, dependency on doles and begging. Inspired by Edward Denison (an Oxford graduate who lived and worked among the poor of East London), who Henrietta Barnett later called the 'first settler', going to '[breathe] the air of the people [where] he absorbed something of their sufferings' (Barnett and Barnett, 1915, 107), the Barnetts began to take in other recruits from Oxford willing to follow his example. In Whitechapel, they met a young Oxford student, Arnold Toynbee. Due to ill health this charismatic young man was unable to stay in the area as long as intended. However, deeply affected by his experiences he invited the Barnetts to Oxford to speak to the undergraduates about the problems of East London (Barnett and Barnett, 1915, 112). They found enthusiastic and responsive audiences. This was partly because Toynbee and other undergraduates had been influenced by a number of thinkers, notably T. H. Green and Ruskin who emphasised the importance of active citizenship and social service. This combination of inspirational thinking and youthful enthusiasm linked to the hard work of the Barnetts led to the founding of Toynbee Hall.

Ruskin may have been an erratic thinker and personality, but it is undeniable that he possessed great charisma. In his writings Ruskin combined art criticism with social criticism. He argued that the material poverty of the poor, their uncertain prospects, and the repetitive, inhuman nature of their daily toil created not just physical hardship, but ensured that both 'soul and sight be worn away, and the whole human being be lost at last' (Ruskin, 1985, 85). It is easy to suppose he annoyed many members of the middle class who blamed the poor for their own condition. Ruskin contended that 'in most cases it is all our own fault that they are tardy or torpid' (ibid, 84) and condemned the wealthy as 'slave-masters' (ibid, 85). In contrast to those seeking a revolutionary solution to national inequality, Ruskin believed that a change in the morality of the people would eventually produce a desirable society.

Green also believed in the need for people to define themselves in relation to society as a whole. He argued that individuals should, of their own volition, regulate their behaviour in order to take into account the common good (1907, 157–159). Green claimed that society bestowed rights upon individuals on the assumption that they would act in accordance with the common good (ibid, 159, 209). The obligation of individuals was to promote the best society possible for the good of all. As people's conception of the common good would be influenced by what they understood to be a good life, their experiences of education, religion and culture were capable of altering how they acted towards those around them. Therefore, individuals had the responsibility to develop themselves and their abilities to the utmost (Jeffs, 1998, 13). These ideas left Green somewhat unsure about state coercion even towards the achievement of good, as only actions born of the free volition of individuals were of real moral worth.

While there are parallels between the thinking of Ruskin and Green the former tended more towards the idea of the state as provider for the individual (Kadish, 1986, 37; Ruskin, 1985, 21, 22). However, Green felt that the state's role was one of removing the obstacles preventing people from cultivating their best selves; obstacles such as a lack of access to schooling, hunger and disease. In this sense Barnett seemed more closely allied to Green's line of thinking. As Barnett grew older he developed the idea that the apparent moral and spiritual poverty of the poor was related to their social and physical environment. Both of which could be changed (Meacham, 1987, 23). For those such as Barnett, the tackling of social problems became essentially a matter of educating both rich and poor. The rich needed to understand the issues of poverty and use their position to help change the environment of all. There was a parallel need to raise the sights and spirits of the poor through bringing to them the culture, knowledge and ideas ordinarily reserved for the middle and upper classes (ibid, 55).

In November 1883 Canon Barnett gave a talk entitled 'Settlements of university men in great towns' in St John's College, Oxford. In this, he outlined a project whereby the 'life of the university [would be brought to bear on] the life of the poor' (Barnett and Barnett, 1915, 98). The idea was that this would be a venture in which enthusiastic volunteers of any religious persuasion (including agnostic) could take part. The purpose would be educational, and seek to associate the rich and the poor on a personal level. To achieve this a suitable building would be purchased with accommodation for university undergraduates and graduates and rooms in which lectures, social gatherings and all kind of workshops and classes would be held (Barnett and Barnett, 1915, 7). It would become a place where people of all kinds, rich and poor, high and low would meet and get to know each other (Meacham, 1987, 33). The settlers would be guided in their endeavours to reach out to the poor by the warden, a person of learning, an amiable and enthusiastic personality to whom people could easily relate (ibid).

There was from the beginning an unwillingness to be tied down to any specific way of doing things. Picht probably best describes what might be called the attitude, rather than the method:

He [the settler] mistrusts dead organisations, and would replace them by personal relationships. Not as an official but as a friend does he approach the poor, and he knows that he is thereby not only the giver but the receiver. Life instead of machinery, exact knowledge of the conditions to be improved, in the midst of which he must place himself instead of trusting to an unreliable judgment from a bird's-eye view. . . . Crystallisation would have meant . . . immediate death, and denial of its most characteristic ideals.
(Picht, 1935, 2)

With the opening of the settlement, named after Arnold Toynbee following his death the previous year, the movement was born. The *List of the Settlements in Great Britain* supplied by Picht (1914) indicates the rapidity of the dissemination of the idea. By 1914 the settlement idea had spread throughout Britain and made its mark upon American industrial towns and cities. All settlements were not entirely faithful to the original concept. For example, not all were linked to universities. Some were religious, others were not, some were women's settlements, and so on. The settlements were generally eclectic, seldom tying themselves to goals other than association and the provision of opportunity for personal contact and service. They also researched the local environment in order to be more effective in their work and sought to adapt their goals and work according to the needs of the locality (Meacham, 1987, 8).

Settlements in the north east

North east England had a number of educational settlements, including Lemmington just outside Newcastle, Bensham Grove, Gateshead, and later Rock House, Seaham and Spennymoor (Gilchrist and McGimpsey, 2000, 35). The industrial north east in the 1930s was experiencing economic difficulties. According to W. G. Farrell, Spennymoor Settlement's first warden, the town was 'but one little part of the wreckage left on the verge of civilisation's shore by the receding tide of economic prosperity' (Farrell, 1938). The story was little different in Durham City. The situation described by Farrell was clearly viewed with serious concern by settlers in London. J. J. Mallon, then warden of Toynbee Hall, was keen to see such disquiet translated into activity. He later wrote:

> It is worth while briefly to compare Spennymoor on the dark wet day on which Mr Farrell and I first saw it with Spennymoor as it will be on the perhaps radiant day on which we shall celebrate the 21st birthday of the settlement . . . Spennymoor had lost heart. Spennymoor was weak and shaken and spent and nearly dead . . . [Now,] dignified by work, unpestered by hunger and poverty, and the degrading inability to sustain those who depend on us, we can meet [new challenges] 'with a heart for any fate'.
> (Spennymoor Settlement's 21st Birthday Commemorative Magazine, 33)

In 1931 the British Association of Residential Settlements (BARS) opened Spennymoor Settlement and less than two years later a settlement in Durham. This work was a part of the pioneering work of BARS in 'depressed areas'. The focus was on social service, education and cooperation with organisations already involved in the field, especially the National Council of Social Service and the Educational Settlements Association (Pimlott, 1935, 240–241). It was believed that the settlement approach would be effective in bringing renewed hope, spirit and opportunities to individuals and communities in depressed areas (Briggs & Macartney, 1984, 116).

The planned launch of Durham House Settlement gained unanimous approval from the Coalfields Settlements Committee of BARS in July 1933. A letter from Barbara Murray of BARS to Dr Pace, (24 July 1933) made recommendations based on the London experience which included coordinating work for the welfare of the unemployed, becoming a neighbourhood centre for the city, and the furtherance of the 'educational and social work' in the surrounding villages.

There is continuity between this and the first recorded constitution written by the Settlement Committee six months later. The subtitle of the organisation was 'University, City and District Settlement' which reflected the institutions and geography mentioned in the recommendations from BARS. It aimed to promote adult education through the provision of classes for those over 18. It also sought to become a focal point for the provision of adult education in the city itself, while linking organisations involved in the district to make more effective the provision beyond the city. There is also mention of aiming to become a centre for the study of social problems in the area. This final point, although not mentioned by BARS, remains consistent with what was happening elsewhere in the settlement movement (Constitution of Durham House Settlement, January 1934).

Durham House is often referred to in different ways, sometimes as an educational settlement, but also as a residential and coalfield settlement (Warden's Report, 2nd May, 1936). The latter title reflected the geography and administration. Durham City and its surrounding villages' populations were then heavily involved in coal mining. Importantly Spennymoor and Durham Settlements were both dealt with by the Coalfields Settlements Committee.

One of the descriptions most frequently used was university settlement. The links with the University of Durham were close. The main building of the settlement and the warden's residence was 3 Queen Street (now Owen Gate) provided by the university free of charge for almost nine years. This site was close to where most of the Durham university colleges were then situated. Many members of the Durham House Settlement Council were lecturers or administrators at the university (for example, see 'Members of Council of Durham House Settlement', 4th July 1934). In addition, many of the events that the settlement organised took place on university property (for example, see 'Durham House Settlement Musical Group's First Concert' Programme, 19th March 1934 which was held in Hatfield College Hall). Durham House was in a prime position to attempt to bring the life of the university to bear on the lives of the people who surrounded it, as had been Canon Barnett's wish. Durham House, like many other settlements, had no student residents. The settlement, unlike Toynbee Hall, was located in the heart of the university. At the same time it was close enough to the ordinary people it was trying to reach.

The success of settlements seems traditionally to be dependent on the charisma, ingenuity, determination and energy of their leaders. Durham House was no exception. The Settlement Council was chaired by a man not to be intimidated by circumstance or task, and who remained chairman until the end, The Reverend Canon Dr E. G. Pace. Pace was a reader in divinity at Durham University for 26 years, and vice-master of the Durham College of Hatfield from 1917 to 1947. He was also director of extra-mural studies in the Durham Division from 1925 to 1947. He was, by all accounts, a popular figure in his college and the university (Hatfield Record, Vol 1, No 1, 7–8) and his obituary highlights his 'personality and strength of character' (Hatfield Record, Vol 1, No 1, 194). Durham House benefited from these qualities in his time there and despite having retired from his university responsibilities, partially on health grounds, Pace remained chair of the Spennymoor Settlement Council for at least a further four years. He was credited, along with Farrell, as having ensured the survival of the Spennymoor Settlement (Mallon in Spennymoor Settlement's 21st birthday commemorative magazine).

The first warden of Durham House, Eric S. Barber, was appointed in August 1933 (Durham House Settlement Provisional Council Meeting minutes, 24th July 1933). Two months after his appointment, a leaflet appeared advertising the programme of the settlement.

In it is a list of classes, covering an impressive range of subjects, included languages, basic sciences, drama, choral singing and orchestral groups, economics and current affairs. By April 1934, the first dramatic production by members of Durham House, *As You Like It*, produced by Eric Barber, was performed.

The settlement, if numbers are any guideline, was initially very successful. The warden reported 250 individuals using the settlement by January 1934 (Durham House Council Meeting Minutes, 24th January 1934). It is difficult to know the impact upon the lives of the people who participated. However, all indications are that through dramatic, choral and orchestral classes and productions, the settlement enabled people to access art and culture that otherwise would have been out of reach. Early in the settlement's life there were attempts to undertake a 'sociological survey' (Durham House Council Meeting Minutes, 10 October 1933). However, this was not subsequently discussed in any great detail in later minutes. There is evidence of work in the wider district with the warden reporting on attendance at meetings held in surrounding villages (ibid).

In this profusion of activity, there were commonalities and crossovers in the work and life of Durham House and Spennymoor Settlements. Farrell sat upon the Durham House Settlement Committee. Both settlements and their wardens had a preoccupation with drama; indeed each put on similar plays (for example, both staged plays by Ibsen). In addition, the literature of each settlement described its visions and goals in similar terms:

Durham House is a settlement – that is to say, a meeting place for men and women of every description who would like to increase their knowledge, widen their interests and make new friends. It is attached to no political party or religious denomination. Membership, at a very moderate fee, is open to anyone over the age of 18 in the city and district.
(Eric S. Barber in a programme for Durham House Settlement Members' performance of *As You Like It*, 26–28 April 1934)

Spennymoor Settlement's first syllabus stated that:
The settlement seeks to encourage tolerant neighbourliness and voluntary social service, and provides for its members opportunities to increase their knowledge, widen their interests, and cultivate their creative powers in a friendly atmosphere.
(Farrell, 1938)

The similarities are obvious. It was not long before a combination of perceived need related to the prevailing economic conditions and the evident levels of cooperation between settlements in the area resulted in an expanded vision. May 1934 saw a Durham House council meeting attended by a representative from BARS mooting an ambitious plan. This was the possibility of setting up a number of new settlements in the region. The idea was to make Durham a regional centre for the cooperation of local settlements and the establishment of a Settlements Regional Council, based at Durham House (Durham House Council Meeting Minutes, 14 May 1934). Three years later a draft constitution appeared for a County Durham Joint Settlements Council which incorporated these aims (County Durham Joint Settlements Council Draft Constitution, undated). It proposed to involve Spennymoor,

Rock House and Durham House but Rock House quickly dropped out of the process, thereby damaging the chances of success. After 1938 documentation refers instead to a Joint Council for Durham House and Spennymoor Settlements. Having established a number of settlements in deprived areas and observed their early success, Mallon clearly had plans for expansion. In the Toynbee Hall Jubilee Report of 1935, he mentioned that Durham House had 'aroused a new interest in social work' in both the city and 'neighbouring villages'. He went on that for the stimulating effect to continue, 'the founding of further settlements in these areas and elsewhere may soon be expected' (cited in Briggs and Macartney, 1984, 116).

Decline

By 1937, despite these ambitious plans, BARS may have detected signs of a terminal decline in the fortunes of Durham House. Barber had already resigned as had the sub-warden, Mr Roy H. Blew-Jones (letter from Eric S. Barber to Dr Pace, 10th May 1935 and letter from Roy H. Blew-Jones to Dr Pace, 25th April 1935). No reasons were given.

The new warden, E. G. Mawson was a graduate of Liverpool University who prior to appointment lectured in economics, social problems and the social sciences for the WEA and Fircroft College. Taking a break from lecturing in the 1930s he worked for the Federation of Prison Aid Societies, and the Friend's Unemployed Welfare Centre in Manchester. He applied while in post with the FUWC saying that he desired to have a job that would offer him scope for his 'educational and social interests' (letter from Mawson, 11th June 1935).

Evidence that there had been a decline in the settlement's fortunes could be inferred by Mawson's report to the Coalfields Settlements Committee in 1936. In it he recommended for the future health of the settlement the continuation 'of all activities which seemed to have been successful, and only introducing new ones when there appeared to be a real demand'. At this stage it is noted that Durham House is now only open on weekday evenings, as opposed to the 10am to 10pm six days a week previously (Durham House Settlement warden's report as delivered to the Coalfields Settlement Committee, 2nd May 1936). Numbers appear to have fallen rapidly, although Farrell was trying to reorganise the Durham House Players (successfully, at least for a time) and new activities were still being tried.

The settlement movement in Britain as a whole was struggling due to the economic difficulties of the late 1920s and the 1930s (Glasby, 1999, 14). However, for Durham House, problems came to a head in 1941 when the university decided to take back the property due to an 'acute shortage' of space caused by the military occupation of all available buildings. The settlement was given eight months to find alternative premises (letter to Dr Pace written on behalf of Durham University, 3rd November 1941).

With three months left before eviction, a letter was received by Pace from the National Council for Social Service (NCSS) complaining of incoherence and a lack of cooperation on the part of the warden (letter from G. Haynes on behalf of the NCSS to Dr Pace, 18th

March 1942). The NCSS were crucial to the settlement's economic viability. Durham House was already in debt at this stage and things were clearly in a state of some confusion.

Pace successfully applied for funding on behalf of the settlement (letter from G. B. Stow on behalf of the NCSS to Dr Pace, 10th June 1942), but failed to acquire alternative property. As an alternative he hoped to survive by using on an occasional basis small rooms that the settlement had previously acquired, by selling off equipment to settle debts and by reorganising the staff. The most interesting feature of the reorganisation was the decision that the warden be 'advised to seek alternative employment due to the uncertain nature of the future of the settlement' (letter from Dr Pace to Mr Haynes of the NCSS, 2 June 1942). Mawson's resignation was duly tendered (letter from Dr Pace to Mrs Caillard of The Pilgrim Trust, 12th May 1942).

Despite Farrell's commitment to do his best to help, the lack of a warden, traditionally the rudder of any settlement, was addressed in a fascinating and heartening way. Such was the commitment to the institution, that members agreed to take on the running of the settlement themselves (letter from Dr Pace to Mr Haynes of the NCSS, 2 June, 1942). This is probably unique in a movement so committed to the idea of leadership. Unfortunately, there was no arresting the decline. In 1947 Pace retired from both the university (*The Durham University Journal*, March 1953) and the settlement. With his withdrawal the settlement appears to have breathed its last. The optimism that the solution to many of the problems would come with the end of the war was unfounded, no record of Durham House Settlement can be traced after 1947.

Conclusion

Durham House was initially a central part of the settlement movement's ambitions to make a difference to an area of acute deprivation. Questions must be asked as to why it floundered, why others in similar circumstances did not, and what, despite its relatively short life span, it achieved. In its lifetime, Durham House showed an ability to pour itself into the city, filling cracks and holes in provision. This is probably its principle 'settlement' characteristic. Its concern with the democratisation of the knowledge, culture, and other advantages that the university possessed, but which working–class and unemployed men and women in the surrounding areas lacked, remained faithful to the settlement ideal, as did its commitment to serve as a meeting place for all.

Durham House was also concerned with research into the lives of local people. However, the research undertaken was on a much smaller scale that that encountered in some other settlements, especially Toynbee Hall. Durham House's priorities simply appeared to lie elsewhere and the sociological surveys fell by the wayside. This may have contributed to its downfall. Around the time of the change of warden, Durham House appears to have become complacent, failing to find a new focus when it was most needed, wasting resources and losing effectiveness and popularity as a result. The dynamic of intimate and personal knowledge of the people feeding directly back into practice that existed to such good effect at Toynbee Hall was simply not in evidence at Durham House.

Finally, Durham House relied on individual personalities. This is characteristic of the movement. Key individuals (with the exception of Pace) seem to have let the venture down. When Mawson replaced Barber, what was demanded was a reorganisation of provision, a change of ideas and a better use of resources. A new person at the helm generally brings new ideas. Mawson seems to have let the settlement down albeit in unforgiving times. The manner of his departure was ignominious, and thereafter it fell to an ageing Dr Pace to carry the settlement forward, a task he performed with stoicism. Despite a dogged enthusiasm to keep going, shared by his co-workers, the settlement perished, leaving Durham City and its people the poorer for its passing.

Bibliography

Primary Sources

Appeal pamphlet, W. G. Farrell, Spennymoor Settlement (1938). *The First Seven Years at Spennymoor Settlement – A historical sketch and appeal.* Produced by the Joint Settlements Council (Durham House and Spennymoor).

Concert programme, Durham House Settlement Musical Group's *First Concert*, 19th March 1934. Durham County Hall, Records Office.

Concert programme, *Durham House Settlement – A dramatized concert programme of Old English music entitled 'When George III Was King'*. 15th & 16th June 1937. Durham County Hall, Records Office.

Constitution document of Durham House Settlement. January 1934. Unpublished document. Durham County Hall, Records Office.

Constitution document (draft) of the County Durham Joint Settlements Council. Undated. Unpublished document, Durham County Hall, Records Office.

Council Members list, *Members of Council of Durham House Settlement*, 4th July 1934. Unpublished document, Durham County Hall, Records Office.

Letter from Miss Barbara Murray, representing BARS, to Dr Pace of Durham House Settlement, 24th July 1933. Unpublished correspondence, Durham County Hall, Records Office.

Letter from Roy H. Blew-Jones, subwarden of Durham House Settlement to Dr Pace of Durham House Settlement, 25th April 1935. Unpublished correspondence, Durham County Hall, Records Office.

Letter from Eric S. Barber, warden of Durham House Settlement to Dr Pace of Durham House Settlement, 10th May 1935. Unpublished correspondence, Durham County, Records Office.

Letter from Dr Pace of Durham House Settlement to Mr C. Watson, 3rd June 1935. Unpublished correspondence, Durham County Hall, Records Office.

Letter from Mr Eric G. Mawson to the Chairman of Durham House Settlement, 11th June 1935. Unpublished correspondence, Durham County Hall, Records Office.

Letter from Hon. Asst. Secretary of Durham House Settlement to Mr E. G. Mawson, 6th July 1935. Unpublished correspondence, Durham County Hall, Records Office.

Aldham Roberts L.R.C.
TEL. 051 231 3701/3634

Letter from J. H. Richardson (Hon. Secretary) to all members of the Joint Council for Durham House and Spennymoor Settlements, 6th May 1939. Unpublished correspondence, Durham County Hall, Records Office.

Letter on behalf of Durham University to Dr Pace, 3rd November 1941. Unpublished correspondence, Durham County Hall, Records Office.

Letter from G. Haynes on behalf of the NCSS to Dr Pace, 18th March 1942. Unpublished correspondence, Durham County Hall, Records Office.

Letter from Dr Pace to Mrs Caillard of The Pilgrim Trust, 12th May 1942. Unpublished correspondence, Durham County Hall, Records Office.

Letter from Dr Pace to G. Haynes, 2nd June 1942. Unpublished correspondence, Durham County Hall, Records Office.

Letter from B. G. Stow on behalf of the NCSS to Dr Pace, 10th June 1942. Unpublished correspondence, Durham County, Records Office.

Minutes of a meeting of the Durham House Settlement Provisional Council, July 24th 1933. Unpublished minutes, Durham County Hall, Records Office.

Minutes of a meeting of the Durham House Settlement Council, 10th October 1933. Unpublished minutes, Durham County Hall, Records Office.

Minutes of a meeting of the Durham House Settlement Council, 24th January 1934. Unpublished minutes, Durham County Hall Records Office.

Minutes of a meeting of the Durham House Settlement Council, 14th May 1934. Unpublished minutes, Durham County Hall, Records Office.

Newspaper article, *'Wild Decembers' staged in Durham*, *Durham County Advertiser*, 7 May 1937. Copy of article found in Durham County Hall, Records Office.

Production programme, *Durham Shakespeare Birthday Production of 'As You Like It' by William Shakespeare*, 26th, 27th and 28th April 1934. Durham County Hall, Records Office.

Production programme, *The Durham House Players in 'Peer Gynt' by Henrik Ibsen with incidental music by Edvard Grieg*, 1934. Copy found in Durham County Hall, Records Office.

Publicity leaflet, *Classes at Durham House Settlement*, October 1933. Durham County Hall, Records Office.

Warden's report, Durham House Settlement (as given to the Coalfields Committee of BARS), 2nd May 1936. Unpublished report, Durham County Hall, Records Office.

Secondary Sources

Anthony, P. D. (1983). *John Ruskin's Labour: A study of Ruskin's social theory.* Cambridge, Cambridge University Press.

Barnett, Canon S. A. and Barnett, Mrs S. A. (1915). *Practicable Socialism (New Series).* London, Longmans, Green and Co.

Briggs, A. and Macartney, A. (1984). *Toynbee Hall: The first hundred years.* London, Routledge and Kegan Paul.

Carson, M. (1990). *Settlement Folk – Social thought and the American Settlement Movement, 1885–1930.* Chicago, University of Chicago Press.

Durham University Journal, The, March 1953 in *Durham University Journal,* The, Vol XLV, 1952–1953 (1954). Durham, The University of Durham.

Farrell, W. G. (1938). *The First Seven Years at Spennymoor Settlement.* Spennymoor, Spennymoor Settlement.

Glasby, J. (1999). *Poverty and Opportunity: 100 years of the Birmingham Settlement.* Studley, Brewin Books.

Gilchrist, R. and McGimpsey, I. in J. Glasby, (ed) (2000). *'Back To The Future': The history of the settlement movement and its relevance for organisations today.* Birmingham, University of Birmingham.

Green, T. H. (1907). *Lectures on the Principles of Political Obligation.* London, Longmans, Green and Co.

Hatfield Record, Vol 1, 1947–1953. Durham, Hatfield College.

Jeffs, T. (1998). *Henry Morris: Village colleges, community education and the ideal order.* Nottingham, Educational Heretics Press.

Kadish, A. (1986). *Apostle Arnold – The life and death of Arnold Toynbee 1852–1883.* Durham N. C., Duke University Press.

Meacham, S. (1987). *Toynbee Hall and Social Reform 1880–1914: The search for community.* New Haven, Yale University Press.

Picht, W. (1914). *Toynbee Hall and the English Settlement Movement (Lilian A. Cowell, trans.).* London, G. Bell and Sons.

Pimlott, J. A. R. (1935). *Toynbee Hall: Fifty years of social progress 1884–1934.* London, J. M. Dent and Sons.

Ruskin, J. (1985). *Unto This Last And Other Writings.* London, Penguin Books.

Twenty-First Birthday Commemorative Magazine (1957). Spennymoor Settlement.

WOMEN'S CONTINGENT
MARCHING
TO LONDON
AGAINST
THE MEANS TEST

Social action in the 1930s

Chapter eleven

Fellowship and Reconstruction: Social action and unemployment in the 1930s

Crescy Cannan

As Malcolm Muggeridge wrote in his survey of the 1930s, these years were a time of rival 'heavens on earth'; there were intense cleavages of opinion and few were immune to debates about religion and aetheism, communism and fascism, dictatorship and democracy (Muggeridge, 1940/1967, 42–45). In this atmosphere many young people brought their ideals to areas of great poverty, not only as a form of service, but as part of a wider scheme of reconstruction of an unjust world.

This chapter looks at the Government's reliance on the voluntary sector, coordinated by the National Council of Social Service (NCSS), to cope with the effects of unemployment. I will then focus on the work of the Quakers in south Wales, especially the work of Hilda Jennings and Peter Scott, relating them to other contemporary activists including Rolf Gardiner. I hope to show that their projects have a lasting relevance, stressing as they do the importance of connecting social and economic development and central principles (in the case of the Quakers) of the common good and the inclusion of all sections of society in community building. If today's concerns in youth and community work are the combatting of exclusion and the creation of new forms of work, then the thirties have a good deal to teach us.

The background: Government responses to unemployment

While high unemployment is generally associated with the 30s, the roots of what was to come lay in the early 20s. A brief post-war boom had been quickly followed by a slump, wage cuts and industrial strife, culminating in the General Strike in 1926. The 1929 Wall Street Crash deepened the depression in which the 'older' industries of coal mining, ship building, iron and steel, and textiles already bore the brunt. Long-term unemployment was concentrated in south Wales, the north east of England, and Strathclyde, regions where conditions differed markedly from the increasing prosperity of the Midlands and the south east of England with their new industries, new suburbs and rising car ownership.

The Labour Government, and the National Government which succeeded it in 1931 under the leadership of Ramsay Macdonald, conformed to the prevailing economic orthodoxy that the correct response to a depression was to cut public expenditure, reducing the level of benefits. This meant that for many unemployed and their dependents, the stigma of the Poor Laws continued in the new local authority Public Assistance Committees (PACs) with their hated means tests. In 1934 the Unemployment Assistance Board (UAB) was established to administer benefits (which were often lower than the PAC benefits) to the unemployed, and to run limited training schemes, help for those who wished to transfer to more prosperous areas, and allotment schemes (Bruce, 1961, 243). The UAB often put pressure on young men to attend its training camps whose officials were explicit about their objectives of 'reconditioning human material' and 'toughening the fibre of men who have got out of the way of work' (cited in Colledge and Field, 1983, 156). The National Unemployed Workers' Movement (NUWM) protested about conditions in these 'slave' camps, the regimentation of the men, and the lack of skills training or education, and of useful public works (Hannington, 1937).

As unemployment continued to rise and its regional aspects became clearer, a Special Areas Commission was established in 1934 to look at economic development in areas variously designated as distressed or depressed. The £2 million allocated was seen as niggardly by the labour movement compared to other subsidies, for instance, Hannington, Communist leader of the NUWM, showed that £4.5 million was given to Cunard for the luxury liner the Queen Mary (Hannington, 1937), and Lloyd George spoke for Labour as well as the Liberals when he pointed out that it would take a miracle for £2 million to solve a problem costing the country £100 million a year (cited in Jones, 1991, 112). Bruce (1961, 244) describes the approach as 'altogether . . . too cautious to achieve much', lacking the dynamism and imagination of the public works projects in America, and the Commissioner for Special Areas in England, Sir Malcolm Stewart was to resign in 1936 over the limited scope he was allowed.

British social policy in the 30s then saw an inadequate system of cash benefits, dismally limited resources for economic development, and indignation in the labour movement about the 'slave camps' and the failure of the Government to instigate public works programmes. While these policies emerged from the economic theories of the day, 'inter-war governments were also influenced by a number of other ideas about the boundaries of public responsibility and the importance of voluntary initiative' (Harris, 1995, 533). Thus the Government matched pound for pound the Lord Mayors' Fund for the Relief of Women and Children in Distressed Mining Areas in 1928–9. In 1932, in response to increasing public concern about unemployment, the Government identified the NCSS, an umbrella organisation for voluntary social action, as the body to coordinate the huge charitable donations and to oversee and stimulate local projects which were often run by, or in partnership with, other voluntary organisations (Harris, 1995, 533–35; Tait, 1995, 57–58; Brasnett, 1969, 59–92). The Government reiterated their refusal to set up a public works programme, instead hoping to combat the deterioration and the loss of morale in the labour force through voluntary occupational centres.

The National Council of Social Service and occupational centres

Voluntary initiatives, in the shape of centres for unemployed men, did indeed dwarf state responses. By 1933, 2,300 centres were opened, catering at their peak for a quarter of a million men and women, with Ministry of Labour grants to the NCSS (Brasnett, 1969, 70–1). They were variously called occupational centres, social service centres, unemployed centres, with some located in already established settlement houses and local voluntary premises.

Criticisms of the centres were that they were too paternalistic, that they were being used to subdue the unemployed, and that they were disgracefully limited in facilities. The socialist George Orwell's *The Road to Wigan Pier* (originally published in 1937) described them as having 'a nasty YMCA atmosphere' (1967, 74). This is quoted by both Harris (1995, 539) and Tait (1995, 62), but neither add his subsequent sentence:

> *Yet even here you feel yourself torn both ways. For probably it is better that a man should waste his time even with such rubbish as sea-grass work than that for years upon end he should do absolutely nothing.*
> (1967, 74)

Hannington, who visited a number of projects for the NUWM, saw the centres as the outcome of Ramsay MacDonald's appeal in 1932:

> *To all friends and people of 'social standing' to come to the aid of the poor unemployed, not by helping to stop the means test and restoring the benefit cuts – oh no! – but by helping forward social service centres which would occupy the spare time of the unemployed with games and lantern lectures, and organising the distribution of somebody's cast-off clothing.*
> (Hannington, 1937, 196)

He argued that it was the hunger marches and increasing unemployed militancy that provoked the Government into giving the NCSS greater funding (ibid, 196–7). Hannington reminded the Government that the NCSS had no trade union on their council except the National Union of Teachers, and that in most distressed areas trade unions and the Labour Party viewed social service schemes as a side-tracking of the real issue of providing work and wages for the unemployed (ibid, 201). Further, he asserted that where the centres were providing work they were either forcing men to work as a condition of receipt of benefit, or were undercutting union rates by working for benefit or payment in kind (ibid, 204–7).

J. B. Priestley, in his *English Journey* (originally published in 1934) gives a vivid picture of the grim dereliction unemployment brought to the north east. Visiting settlements and Council of Social Service centres in Blackburn, Gateshead, Hebburn and Seaham Harbour in the north of England, he both praises their effort and is appalled by the limitations of the projects. He went to Seaham Harbour, a mining town, because he had heard that Miss Jowitt 'ran a particularly good settlement', having worked in another in Gateshead for 10 years. He describes the young people who have come to share in the life of the settlement as 'the storm troops of decency and justice and knowledge and civilization. These settlement houses are their advance posts' (Priestley, 1977, 305–6). They bring adult education classes, music and drama to men and women 'on the razor-edge of life' (ibid, 313).

In the neighbouring town of Hebburn he visited the Council of Social Service centre:

. . . which after some difficulty we found in a couple of huts by the side of a derelict shipyard . . . There were places for carpentering and cobbling, a tattered library, and a newly-finished hut for their twopenny whist drives and dances . . . This centre possesses a boat of its own that has already achieved some fame . . . She was an old ship's boat and as she was in poor shape, she was bought for the social centre for four pounds. The men themselves patched her up. She carries a sail and ten men usually go out in her, working three lines. The fish they bring back – and they had had some good catches . . . is not sold but distributed among the unemployed men's families.
(ibid, 97–8)

While Priestley applauds the effort in this he draws attention to the shame it casts on the country when its skilled men are reduced to the simplest forms of survival.

In Community House, Blackburn, a cotton town, Priestley found men cobbling boots, woodworking toys and things for their homes with an instructor paid by the voluntary society who spent much of his energy finding wood that was cheap or free. There were clubs, table tennis, and a separate public assistance woodwork class which appeared more disciplinary. Again Priestley praises the voluntary effort, and stresses that his criticisms are directed rather at the nation:

Community House is doing all it can within the limits imposed upon it, and it is the country at large that is responsible for the fact that those limits are so narrow. The work here was going forward in a building that had once been an elementary school but had recently been condemned . . . It was a dismal hole in a dark back street.
(ibid, 266)

There was something being done for these unfortunate men . . . under that greasy old roof of the condemned school; but on what a pitifully small, cheese-paring, niggling scale and in what a dismal hopeless atmosphere of disorder and shuffling and cadging!
(ibid, 268)

Ann Oakley gives an interesting illustration of such centres in London, describing her mother Kay Titmuss's work at the Fulham Unemployed Centre. This work involved huge expenditure of her (unpaid) time in raising funds for the centre, in administration and keeping its premises functioning, confirming Priestley's picture of the exploitation of voluntary workers and the often limited premises (Oakley, 1997, 38–41).

While the Government saw the primary objective of the occupational centres as alleviating the psychological effects of unemployment, many in the voluntary sector argued that voluntary organisations should pioneer and experiment with the aim of getting the state to take on new roles or to provide services in new kinds of ways. Those working (paid or unpaid) in voluntary organisations were now less likely to be from the 'favoured classes' and more probably the 'ordinary citizen' seeing their work not as relief but as developing the civic life of the community as a whole (Brasnett, 1969, 13–14). Voluntary workers then were troubled at the assumption that their role was mere relief or temporary morale boosting. The NCSS recognised that it was the Government's role and not theirs to cure unemployment and they were clear about the limitations of their actions (Harris, 1995, 538). They were keen to avoid a return to the 'discredited tradition of soup kitchens and indiscriminate charity', rather seeing themselves as meeting an immediate need which could not be met by the dole alone, the need for 'a place in the community, the sense of being wanted', and the need to 'prevent the unemployed from becoming unemployable' (Brasnett, 1969, 68–70).

At the local level, then, experience is clearly mixed – and not fully researched – but there is a discernable move from the earlier patronising approach in voluntary service of doing 'something for the unemployed' to doing things 'with the unemployed' (Brasnett, 1969, 71). Certainly the NCSS stressed it did not wish to undermine the trade unions, and took care that its schemes should not displace employed or skilled labour and that any work in the centres would not otherwise have been done (Brasnett, 1969, 74).

The left's hostility to the NCSS may have hardened over the 30s, but this hostility was probably more directed at the Government for divesting themselves of responsibility than at the voluntary schemes themselves (Harris, 1995, 543–44). Indeed the social service movement contained many who wished for more collaboration with the labour movement and who hoped to bring change to a society perceived to be grossly unjust. While many local authorities, especially those under Labour control, were dismayed that government funds to tackle unemployment went through the NCSS and not themselves, the NCSS claimed that some initiatives came from the unemployed. An example was the club at Garth in south Wales where unemployed men started their own club after hearing a NCSS radio series in 1934. The club was self-governing, men cobbled shoes, made furniture, drew up their own educational programme, organised their own activities, and the NCSS grant enabled them to expand and move to bigger premises (Brasnett, 1969, 71). Another example of a grass-roots scheme is the People's Service Club in Lincoln. This club had the usual metal and wood workshops and boot repairing schemes, as well as social and educational activities, but was distinctive in its origins in a Workers' Education Association (WEA) class. It kept good relations with local trade unions through its strong identification with the working-class movement, and would only take on contracts when it was clear that the need would not be met in another way. Members would visit other organisations when assessing orders for goods the club might make, and typically these orders might come from settlements, nurseries, or from projects in the special areas (Pilgrim Trust, 1938, 371–3).

The challenge of respecting trade unions and the labour movement while trying to find a new response to unemployment and to community regeneration is exemplified in the Quakers' social action in south Wales, projects which moved ahead of mainstream social service thinking in ways which have a lasting relevance for us.

Experiments in reconstruction: 'Friends lend a hand' in south Wales

Unemployment brought enormous suffering (and had done so since the early 20s) to the south Wales mining communities. Here the Quakers, or Society of Friends, who had been active in the area since the 1926 coal dispute, conceived and realised projects based around nine educational settlements. These became widely admired, not only for the immediate help they brought, but for their new thinking on how the effects of unemployment might be tackled in areas where the old industries were unlikely to return and new ones unlikely to settle. I shall focus on the work of Peter Scott and draw on the writings of three people, Hilda Jennings, Margaret Pitt and Joan Fry who were involved in these projects in giving a picture of their aims and experiences.

The Pilgrim Trust report in 1938 described the educational settlements in south Wales as a new form of social institution, as much more than a centre for relief work, as a 'spiritual power-house' for the valleys (p 304). '(T)hey seem to provide the most successful response to the unemployment problem . . . this is partly because unemployment is to some extent an opportunity for educational work' and because the associated clubs are run by elected committees (ibid, 306). The report showed how the settlements were a point for beleaguered communities and individuals to contact the official world, providing links with organisations such as the NCSS (and thus charitable funds), the South Wales Council of Social Service, the UAB, the whole field of education, the Commissioner for the Special Areas, and so forth. It argued that their success also depended upon their lack of paternalism, and the experience of democracy in the clubs. However, and importantly, the settlements respected trade union principles – any work done in clubs and centres would not be done for non-members to avoid competition with the trade (ibid, 309). Despite some concern from the trade unions and the Labour Party, the Quaker initiatives were to win more approval than the NCSS because of their clear insistence that, while working to counter the effects of unemployment, they were nevertheless far from passive or unwitting agents of government policy (Harris, 1995, 543).

In 1926 the Quakers established the Friends Industrial Crisis Committee; in 1928 this became the Coalfields Distress Committee of which Joan Fry was a leading member. The Society of Friends became involved in the collection, reconditioning and distribution of large amounts of money and clothing from more prosperous areas. Friends financed feeding centres, and between 1926–27 67 boot repair centres were opened with Friends supplying the leather. Despite this, terrible need continued, and the Friends began to consider a different approach (Fry, 1947). They established training clubs to meet spiritual as well as physical needs, giving meals and the opportunity to work at trade union rates, without displacing other labour, and paying insurance for young men so that they could later claim unemployment benefit. The clubs employed one man to cook the daily meal, took on useful local work such as creating playing fields, and the leader arranged classes and activities. At the end of 1929 there were 49 such clubs in south Wales with a membership of 2,397; the Friends found them to be successful in improving health and morale and in enabling many men to go on to Government Training Centres or to transfer to more prosperous parts of the country (Fry, 1947, 16–19). These approaches were the core of the educational settlements, which also drew on the longer history of Quaker adult schools. I now turn to two such settlements which exemplify the range of ideas and action the Friends brought together in south Wales.

Maes-yr-haf

This educational settlement was run by William and Emma Noble. Dr (Lord) A. D. Lindsay, Master of Bailliol College Oxford, (and chairman of the NCSS Unemployment Committee), was chairman of the committee for 21 years. Lindsay's philosophy stressed social solidarity, and the importance of providing opportunities to prevent class or sectional interests prevailing over the common good (Tait, 1995, 59). Willian Noble, while sharing the Quaker view on the need to reconcile differences, nevertheless stressed in 1933 that:

> The (settlement) workers themselves feel they are only able to touch the fringe of the thing and are as anxious as others are for a permanent solution . . . We are rendering first aid when a big surgical operation is necessary.

(quoted in Harris, 1995, 539)

Emma and William Noble both had backgrounds in Methodism, had left school early, had been keen WEA members and had graduated from Ruskin College, Oxford. They joined the Quakers, and in Swindon William was a trade union official in the railway works. Their background meant that adult education was a priority in their work.

Emma Noble had gone to the Rhondda Valley in 1926 to investigate need for Friends in Oxford and London. She lived in a miner's cottage doing relief work at Tonypandy, but stopped this when it was planned to found a social and educational centre which should not be associated with relief. An adult school was started by Rowntree Gillett at Porth in 1926, transferring to Maes-yr-haf in 1927, with Emma and William Noble as wardens for nearly 20 years (Pitt, 1982, 2–4).

At Maes-yr-haf Friends lived in a house from which they worked to alleviate the distress of local people, looking into local social conditions and history in order to frame policy (Fry, 1947, 20). From this centre there grew a network of 52 clubs in the Rhondda Valley, including training clubs, adult educational classes, weaving and craft clubs for women, girls' clubs, furniture making, public amenity work in building playgrounds, sports grounds and swimming pools and a holiday camp by the sea (Pitt, 1982, 5). The clubs were self-governing, and after 1930 when unemployed men were permitted to work voluntarily, they built their own club houses, specially designed by Paul Matt (see below) (Pitt, 1982, 5). Emma Noble developed a small weaving industry, with rugs for sale with traditional Welsh and Celtic designs. There was a nursing association and help from Friends' Allotments Committee (led by John Robson) to help men develop their gardens and allotments. The Quakers persuaded the Government that men should not have their dole reduced if they were to sell a small amount of produce from their allotment, and this increased the acceptability of the scheme and of Friends' donations of seeds and tools in other distressed areas, notably in Durham (Fry, 1947, 24). The clubs were supported by the University of Wales, National Council of Music for Wales, NCSS, the Welsh Council of Social Service and the Carnegie Trust. There was cooperation with the WEA, music, drama, dance, and lectures given by Oxford graduates on international affairs, history, economics, literature, art, science, local government and so forth. These classes enabled some to attend Coleg Harlech, Fircroft College, The Beeches (Birmingham) and Ruskin College, linking the unemployed with the outside world (Pitt, 1982, 4–7).

Brynmawr: Towards a new social structure

While Maes-yr-haf is an example of a very well conceived and run educational settlement, Brynmawr was to become famous as an experiment, 'unique in Britain, to encourage a community afflicted by desperate levels of unemployment to fight back on a number of fronts'. The Friends' national network and links with the establishment (there were messages of support from the Prince of Wales, Ramsay McDonald and Lloyd George) gave the project management, money, volunteers and technical skills (Pitt, 1982, 93) and publicity.

A group of Friends, including Peter Scott, went to Brynmawr in 1928 initially lodging with unemployed families but then sharing a house in the town of about 7,000 people. They were sponsored by the Friends' Coalfields Distress Committee, and although they wanted to distance themselves from relief work, the sheer scale of charitable donations meant that the house became a centre for the local organisation of relief. Scott aimed to counter this by looking at ways of creating work (Pitt, 1982, 8–10).

Born into a Plymouth Brethren family, Scott became a student at the Liverpool School of Architecture but his education was disrupted by military service in the war. He joined the Society of Friends in Birkenhead in 1924 and became involved in the Beechcroft Educational Settlement and the Friends' Home Service Committee. He was influenced by John MacMurray's vision of the 'creative life'; and was always searching for new ways of people living and working together, stressing the fundamental equality of everyone (Pitt, 1982, 62–63). A powerful and persuasive speaker:

I think he was happy leading the youngish group of Friends and fellow travellers at Brynmawr, when we all felt we were doing a useful job and really helping people . . .
(Pitt, 1982, 63–64).

Scott was to continue his work without official Quaker support after a rift in 1929 but he became well known as an inspiring and radical, though somewhat headstrong, figure. Even the Government 'thought he had exceptional knowledge and wisdom, and succeeded where others failed' (ibid, 64). He was judged to be 'one of the most vital social innovators of our time' by the NCSS and COS (ibid, 64–68), and clearly there was something charismatic about him:

A girl in Brynmawr recalls Peter, tall and bronzed, striding about the town in shorts, the group having arrived as from another planet, calling people by their first names, bringing out the best from men who had previously been demoralized and apathetic. He was good looking, although short-sighted, athletic, and sat well on a horse, and was adventurous so that he had many admirers.
(Pitt, 1982, 63)

Peter Scott and his fellow activists wanted, as we have seen, to move on from mere relief work to the creation of a new social structure without confrontation in industrial relations. They asked whether it was not:

possible to devise a way in industry which would release the constructive forces latent in human relationships and substitute free cooperation for autocracy or manoevring for strategic position?
(Jennings, 1934, 209–10)

Accordingly, in 1930, they started small cooperative industries, of which the most successful were Brynmawr Furniture and the resurrected Brynmawr Bootmakers, under the umbrella of the Brynmawr and Clydach Valley Industries Ltd. Peter Scott wanted to help the community avoid reliance on a single industry or employer, making it less vulnerable to market trends, and promoting initiative and interdependence. A disused factory was used for these ventures and for a weaving project in which there were hopes that traditional Welsh craftsmanship would be revived, with associated ventures in quilt making, small-scale mining and poultry keeping. The industries were started with funding from a national appeal, and once the loans were paid off the schemes were owned and controlled by their workers with a central organisation providing the business management and services. The goods were sold on the open market, and a shop was opened in London, enabling more workers to move from part-time into full-time work. It was the success of this scheme which persuaded the Government to do more to encourage small trading estates in distressed areas; nevertheless, the scheme only dented overall unemployment in the region where it remained at about 70 per cent (Pitt, 1982, 46–48).

The furniture project was particularly successful; its inspiration and leadership came from Paul Matt, originally from Germany, who had come to help in Brynmawr in 1929, organising clubs for young unemployed men. The success of the project lay in the high quality of his designs which were sturdy, practical and attractive, with cheap materials and imaginative construction methods which less skilled craftsmen could use. The furniture was exhibited in national centres and was quickly in demand, and became sought after by collectors (Pitt, 1982, 42–45; Society of Friends, 1934, 21–22).

The Brynmawr and Clydach Industries were cooperative enterprises which became self-sufficient after start-up donations, grants and volunteer expertise. A somewhat different and, to Peter Scott, more radical and utopian scheme was the Eastern Valley Subsistence Production Society, not far from Brynmawr, in which groups of members were provided with seed, fertilizer, land and tools which would enable them to produce food for their own consumption. Each group elected a leader, responsible to the elected council. The schemes visualised self-contained, democratic, economic communities with a restoration of the fellowship of work and a revitalised community life (Pilgrim Trust, 1938, 354–57).

Peter Scott gradually developed the idea of getting the unemployed men to produce things for their own consumption and for exchange amongst themselves, so supplying their families with necessities, while still drawing their unemployment pay. This could be said to be based on the old barter idea of exchanging goods without money. A professor at Cardiff University worked out a system of credits for hours of labour, which could be exchanged for goods produced . . . It was not an economic enterprise and could not be self-supporting, as the members would need some cash from the State . . .
(Pitt, 1982, 48)

For those who joined the scheme, which covered dairy, poultry and pig farming, fruit and vegetable growing, bee-keeping, flour-milling and bakery, and workshops for necessary equipment and materials (carpentry, brick making, blacksmiths, boilermen and so forth), it appears to have been a success. Participation in the scheme meant a much better quality and more varied diet. This was particularly appreciated by women, for whom, in the case of the associated Wigan scheme, there was direct benefit in that the 'wages' could not be spent other than on necessary goods for the family, and families had an extra allowance, thus offsetting child poverty and ill health (Pilgrim Trust, 1938, 362–66). The Friends ensured that members could receive benefit without having to sign on at a labour exchange, and without the fruits of the scheme being taken into account by the means test. There was hostility from trade unions, shop keepers and some local people who feared a return to the old 'task work' of the Poor Law – views carefully explored in Hannington's report after his visit to this and other subsistence production schemes but even he conceded that we 'parted friends, but without having reached any agreement!' (1937, 210–11).

With a grant from Lord Nuffield and some government funding, the Eastern Valley scheme reached a membership of 400 in 1937, covering 25 groups in eight units, with a general store and canteens where social events were held as well as mid-day meals (Pitt, 1982, 52–60). Size was a problem: Scott estimated 500 members as the optimum for each unit, but neither the Eastern Valley nor the Wigan schemes were able to reach that level, and the more capable men were the ones most likely to move on to other employment (Pilgrim Trust, 1938, 361). But for those unlikely to work again '. . . by pooling effort on a large scale, with a complex organisation behind it, the scheme makes unemployment assistance go much further' (ibid, 354–5).

Perhaps it was this point which attracted the Government:

Sir George Gillett, the commissioner for the special areas visited (the scheme) . . . and he was most impressed by the wonderful organisation and the range of skilled activities that went on in a single building by men who received no cash reward.
(Pitt, 1982, 57)

Peter Scott resisted pressure from the Ministry of Labour which urged him to start five more schemes, each of five hundred men. The projects declined when anticipation of war in 1938 meant resumption of employment in the 'old' industries, but have much interest for us today as cooperatives, local exchange schemes (LETS), social enterprises and various types of subsidised employment for those on benefits are on the increase.

The Brynmawr Community Study: a new role for research

In 1928 when the Friends began to look for an alternative to relief it was decided that future policy and action should be based on a study of the area from historical, social, political and industrial perspectives. To some extent this reflects the mania for research in the 30s which Muggeridge describes as an attempt to find comfort in the face of chaos by counting, measuring, classifying, and quantifying:

> From the London School of Economics and other places went annually many earnest persons, male and female, to plant their tents in depressed areas, housing estates, malnutrition belts . . .
> (Muggeridge, 1949/67, 280–81)

Ann Oakley (1997), describes the inter-war world of young, progressive liberals, involved in international movements for peace and social reform, and, like her father Richard Titmuss, passionately committed to researching social problems so that a planned and humane world might be constructed. The 30s saw novel forms of research on 'ordinary people', for instance at the Peckham Health Centre in London, or through mass observation. These young middle-class pioneers were deeply sympathetic to the needs of working-class people yet stood apart from (above) them in their plans for reform. Yet occasional activists avoid the 'us and them' of so much of this research, and Hilda Jennings, who would later become warden of Bristol University Settlement, was outstanding in her involvement of local people (see her *Brynmawr: A study of a distressed area*, 1934).

The survey was sponsored by the University College of South Wales but its organisation and inspiration were Hilda Jennings. The survey anticipated modern participatory community studies and needs audits, not only in finding out what local people see as the problems of their area and how they would like to see it changed, but in developing the community through the process of inquiry and planning:

> Unlike other social surveys, the work was planned as a piece of community self-study, in which educated and uneducated, workers, unemployed, shop-keepers, teachers, transport officials, bank managers, and nurses were all invited to take part on equal terms . . . The constitution of the groups ensured the use of expert knowledge and also brought together representatives of the management or employers and the wage-earners. In order to ensure that the facts obtained were considered, not only from the specialist point of view but from that of the community, the members of all the groups were invited to join a Community Study Council where the results of their enquiries were discussed at regular meetings. In this way, many questions were considered as factors in the common welfare instead of sectionally.
> (Jennings, 1934, 200–1)

The Community Study Council met in Community House every month, and aimed:
. . . at a new relationship – a coordinating of varied interests, as parts of a whole rather than as opposing and self contained units. Experience is thus pooled for the common good and neighbourliness becomes a reality. It depends upon 'the power of a right idea', the seeking of right personal relationships, and is concerned not so much with eventual completeness, as with continual growth and progress in action.
(Society of Friends, 1934, 7)

The Community Study Council was not uncontentious for despite the Friends' aim of bringing people together and breaking down barriers, the trade unions and the Labour Party, and therefore the local district council, resented interference in what they perceived as their domain. The Quakers were clear that the Community Study Council was not intended to usurp the functions of the local authority, rather it was to work in experimental ways where official bodies did not function. The Quakers insisted that they brought a different conception of democracy, which operated by bringing diverse interests and groups together, arguing that only thus could a spirit of self-help, cooperation and initiative (rather than jealousy and suspicion) grow within the community (Jennings, 1934, 199). Here again there is a relevance for community workers today, working in communities which have become much more heterogeneous in terms of culture, ethnicity and interests, where the prevention of exclusion is a major aim of public policy (Cannan, 1997).

The Community Study Council considered the findings of the various groups, which had involved about two hundred people, dealing with population, transport, education, health, housing, finance, commerce, municipal services and industry. The Community Study Council decided on projects to be undertaken, which included play schemes for children, a library and children's book scheme, action on illegal child labour, boys and adolescents' clubs, arts and crafts clubs, and classes which responded to the keen interest in music and in the history of the coal and steel industries (Pitt, 1982, 32).

The Development Group grew out of the survey committee's view that the town needed a facelift as it was dirty and dilapidated with rubbish dumps in the streets, and very poor housing. Volunteers, local people and outsiders, were to clear land and a rubbish dump to make a garden, woodland, a swimming pool and a paddling pool, a small park, a children's playground, and a nursery school. Houses were to be colour washed and a Community House acquired and renovated. Much of this work was to be achieved by young people who came to the project from other parts of England as well as from other countries.

The International Work Camp and the wider youth movement

The work of the local volunteers to clear the land for a swimming pool had dragged on for two-and-a-half-years, partly because of a degree of local criticism. But in 1931 Peter Scott invited a multi-national group of students to Brynmawr under the auspices of International

Voluntary Service, or *Service Civile Volontaire*, formed in Holland in 1920 as an alternative to compulsory military training. The 12-week Brynmawr work camp was led by the Swiss Pierre Céresole, who worked with representatives of Brynmawr Community Council, Welsh Students Self-Help Council, the Student Christian Movement, and the Young Friends' Committee. There were some 70 students from English colleges, and 37 more came from other European countries and the USA. The days of work were followed by evenings of discussion and singing with local people (Pitt 1982, 35–36).

Contemporary accounts suggest that the work camp did much to break the isolation of Brynmawr by linking it with an international movement. It is well known that the 1930s were a time where the outdoors, cycling and youth hostelling were part of popular culture. Behind these lay an internationalism, with roots in the early 20s, that sought reconciliation and understanding rather than the confrontation and prejudice that led to the pointless waste of the First World War. Some of those who were most active in the new youth movements were people who had broken away from the Scouts which had become more militaristic during the war. John Hargrave had formed the Kibbo Kift Kindred in 1920, and Leslie Paul had became leader of the Woodcraft Folk in 1925, at the age of 18. Both hoped to start a left-wing, co-educational, and non-religious scout movement, and both saw the outdoor life as an antidote to the city, and as a means of reconstruction of a world corrupted by the forces of industrialism and war (Springhall, 1977, 110–120). Leslie Paul was one of the few voices on the left to express reservations about Stalin's Soviet Union, drawing his inspiration rather from the craft guilds, Edward Carpenter, William Morris, H.G. Wells and the German and Austrian youth movements with whom he had good links. In his autobiography he gives a vivid description of the impatience of youth with the older generation's programmes and organisations:

Despite the socialist dressing we gave to everything . . . we believed in, every kind of future reform or revolution paled beside our concern for the content of the actual life we were living at that moment . . . For this reason we were bitterly attacked by Communists and doctrinaire Socialists who wanted only immediate and unconditional sacrifice for a hypothetical future revolution . . . There was nothing one could do by oneself. How supine and ignoble a surrender of one's vitality this seemed to us!
(Paul, 1951, 68–69)

John Hargrave's 'informal commissioner' abroad from 1923–25 was Rolf Gardiner (Wright, 1995, 183) who was to join the camp in Wales, and who admired Peter Scott's 'courageous experiment' (Gardiner, 1943, 67). Influenced by guild socialism, and by D. H. Lawrence, Gardiner is an important English link with progressive German, Dutch and Scandinavian youth movements and centres. After Cambridge University, he started a folk dancing team that toured Germany in the 20s and he was deeply inspired by the youth Bünde with their blend of the outdoor life, intellectual debate, folk song and dance, work service and a disdain for urbanised mass societies. He admired their pacifist internationalism and the ardour for a socialism which stressed the individual and diversity rather than communist dogma. Gardiner edited *Youth* to disseminate these new ideas in England

(Gardiner, 1943; Wright, 1995, 181). Leslie Paul gives an idea of his importance:

Gardiner's role during the twenties and early thirties had been to bring German and British youth closer together, and in this he had many extraordinary achievements to his credit, one of which was the bringing of German youth choirs to England to sing Bach cantatas in our cathedrals . . . (H)is authority in Germany was even greater than his prestige in England. (Paul, 1951, 205)

Gardiner dreamt of reviving depressed rural Wessex with a small circle of comrades. He envisaged his farm, Springhead, as a centre around which cooperative rural industries could be regenerated, with links with similar centres in Holland, Scandinavia and Germany, all combining musical and cultural activities with work on the land. Gardiner's project owed its form to the German examples he knew; he particularly admired Eugen Rosenstock-Hussey's Boberhaus in Silesia, which aimed to generate common understanding among students, workmen and peasants of divergent outlook and religious faiths. The other centre which inspired Gardiner was the Musikheim in Frankfurt-an-der-Oder. This was a 'college of the social arts', directed by Georg Goetsch, which brought together music and the arts as a basis for 'human and community health and wholeness' (Gardiner, 1943, 130–31; Gardiner, 1937, 113).

These German centres combined a form of communitarian socialism with educationalist ideas, seeking to reach wider groups through work service camps. Céresole's *Service Civile Volontaire* shared the idea that voluntary manual work, intellectual discussion and music and drama could be a practical means of reconciliation of different groups and interests. Gardiner, through his links in Germany and his active involvement in the International Works Camps conferences in Switzerland, brought both ideas and people from other European countries to camps in Britain from the late 20s. He had first put these ideas into practice in East Cleveland in North Yorkshire where the iron pits had declined after the First World War, leaving poverty and entrenched unemployment. A local squire, Major James Pennyman, had established a mutual aid system of small scale agriculture, furniture making and boot repairing. Gardiner recognised its similarity to existing schemes in the distressed areas, but a distinctive feature in Cleveland was the work camps of young men and women helping to clear and dig the land (Gardiner, 1943, 67). The majority of students (in reality young people from many professions) were English, with some Danes, Norwegians, and Germans. They, and local unemployed miners were joined by miners from Silesia and the Ruhr. After work in the mornings there would be discussions – often started by the method he had observed in German centres of one person telling his life story, or lectures on the history of the region and prospects for the future – and social activities, music, singing and dancing.

At Springhead Gardiner ran two series of land service camps, 1934–36 and 1938–40. Held in the context of unemployment, they were 'experiments in community', falling 'into the category of national (and international) education rather than of reconditioning and social recreation' (Gardiner, 1943, 39). The camps, of around 70 people would include teachers, university lecturers and people engaged in social service, with a 'sprinkling of hard-worked women helpers' as well as unemployed men from labour exchanges and groups of miners from Germany. There were people who had attended NCSS centres and courses, and members of Grith Fyrd, another independent body which ran its own camps for young unemployed men in the New Forest and Derbyshire, and which, like Gardiner, stressed the manliness of outdoor living and working. The camps had ceremonies to start and end the day, with runs, flag waving, dancing and singing, flaming torches (Gardiner, 1943, 39–49). Not everyone found this to their taste – Michael Tippett, the composer, who had participated in the Cleveland camps, found it hard to take seriously the atmosphere of nature worship, chivalry and woodcraft (Wright, 1995, 186). Less amusingly, as the Nazi regime in Germany became established, Gardiner was to be much criticised by the centre and left for failing to distance himself from developments in Germany, and for his Anglo-Saxon nationalism and veiled anti-Semitism, and his links with right wing appeasers (Griffiths, 1980, 40, 74–75, 142–46; Chase, 1989, 141–42; Paul, 1951, 196–206).

Conclusion

It is easy to dismiss some of these ideas and people. I have not drawn out the obvious sexism in projects where women were often the unpaid helpers, overshadowed by men with apparent glamour and charisma. And the sheer crankiness of the English movements in the thirties, captured by George Orwell (1967, 152), means it is too easy to mock and forget. Over the decade from the late 20s we have seen activists start from common ground in an anti-militiaristic, leftish internationalism and a desire to find ways of overcoming (urban and rural) unemployment and its social effects. By the late 30s there are clear splits in this movement, centring on attitudes to Nazi Germany. Gardiner's (and Hargrave's) mysticism, moral authoritarianism and disdain for urban life link him with some of the more conservative strands in today's deep greens with their nostalgia for an imagined harmonious past, and their suspicion of the state (Chase, 1989). In contrast, Peter Scott and the Quakers' educational settlements in south Wales, the WEA in Lincoln, and Leslie Paul resemble today's democratic socialist community activists with their desire to construct communities knitted together by many forms of democratic participation and by a variety of types of work. Gardiner and Scott sought reconstruction through bringing together different groups, but while Gardiner's project rested on an élite imposition of rituals and ideals, Scott and Jennings emphasised the educational and political importance of the *process* of involving all sectors of a community in its regeneration. And the third strand we have seen lies in the leadership of the NCSS movement which foreshadowed the pluralism of a rather more minimalist and paternalistic welfare state which middle way Conservatives or Liberals might have established had they won the 1945 election.

As it was, the Labour Party's post-war policies of state welfare and nationalisation pushed these initiatives on to the back burner, but now, as we search for a third way, these activists have something to tell us. Firstly, they were all concerned with the bringing together of different groups, and this is of great importance when strategies to reduce social exclusion and conflict are becoming more crucial. Secondly, they are concerned with the relationship between social and economic development, and recognise that if a community is to be viable then it must have a diversity of employment and not be overly dependent on a single employer and the global market. And thirdly, they remind us that the quality of work matters, that work should not be just a job but that good design and craftsmanship have an importance for the human spirit. Furthermore work needs to be about more than the satisfaction of private needs; we need forms of employment which leave space for participation in a public sphere of neighbourhoods, the countryside and cultural activities. Such employment might be in cooperatives, subsidised schemes based on barter or exchange, or in other kinds of social enterprises – a sector which is of great relevance today – and which still needs much of its history to be told.

Bibliography

Brasnett, M. (1969). *Voluntary Social Action: A history of the National Council of Social Service 1919–1969*. London, National Council of Social Service.

Bruce, M. (1961). *The Coming of the Welfare State*. London, Batsford.

Cannan, C. (1997). 'Social Development with Children and Families in France' in C. Cannan and C. Warren (eds) *Social Action with Children and Families: A community development approach to child and family welfare*. London, Routledge.

Chase, M. (1989). 'This is no claptrap, this is our heritage', in C. Shaw and M. Chase (eds) *The Imagined Past – History and nostalgia*. Manchester, Manchester University Press.

Colledge, D. and Field, J. (1983). ' "To Recondition Human Material . . ." an Account of a British Labour Camp in the 1930s, an Interview with William Heard', in *History Workshop Journal*, Issue 15, pp 152–166.

Fry, J. M. (1947). *Friends Lend a Hand in Alleviating Unemployment – The story of a social experiment 1926–1946*. London, Friends' Book Centre.

Gardiner, R. (1943). *England Herself: Ventures in rural restoration*. London, Faber and Faber.

Gardiner, R. (1937). 'The Triple Function of Work Camps and Work Service in Europe from North Sea and Baltic', reprinted in A. Best, (ed) *Water Springing from the Ground – An anthology of the writings of Rolf Gardiner,* Springhead, Shaftesbury, pp 109–125.

Griffiths, R. (1980). *Fellow Travellers of the Right – British enthusiasts for Nazi Germany 1933–9*, London, Constable.

Hannington, W. (1937). *The Problem of the Distressed Areas*. London, Victor Gollancz.

Harris, B. (1995). 'Responding to Adversity: Government-Charity Relations and the Relief of Unemployment in Inter-War Britain', in *Contemporary Record*, Vol 9, No 3, pp 529–561.

Jennings, H. (1934). *Brynmawr – A Study of a Distressed Area*. London, Allenson and Co.

Jones, K. (1991). *The Making of Social Policy in Britain 1830–1990*. London, Athlone Press.

Muggeridge, M. (1940). *The Thirties: 1930–1940 in Great Britain*. London, Hamish Hamilton.

Oakley, A. (1997). *Man and Wife – Richard and Kay Titmuss: my parents' early years*. London, Flamingo.

Orwell, G. (1937). *The Road to Wigan Pier*. Harmondsworth, Penguin.

Paul, L. (1951). *Angry Young Man*. London, Faber and Faber.

Pilgrim Trust (1938). *Men Without Work*. London, Cambridge University Press.

Pitt, M. R. (1982). *Our Unemployed – Can the past teach the present? Work done with the unemployed in the 1920s and 1930s.* London, Friends' Book Centre.

Priestley, J. B. (1934/1977). *English Journey*. Harmondsworth, Penguin.

Society of Friends (1934). *The Brynmawr Experiment 1928–1933*. Community House, Brynmawr, South Wales.

Springhall, J. (1977). *Youth, Empire and Society – British youth movements 1883–1940.* London, Croom Helm.

Tait, I. (1995). 'Keeping the Jobless Occupied: Voluntary welfare and unemployment in 1930s Britain' in *New Directions in Economic and Social History*, I. Blanchard (ed). Avonbridge, Newlees Press.

Wright, P. (1995). *The Village that Died for England – The strange story of Tyneham*. London, Jonathan Cape.

Henry Morris

Chapter twelve

Henry Morris and the Cambridgeshire Village Colleges

Tony Jeffs

Henry Morris, some claim, invented the community school. This is an exaggeration; but it is not hyperbole to identify him as a major figure in the development of community education. A brilliant administrator who venomously loathed bureaucrats; an educator with virtually no teaching experience, a man oft recalled for the great buildings he endowed and inspired who could not be trusted to hammer a nail into a wall, a passionate champion of local democracy and implacable enemy of intolerance yet an office tyrant to many and habitually contemptuous of elected councillors and politicians, a city and suburban dweller all his life who fought for the regeneration of the countryside – Morris was certainly not devoid of contradictions.

Morris spent almost his whole working life as chief education officer of Cambridgeshire. Joining the county in1922 he remained until retiring in 1954. Other jobs were offered but Morris, unlike his modern counterparts who usually abscond every few years leaving others to rectify and endure their failures, stayed to create something of lasting value – the village colleges of Cambridgeshire. Conceived on a grand scale they were an educational and community resource inspired by a unique vision. They were places that would:

Take all the various vital but isolated activities in village life – the school, the village hall and reading room, the evening classes, the agricultural education courses, the Women's Institute, the British Legion, Boy Scouts and Girl Guides, the recreation ground, the branch of the county rural library, the athletic and recreation clubs – and, bringing them together into relation, create a new institution for the English countryside.
(Morris, 1925, 11)

To create these community centres for the neighbourhood able to 'provide for the whole man and abolish the duality of education and ordinary life' (op cit) was Morris's ambition.

A Cotswold holiday

Henry Morris never learned to drive. So he probably went by train from his Cambridge home to Kingham before travelling on by taxi to the Cotswold village of Idbury where in August 1924 he spent his summer holiday. However, given his passion for poetry Morris may have gone the extra four or five miles to Adlestrop before alighting; to linger on the platform of that small halt and reflect, like so many others, on the lines by Edward Thomas that immortalised it. The poem was the result of a fleeting experience Thomas had had weeks prior to the outbreak of the Great War. *Adlestrop*, a poem of just 16 lines came to symbolise for many a lost tranquillity and a rural idyll fast fading from view (Thomas, 1920). Our traveller would certainly have been familiar with the poem. It would have resonated with his experiences. Thomas and Morris shared more than a passion for poetry. Both were born 'townies' destined to become vocal advocates for the preservation, protection and rejuvenation of the countryside. Each adored spending Sundays indulging a predilection for energetic literary hikes with congenial company that incorporated at some point a visit to a country pub. Despite humble backgrounds and low incomes, both secured a place at Oxford. Finally each volunteered for the army, secured a commission and served at the front. Morris returned; Thomas, like most of Morris's student friends, did not.

As the newly appointed Secretary for Education for Cambridgeshire (today he would be called a director), Morris had been invited to Idbury by the journalist and writer J. W. Robertson Scott. His host was the founder and editor for 20 years of the quarterly magazine *The Countryman*, a radical campaigning journalist and a prolific writer who for over 60 years tirelessly promoted policies designed to revitalise the countryside. Robertson Scott was, among other things, an energetic supporter of the National Union of Agricultural Workers and enthusiastic advocate of self-help community organisations such as the Women's Institute, of which he wrote the first history (Robertson Scott, 1925 (b)). He also believed the root and branch reform of rural education to be an essential first step if the long-running economic and social decline of the countryside was to be halted. It is impossible to ascertain to what extent the guest borrowed from the thinking of his host, not least because the latter was always reluctant to acknowledge the contribution of others. Certainly in subsequent writings both were adamant that no sustainable movement for the economic and social regeneration of the countryside would emerge until a new cadre of community leaders was created. Dismissing the clergy and squirearchy as lost causes, relics of an old order in terminal decline, who having presided over decades of retreat were now incapable of providing a credible leadership to a rural population that lacked the confidence as well as the financial and educational resources to fight back, they knew they had no alternative but to seek salvation from another quarter. According to both only one viable option was available. Robertson Scott, like Morris, pinned his hopes on what he saw as the only professional grouping with a substantive presence in rural areas – schoolteachers. As the former noted:

In hamlets I know best, the standard-bearers of progress, civilization, evolution, well-doing, the

higher-life, better living, true religion – call it what you like – have been, without doubt, teachers at the schools.
(Robertson Scott, 1925(a), 71)

Idbury Manor remains a bleak three-storey 15th century building set, with scarcely a garden to protect it, on a bend in the lane that meanders through the hamlet. Robertson Scott, the owner, offered Morris the use of an adjacent house for the summer. Morris, who needed a retreat where he could formulate his plan for the reform of rural education and rejuvenation of the English countryside, accepted. By the end of the holiday an ambitious manifesto had been almost completed. Within weeks of his return a draft was circulated to the elected members of the Cambridge County Council. Following minor modifications this was published a few months later at his own expense, by the Cambridge University Press. It was to be the only work of any significant length Morris wrote.

Somewhat portentously entitled *The Village College: Being a memorandum on the provision of education and social facilities for the countryside, with special reference to Cambridgeshire* (Morris, 1925) it comprised barely 7,000 words. What it lacked in quantity was amply compensated for by quality. Those weeks at Idbury proved astonishingly fruitful, producing a manuscript destined to become a classic community education text. It is still capable of providing us with a conceptual framework for that nebulous creature the 'community school' and an inspirational vision of what education might achieve if only it were dedicated to the 'pursuit of goodness, of truth, of beauty' (Morris, 1946, 109). Given Morris's self-evident dexterity as a writer and his previous employment as a working journalist the paucity of his output is sometimes bewildering. In mitigation it should be recognised that having once assembled this blueprint for reform he returned from Idbury to dedicate the remaining 37 years of his life to securing its implementation. Henceforth everything written, comprising a mix of conference papers, transcripts of radio broadcasts, a book review, the odd article, a solitary book chapter and briefing papers (the bulk of which are re-printed in a slim volume edited by Harry Ree, 1984), embellished the key themes set forth in the memorandum. At Idbury Morris literally penned the raison d'etre for his professional life. It was a powerful tide that bore Morris onwards. Many, like a teacher who first worked with Morris in the 1930s, recognised this single-mindedness of purpose, sensing in his manner that 'always in his head was a great plan. This frightened a lot of people. They didn't understand what was growing there' (interview).

Journey to Cambridgeshire

Born in Southport in 1889, Morris was one of a family of eight. His mother died when he was 12; his father was a plumber. Leaving school at 14, he became first an office boy, then reporter with *The Southport Visitor*. Profoundly religious, his spare time appears to have been divided between the Anglican Church and studying. In 1910 he secured a place to read theology at St David's University College, Lampeter. The intention was to secure ordination prior to entering the church. The subsequent university career proved extraordinarily chequered. Departing St David's after two years, following an altercation with fellow students and staff over a petition opposing the disestablishment of the Church of Wales, Morris transferred to Oxford. He remained there until enlisting in November 1914. After demobilisation in 1919 he returned to complete his degree but had lost his zeal for both theology and the ministry. Wartime experiences had shattered his faith. While incessant reminders of 'the golden hours there years ago, and all my dear friends . . . killed in the war' (letter quoted Ree, 1973, 10) made life in Oxford unendurable for Morris. So he transferred to Cambridge to read philosophy and 10 years after embarking on a university career finally graduated in 1920.

Much remained of the Oxford years, not least the lasting influence of his tutor Hastings Rashdall, a scholar from whose works Morris apparently never tired of quoting (Palmer, 1976, 243). The friendship was influential. Rashdall provided the references for his job applications, but of greater significance was the impact the relationship had on Morris's intellectual development. Enthusiasm for educational and social reform on the part of Rashdall reflected deeply held religious and political beliefs. Like so many of his background and generation Rashdall was a neo-Hegelian, an affiliate of the philosophical movement known as British Idealism. During the late 19th and early 20th centuries this movement dominated the philosophy departments of British universities and eventually came to shape a great deal of public policy. In particular many adherents of the movement became key figures in the fields of education and welfare (Vincent and Plant, 1984) and via the settlement and club movements in youth and community work (Jeffs, 2000; Rose, 2000; Smith, 2000). T. H. Green, who Rashdall assures us, was one of two writers to whom he owed his greatest debt (the other was Sidgwick) (Rashdall, 1907), is usually viewed as the founder of the movement and the most influential British Idealist. Rashdall became part of a coterie of philosophers and theologians somewhat unfairly dubbed by their opponents the 'Green Parrots' (Nicholson, 1990, 1).

Morris was a habitué of the British Idealist tradition, maintaining that the transformation of society and the promotion of the 'good life' flowed as much from changing the moral attitudes of individual citizens as it did from securing parliamentary reforms. Active citizenship, allied with the need to create vibrant communities, lay at the heart of this doctrine. British Idealists held that citizenship necessitated much more than the irregular casting of a vote. Rather it imposed on all an obligation to 'cultivate' their 'best self' and pursue the 'common good'. As Green explained, an individual 'bettered himself through institutions and habits which tend to make the welfare of all the welfare of each' (quoted Nettleship, 1888, cxxxviii). Green, like Rashdall, was a devout Christian and according to an early biographer 'held the life of citizenship to be a mode of divine service' (MacCunn, 1907, 220).

Religious faith was not obligatory; many British Idealists, like Morris, had none. However what all shared was a belief in 'an automatic relationship between fulfilling one's capacities and taking on a responsible role in society' (Vincent and Plant, 1984, 27). As Morris explained 'it is as members of a community that the life of action and the conduct is best realised and our souls saved' (1926, 35). Inherent within this tradition is a striving to reconcile the twin ideals of community and individual freedom; to traverse a tightrope linking communitarianism to individualism. Like all Hegelians and Neo-Hegelians these pilgrims refuse to abide a dualism for long. Instead they endeavour to assemble unifying doctrines and solutions to seemingly irreconcilable conflicts. Social harmony, amidst change and confusion, was, they argued, achievable when the individual strove for what Green termed the 'common good'. Unquestioning altruism was not a pre-requisite for all would be beneficiaries. After all the individual was a social animal obliged to exist in the company of others and therefore could ultimately find fulfilment only by living a worthwhile life and helping others to do likewise. Collective action and association as a consequence were essential to bestow meaning to freedom and vanquish social evils such as poverty, ignorance and unemployment. As Green explains all citizens 'ought to be called upon to do that as a body which under the conditions of modern life cannot be done if everyone is left to himself' (1888, 432). Or as another follower explained in terms possessing a distinctly contemporary ring 'the power of the good state empowers the citizen, and the power of the good citizen empowers the state' (Jones, 1919, 89).

The Great War transformed Morris. During military service the bearing and mannerisms of the public school officer were acquired; a persona actively nurtured by the judicious application of subterfuge. Bogus claims were employed to bolster the image, for example, of a young nephew attending Uppingham. Generally it was massaged by the astute suppression of information regarding his humble origins and the promotion of an aura that encouraged friends and acquaintances to assume that here was a product of that 'special class' which assumes an unassailable belief in its right to rule. So triumphant was this performance that a friend commented, one sensed with admiration, 'people were surprised when his brother turned up at the funeral and that moreover he was a mere plumber'. Some colleagues and local politicians undoubtedly hated him. For he easily 'fell out with people [and] had a terrible temper' (interview). If some of the anecdotes related to the author were even partially true, it seems he was capable of immense kindness and generosity as well as spiteful cruelty. He could, for example, sulk in petulant silence throughout a meeting and then climb into a colleague's car, graciously apologise for the boorishness and then act throughout the journey home as if nothing untoward had occurred. Most recall him with great affection. One female headteacher reminisced: 'Morris was a very handsome man whose intelligence and care for humanity came through. It oozed from his face.' Another, a man this time, described him as 'smart and upright, a gentleman in every way. His austerity might have put a lot of people off though.' A third borrowed a line of poetry to summarise the essence of the man – quoting Yeats – 'His mind floats on silence'.

For Morris, hiding his past posed fewer problems than for many. As a close colleague of many years standing explained: 'Henry carefully compartmentalised his life.' This was an essential survival mechanism. As a homosexual holding a senior education post when such acts were illegal, and the mere hint of such a predilection could augur disgrace and dismissal, Morris knew the importance of discretion. Still the mask slipped and secrets got out. His friendship with the son of a local aristocrat towards the end of his reign certainly encouraged scurrilous gossip among teachers about 'the house parties he attended at X Hall'. However, a clerk who worked alongside him for almost two decades was upset that Ree's biography (1973), in his opinion, dwelt on his sexual preference because he recounted: 'Henry's behaviour and conversation never gave any indication of such an orientation.' Nevertheless the interviewee had earlier volunteered that Morris clearly preferred 'male company'. The only close female friend seems to have been Jacquetta Hawkes the archaeologist and wife of J. B. Priestley. During Morris's three decades as director, women secured primary but never secondary headships and with regards to senior administrative or advisor posts the only exception was the redoubtable Nan Youngman, appointed County Art Adviser in 1944. Youngman, a talented artist in her own right, became a close confidante and creative influence on Morris. Through the workshops and training events she organised, as well as via persuasion and leadership, Youngman raised the profile of the arts within Cambridgeshire schools to a degree unmatched elsewhere. All, not merely the talented, were to be offered opportunities for creative expression. She also instigated a revolutionary scheme for the central purchase of works by living artists to be loaned out to schools – 'a policy which obliged the Local Education Authority (LEA) to act as a patron of the arts' (Jones, 1988, 28). Before Youngman and Morris retired such was the success of their purchasing programme that the original works of art gracing the schools were of sufficient quantity and quality as to merit a London exhibition. Moreover there does not appear to have been recorded in over half a century a solitary case of vandalism towards these works of art openly displayed within the schools. Youngman worked with Morris post-retirement, serving as a trustee for his final project, the Digswell Arts Trust.

Cambridgeshire and the rural education crisis

After graduating from Cambridge Morris entered educational administration as a learner with Kent Education Department. Within a year he was back living in his beloved Cambridge having secured the post of assistant secretary for education for Cambridgeshire. Two years on the chief he loathed died. Aged 34 Morris was appointed secretary for education. Russell Scott, a friend 10 years his junior, took over as the deputy.

Morris never taught. One teacher who observed him in action concluded it was probably just as well for he 'was a bit awkward with children'. By way of contrast another colleague, subsequently appointed warden of a village college by Morris, recollected the chief visiting the small village school where his aunt was head. Seventy years on he recalled a kindly man bending down to shake his hand and engaging him in conversation.

Cambridgeshire was then the second poorest English county (the prosperous city was administratively separate). By 1922, 80 years of rural depopulation had devastated the income base (Saville, 1957). Nationally disparities between the quality of services in urban and rural localities were growing, providing an additional incentive for those able to do so, to migrate. All aspects of educational provision suffered. One government report found rural areas poorly served by adult education compared to their urban counterparts (Ashby, 1916).

Likewise with libraries; research undertaken in 1915 found 'only 2.5 per cent of the rural population had access to public libraries compared to 79 per cent of townspeople' (Bourdillon, 1945, 220). Schools fared no better. Declining rolls led to escalating rates of closure, lower capital investment, a growing backlog of set-aside repairs and improvements, pupils travelling longer distances, the retention of all-age single teacher schools, the employment of unqualified teachers, and qualified and unqualified teachers being paid substantially less than metropolitan colleagues. Rural heads, for example, then received on average half the pay of London colleagues (Hurt, 1979). Cambridgeshire became the first rural county to eradicate this disparity. Shortly after doing so Morris addressed a meeting of teachers and upon entering the hall, according to one present, the audience 'as one rose to its feet and cheered him to the echo as he walked to the front . . . he looked most embarrassed'.

The situation in Cambridgeshire on Morris's accession was dire. Firstly it had the worst qualified teaching force in Britain; 49 per cent were uncertified, possessing only a school-leaving certificate compared to a national average of 22 per cent. An additional 8 per cent lacked even that meagre qualification. Known as supplementary teachers these were merely 'vaccinated and over-18' (Wise, 1931). Secondly most schools were small, scattered, isolated and physically substandard. Thirty-three had an average roll of less than 30; 14 between 30 and 40 pupils; 12 between 50 and 60; and 41 more below 100; only 21 between 100 and 250 pupils. In small schools all 3 to 14-year-olds were taught in a single room; in slightly larger units infants were separated off leaving the remainder to be taught en masse.

The memorandum penned at Idbury retains an exhilaratingly radical edge. Endowed with a sense of history and a vision of what might be, it has little in common with the current variant. It exudes the author's belief that 'the ideal order and the actual order can ultimately be made one' (Morris, 1925, 11). The objective was to create in rural localities educational institutions equal to the best encountered elsewhere. These institutions were not to be mere schools. They must be capable of offering country folk the 'social and recreational' life they deserved. This required more:

. . . than the reorganisation of the elementary school system. There must in natural geographical centres be a group and coordination of all educational and social agencies . . . which now exist in isolation in the countryside.

(ibid, 4)

Amalgamating provision was essential to reduce duplication and secure economies of scale, but primarily because integration of welfare, social and educational services would help draw communities together. An excellent summary of Morris's aims can be found in an article written for the house journal of the progressive education movement *New Ideals Quarterly*. It still provides a cogent and accessible account of the aspirations of the community school and community education movements:

At the present moment our state system of education is concerned almost wholly with children and the teachers of children. We ought to see our way to the organic provision of education for the adult community. We must do away with the isolated school. We must so organise the educational buildings of the towns and countryside that the schools of the young are either

organically related to, or form part of, the institutions in which the ultimate goals of education are realised. We must associate with education all those activities which go to make a full life – art, literature, music, festivals, local government, politics. This is as important for the teaching of the young, as it is for the teachers themselves . . . It is only in a world where education is confined to infants and adolescents that the teacher is inclined to become a pundit or tyrant. We should picture a town or village clustering around its educational building, with its hall, library, and recreation grounds, where young and old not only acquire knowledge but are inducted into a way of life . . . We should abolish the barriers which separate education from all those activities which make for adult living . . . it should be the first duty of education to concern itself with the ultimate goals of education . . . Man's life as an economic, social and religious animal – that is the subject matter of education and education the means whereby he achieves the best in all respects . . . It is the life the adult will lead, the working philosophy by which he will live, the politics of the community which he will serve in his maturity that should be the main concern of education.
(1926, 4–5)

How was this vision to be achieved? Morris sought not to reform the isolated school but to fashion a new educational institution – one serving the whole community, the whole person. The memorandum justified the necessity for a radical break with the past along with a blueprint for the future.

Implementing the memorandum

Tinkering with the existing system of rural education would, according to Morris, achieve little – it must be 'recast'. Moreover it was essential the new institutions were set within communities possessing a 'social and recreational life based on stable foundations' (1925, 2). Pale imitations of the urban model would not secure such foundations. Therefore the first requirement for the inauguration of a vibrant rural civilisation possessing 'chronic vigour' was the creation of a 'localised and indigenous system of education' (ibid, 2) based upon a 'many-sided' (ibid, 4) institution which Morris christened 'the village college'. According to the memorandum 10 village colleges would provide a basis for regeneration and the genesis of a network to serve the county. Each college would incorporate as a minimum the following:

- a primary school for those aged 5 to 10 living in the immediate locality;
- a secondary school for 250 to 400 11 to 15-year-olds drawn from surrounding villages and hamlets equipped with specialist rooms and laboratories suitable for day and evening class usage;
- an auditorium for assemblies, mid-day meals, physical education, plays, concerts, film shows, social events, public meetings and lectures;
- a library and public reading room for the whole community;
- a specialist room for agricultural education;

- common and lecture rooms for adult education, village meetings and use by affiliated societies and clubs;
- shower baths and changing rooms for school students and sports clubs;
- an infant welfare centre;
- land for a school garden;
- rooms and facilities for indoor recreation such as billiards; and
- houses for the warden, up to five teaching staff and the caretaker.

In addition he was adamant, success would rely on the recruitment of a new breed of country-bred and university educated teachers 'with a love of and understanding of rural life with the powers of leadership' (ibid, 9). Securing the individuals to staff and the resources to build such lavishly endowed colleges during a period of economic slump and falling rolls was never going to be easy. Surely few who read this prospectus imagined one, let alone 10 colleges, would materialise before Morris retired.

Morris made the task doubly difficult by his resolve that the colleges would be precursors of a new public architecture within rural Britain. He determined that these buildings would enhance:

> . . . *every side of the life of the inhabitants of the district in which it is placed . . . A building that will express the spirit of the English countryside which it is intended to grace, something of its humaneness and modesty, something of the age-long and permanent dignity of husbandry; a building that will give the countryside a centre of reference, arousing the affection and loyalty of the country child and country people, and conferring significance on their way of life? If this can be done simply and effectively, and the varying needs which the village college will serve realised as an entity and epitomised in a building, a standard may be set and a great tradition may be begun; in such a synthesis architecture will find a fresh and widespread means of expression. If the village college is a true and workable conception, the institution will, with various modifications, speed over rural England; and in course of time a new series of worthy public buildings will stand side by side with the parish churches of the countryside.*
> (Morris, 1925, 10–11)

Never before had a local authority administrator set out to create educational buildings for young people and the community aiming for more than mere functionality or embodying a higher aspiration than 'value for money'. Indeed when a philanthropist like Cadbury (Gardiner, 1923) or an architect like Rennie Mackintosh (Steele, 1994) built schools to visually enrich the environment and communicate something beyond the necessity for dull conformity, regimentation and the segregation of pupils from their community, they provoked fierce opposition from the pinchfists managing public education. Politicians and administrators, overwhelmingly feared that such 'extravagance' would inflame expectations and unlock the fiscal floodgates. Apart from the early village colleges, apart from Rennie Mackintosh's Scotland Road School, it is nigh impossible to identify a meritorious state school among the thousands thrown up between 1870 and 1940; one speaking to those entering it, student and teacher alike, of the inspirational power of good architecture, that strove to stimulate not dull the senses, raise aspirations not deflate them, to convey in some small measure the glorious potential of education to release the individual from servitude. Morris was unwilling to compromise. However, the county council stipulated that the memorandum might be implemented only if it did not cost the ratepayers an additional penny, therefore leaving Morris with the mammoth task of financing his vision. This he did by consolidation (the closing of small uneconomic schools) and devoting his spare time to cajoling potential benefactors into making gifts of money, land, equipment or time. In 1929, for example, he borrowed the fare to the United States to spend his holiday cadging money from the Spelman Foundation.

From 1922 to the mid 1940s Morris immersed himself in the task of creating a network of village colleges. At times it must have seemed that everything conspired to defeat him – first the slump, then a World War (somewhat symbolically declared on the day his 'masterpiece' Impington Village College was to open), and of course the unremitting antagonism of those who always considered the second and third-rate good enough. As he told his friend David Holbrook, and anyone familiar with his life would confirm, 'it was crucifixion overcoming the Philistines' (interview). Yet defeat them he did to bequeath us some of the most beautiful and inspirational educational building to be found anywhere in the world. Impington Village College designed by Walter Gropius and Maxwell Fry is described by Pevsener as 'one of the best buildings of its date in England, if not the best' (1954, 318). Morris was adamant that 'the school, the technical college, the community centre, which is not a work of architectural art is to that extent an educational failure' (1945, 103–104). It was a principle to which he held fast.

Sawston, the first village college officially opened in 1930, can too easily be dismissed as a rather lacklustre prototype. Yet this monotone brick building, Ree (1973) rightly reminds us, was by the standards of the time revolutionary. It was the first state school to have a separate hall, an appropriately furnished adult wing, a purpose built professionally staffed library for school and community use, a medical services room, playing fields with changing facilities for pupils and community, and a house for the warden. With his 'sharp eye for beauty and his hatred of the second best . . . his most profound characteristics' (Fenn, undated, 17) it was inevitable that his disappointment with the form and design of Sawston spurred Morris on to achieve even higher standards with those that followed. Sawston was not unique solely as a consequence of the layout and design of the building. Rather it was an educational milestone because no-one since Robert Owen, over a century earlier at New Lanark, had succeeded in creating an institution that integrated a school within a social, welfare, cultural and educational centre serving the whole community. For that reason Morris was adamant that the school must not eclipse the other crucial elements of the equation. In the memorandum the harmonious relationship between the constituent parts was illustrated by Figure 1.

One wing represents adult activities, another the school. Bridging both is social and welfare provision for all.

Achieving the equilibrium between all three firstly meant creating a revolutionary approach to the education of young people; one that treated them at all times with respect

Figure 1.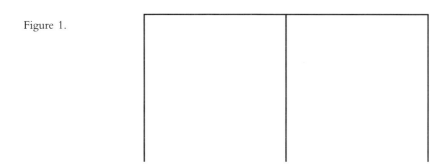

and allowed them the dignity afforded all other users, that would ensure neither they nor their families would be alienated from the village college. It required the elimination of the cruel and humiliating punishments then almost universally employed throughout the education system, the development of a curriculum which they saw as meaningful and valuable, and the integration within the life of the college of social and welfare provision that addressed their needs. Perhaps it was inevitable, therefore, that Morris frequently judged the success of a college according to the degree to which it ceased to resemble a school. He delighted in recounting how, during a visit to Impington, he asked one of the pupils: 'How do you like this?' 'Oh, Sir,' he replied, 'It's fine. It's so much better than school.' Among the worst insults he directed at a colleague was a variant upon that which dismissively summarised the approach of the first warden of Melbourn Village College, namely that 'he acted like a schoolmaster'.

Secondly it required the creation and maintenance of an environment that exalted those using it, confirming their status as citizens, not serfs or customers, speaking to them of their intrinsic worth as equal members of a community. This was required not merely for the buildings to be things of beauty graced with works of art of the highest quality, but that those working there should be men and women of high cultural and educational standing. Rightly, Morris was no more willing to accept average educators working in village colleges than a journeyman architect designing them. Therefore in the early days recruitment was rarely left to chance. Individuals with special artistic or intellectual talents were actively headhunted and persuaded to work in the colleges. Determined to lift the cultural ambience, Morris endeavoured to staff the village colleges with talented people be they poets, philosophers, artists, musicians or writers. Once tipped off regarding the identity of someone suitable he would pursue them, visiting settlements, universities or army camps in order to persuade them to join his crusade. As one young Cambridge graduate, introduced to Morris as a promising poet, discovered, he could be highly persuasive, pleading with the young man 'please join us, our village colleges and schools are crying out for poets'. Such an approach may fly in the face of contemporary recruitment practices and equal opportunities procedures, but it worked.

Nowadays the ignoramuses dictating education policy have decreed that many of those who so enriched the village colleges are not even allowed to enter the teaching profession. They are excluded on the grounds that the subjects they studied at degree or higher degree level don't feature in the national curriculum. Consequently what began as a mean, petty and malevolent attack on sociology by Keith Joseph now extends to philosophers, psychologists, economists, geo-physicists and thousands of other potentially inspiring educators; men and women who, it is feared, might motivate young people to think beyond the limits deemed safe by politicians, and might arouse an interest in uncomfortable ideas. It goes without saying Morris would have held such a policy in total contempt. He had scant tolerance for policies designed to cosset the incompetent, ignorant professional, imposing a third-rate service on the community. In his view only the best was ever good enough. 'Better a dead cat on the wall than a reproduction' was a stance mirrored in his staffing policy. Farnell may be correct in his assessment that Morris was not generally 'a great admirer of school-teachers' (1968, 80). I am not certain this was really the case but he self-evidently viewed the intellectual and cultural vacuity pervading so many educational institutions, not least the teacher training colleges, and shuddered. He knew that the dullards and dolts then running most schools would be incapable of creating the new community orientated institutions outlined in the memorandum. Therefore he took infinite care in recruiting wardens and other staff.

The legacy

How successful were the village colleges? During the period from 1940 to the mid-1960s many independent observers became convinced they were an unalloyed triumph. Bourdillon talked of them achieving with regards rural education 'the highest peak of development' (1945, 228). C. E. M. Joad, philosopher and broadcaster, was equally enthusiastic, as the following extract from an account of a visit to Impington indicates:

> The college, in fact, is a hive of activity, where you can eat, drink, dance, make merry and fall in love as well as learn, attend lectures, talk, and practise the arts and crafts of cookery, metalwork, woodwork, painting, music or whatever else there may be. I could wish that I had the descriptive power to convey the comfort and grace of the environment in which these various activities take place: but the task demands a richer pen than mine. I can only emphasize the general impression of light and air and space, of graceful and harmonious lines, of rich and tasteful furnishings . . . The outdoor amenities are not less remarkable. There are a swimming pool, ample playing fields, swings and a sand pit for small children. There is a terrace where on summer afternoons ancient gents can sit in the sun and ladies gossip over their tea.
> (1945, 131–32)

Others such as Dent (1943), Rowntree and Lavers (1951), Baker (1953) and Farnell (1968) were similarly animated. The latter claimed the villages colleges managed to uniquely dispel the 'peculiarly adolescent ethos of the ordinary school' from the campus (1968, 103). If so, they achieved, and lost, something no other institution catering for young people of school age has since managed. Hard data also lent support to claims that the colleges had 'transformed the conception of education' (Joad, 1945, 134). For example, they achieved exceptional levels of take up of adult education provision, not least among ex-school students. Bracey (1959) estimates that over a quarter of the adults living in the Impington catchment were regular attenders at the college. During this period Morris seems to have created the communities serving the community he dreamt of. Visitors flocked to tour them from all over the world and even in a few cases from elsewhere in the British Isles. Herbert Read, the art critic and poet had no doubts. He asked after a tour if the colleges proved it was possible to not merely:

> . . . *conceive, but to build and introduce into the existing educational system, schools which provide the essentials of an educative environment? The answer is yes; it has been done in at least one instance (Impington), and a model perhaps not perfect in every detail, but practical, functional and beautiful, does exist on English soil.*
> (1958, 136)

Securing the enthusiasm of architects, poets, philosophers, journalists and educationalists was one thing, acquiring political patronage proved a knottier problem. Morris viewed himself as marginalized by the educational establishment. Eustace Percy, or 'Useless Percy' as Morris dubbed the then secretary of the Board of Education, sent him packing in 1929 when he had tried to sell his 'plan' to the Government. Chuter Ede was similarly unimpressed in 1944 endorsing an HMI's memo dismissing the Cambridgeshire plan as unduly expensive and overly demanding of the many sub-standard teachers in post. Soon afterwards a series of documents, including the one on rural education, outlining the policy aspirations of the Ministry of Education, simply ignored the Cambridgeshire model. To add insult to injury the one which mentioned them so misunderstood their ethos and purpose that it informed those LEAs who might opt for this form of provision they must ensure the 'secondary school and the community centre should have separate entrances' (Ministry of Education, 1947, 79). Overall the educational establishment, especially the politicians and senior civil servants, exhibited a wilful indifference to his ideas and achievements.

However, Whitehall was not totally apathetic. The Ministry of Defence co-opted him onto a committee planning educational provision for the RAF. The colonial office asked him, along with Josephine Macalister Brew, to visit West Africa and report on the development of community and further education programmes. Then his friend David Hardman, a junior minister in the Attlee Government, wangled him a two day per week secondment to the Ministry of Town and Country Planning to advise the minister 'on cultural and community aspects of creating new towns'. It was a period of unprecedented growth in the construction of public housing and new towns. Intense pressure to replace war-damaged stock and provide for the growing population created a housing crisis that overshadowed most, if not all, of the problems pressing in on the Government. At last it seemed that Morris had acquired the opportunity he sought to seriously shape policy. Inspired, he threw himself into drawing up grand designs, shooting off memos in all directions and dreaming dreams of towns fit at last 'for the art of living the full life' (Morris, 1936, 49).

But it proved a frustrating and overwhelmingly unproductive sojourn. Local authority officials, civil servants, including those from education, and architects and planners all predominately concerned with delivering bulk not quality ensured his grand designs came to nought. Chastened, he returned to Cambridgeshire to see out the few remaining years to retirement. Even there his visionary scheme for a post-school institution merging further, higher and community education for the county came to nought, blocked by parsimonious officials at the ministry who controlled what could and could not be built. He retired in December 1954, exhausted and disappointed. He left behind the four village colleges opened before the war and the two completed prior to retirement. Four more followed before his death in 1961.

The retirement was not a happy one. The Cambridge home was lost to redevelopment in 1956, the bulk of his furniture and belongings going into store where they remained until his death. A somewhat nomadic existence in rented accommodation followed. However, the old spark returned as he threw himself into bringing the Digswell project to fulfilment. Many close associates, including his long-serving secretary Dorothy Bimrose, Nan Youngman and David Hardman, plus admirers such as Herbert Read became involved. By 1959 Digswell, a charming Regency dwelling alongside a small church on the outskirts of Welwyn, had been re-furbished and 15 artists and craftsmen (etchers, letterers and print-makers) had taken up residence. It was a minor triumph but despite its potential for replication elsewhere it remained, until eventual closure, a lone prototype (Bimrose, 1965). By then he was a very ill man and within little over a year of the official opening he was housebound.

According to a senior county education officer Morris is 'barely recalled or remembered nowadays' in Cambridgeshire. Indeed perhaps little now remains apart from the buildings. Even some of those including Impington have been dangerously overwhelmed by the expansion required to handle a population of school students triple that initially planned for. Growth has stolen the sui generis of the village colleges. Linton and some others still exude a singular elegance and tranquillity but educationally they are all scarcely exceptional. Ree (1980) concluded, following his tour of the county, that those then running the colleges had predominately 'turned their backs on the hopes and ideals of the originator', or as an ex-warden put it they 'regressed to the norm', opting to become typical English schools and typical English teachers obsessed with order, uniformity, league tables and targets, noteworthy only for residing in atypically fine buildings. They became daily evermore 'divorced from creation of all kinds, from play and love and tragedy, from religion and art and discourse' (Morris, 1926, 37) like so many schools. Shamefully some have become grant maintained, thereby making a contribution to the destruction of the local democracy they were created to preserve and enrich, embracing an arrangement that encourages them to 'operate in isolation from the common cause' (Barker, 1997, 32). Adult classes, youth clubs and community groups, in some cases on sufferance, retain a toehold but the contemporary village college is by no stretch of the imagination a 'community centre housing a secondary modern school' (Rowntree and Lavers, 1951, 325).

Why did it all unravel? Outside factors are partially responsible for the damage wrought. First among these has been the impact of the raising of the school-leaving age and increasing willingness of young people to remain voluntarily in full-time education. When the memorandum was published over 90 per cent fled school at the earliest opportunity. Even before 1974 when the school leaving age was raised to 16, more stayed on than left in Cambridgeshire. This numerical growth tilted the equilibrium. A total absence of imagination ensured that all LEAs along with central government, opted for the supposed economies of scale which it was assumed would flow from expanding existing schools, rather than opening new ones, rather than the smaller socially cohesive units the village colleges had shown to be a success. Most village colleges grew like Topsy. Wardens therefore, whether they liked it or not, and some clearly did, were obliged first and foremost to run a school and devote ever less time to serving the community. Second, from the 1950s onwards, the straight-jacket of first external examinations and then the national curriculum and league tables curtailed, almost to the point of extinction, the capacity of staff and community to create a discrete curriculum and institutional persona. As intended, every turn of the centralising screw brought each and every school into line, denying teachers the capacity to be self-actualising creative professionals and transforming them into handmaidens of the state, technicians primed to deliver an externally imposed curriculum. Morris dreamt of an institution that 'would not outlive its function, for the main reason that it would not be committed irrevocably to any intellectual or social dogma or to any sectional point of view' (Morris, 1925, 12). The 1988 Education Act and the thousands of circulars and directives it spawned have made a mockery of that hope. The villages colleges cannot 'intellectually . . . be one of the freest of our English Institutions' (op cit) because no educational institution in England, except perhaps the universities, is allowed to be free.

The village colleges were also victims of their own success. Burgeoning take up of community provision, classes and the demands of community groups encouraged the employment of special community tutors. These released the teachers from their community responsibilities and in seeking to maximise usage and raise income to justify their employment tended to usurp the powers previously devolved informally to 'users' (Dybeck, 1981). This division of labour between school teachers and community staff, full and part-time, created a divisive hierarchy. It enabled teachers to hide from the community and community tutors to avoid the challenge of engaging with the formal educational process. Inevitably a dual use culture followed this fragmentation as Morris predicted it would. The 'classroom-ridden, textbook-ridden, information-ridden, and given over to incessant didactive discourse and discursiveness' (Morris, 1941, 69) mode of education, he always fought against, clawed back what little ground it had lost to secure a seemingly uncontested ascendancy.

In conversation Morris frequently referred to the 'dignities of education'. It is a splendid phrase resonant with meaning, richly capturing what Henry Morris toiled to accomplish. It summarises what is so patently missing within so much contemporary practice. Every attempt to foster those dignities is surely the most fitting of all tributes to his memory; a memory kept alive by the inspirational vision of the memorandum and the knowledge that within one small corner of Britain, for a few decades, an experiment dedicated to the preservation and fostering of those dignities briefly flourished.

Conclusion

Beeching closed Adlestrop Halt in the 1950s. The villages it and Kingham served have lost most, and in some instances all, of those elements required for a corporate life to thrive. Wealthy retirees and commuters have driven up house prices and gentrified this corner of the Cotswolds. Idbury is a cheerless place despite the genteel chocolate box facade. The Norman church remains but the school has gone along with all the other amenities. The school building is identifiable only from the presence of a ludicrous weather vane of a cane-wielding harridan chasing two fleeing pupils. It broadcasts a not very flattering message regarding the intellectual and cultural aspirations of the new occupants. Worse, it reminds us that such a way of conveying the previous usage of the building to a passer-by would be unimaginable elsewhere in Europe or North America. As an example of 'public art' it speaks volumes regarding the widespread support and tolerance in education of a brutal past and oppressive present. The rural poor survive reconfigurated as the new servant class, 'treasures' gardening, cleaning and polishing, clearing up the mess and ferrying the children of the remnants of the landowning class and expanding nouveau riche busy buying up the neighbourhood. Morris and Robertson Scott would be delighted to see the state of the housing but one suspects little else would surely please them.

Bibliography

Ashby, A. W. (1916). *The Rural Problem (Social Reconstruction Pamphlet No. 1)*. London, Ministry of Social Reconstruction.

Baker, W. P. (1953). *The English Village*. London, Oxford University Press.

Barker, B. (1997). 'Who Killed the Local Education Authority – Cambridgeshire 1974–1998?' *Cambridge Journal of Education, 27(1)*.

Bimrose, D. (1965). *Digswell: A matter done. The story of the Digswell Arts Trust*. Digswell, Digswell Arts Trust.

Bourdillon, A. F. C. (1945). 'Needs of the Countryman' in A.F.C. Bourdillon (ed) *Voluntary Social Services*. London, Methuen.

Bracey, H. C. (1959). *English Rural Life: Village activities, organisations and institutions*. London, Routledge and Kegan Paul.

Dent, H. C. (1943). *The Countrymans' College*. London, Longmans.

Dybeck, M. (1981). *The Village College Way*. Cambridge, Cambridgeshire County Council.

Farnell, D. (1968). *Henry Morris: An Architect of Education*. Unpublished thesis, Cambridge Institute of Education.

Fenn, T. (undated). *Recalling Henry Morris 1889–1961*. Private Publication.

Gardiner, A. G. (1923). *Life of George Cadbury*. London, Cassell.

Green, T. H. (1888). *Collected Works Vol 3*. London, Longmans.

Hurt, J. S. (1979). *Elementary Schooling and the Working Classes 1860–1918*. London, Routledge and Kegan Paul.

Jeffs, T. (1998). *Henry Morris: Village colleges, community education and the ideal order'*. Nottingham, Education Now Books.

Jeffs, T. (2000). 'Something to give and much to learn' in R. Gilchrist and T. Jeffs (eds) *Settlements: Social change and community action*. London, Jessica Kingsley Publishers.

Joad, C. E. M. (1945). *About Education*. London, Faber.

Jones, D. (1988). *Stewart Mason: The art of education*. London, Lawrence and Wishart.

Jones, H. (1919). *The Principles of Citizenship*. London, Macmillan.

MacCunn, J. (1907). *Six Radical Thinkers*. London, Arnold.

Ministry of Education (1947). *Further Education*. London, HMSO.

Morris, H. (1925). *The Village College: Being a memorandum on the provision of education and social facilities for the countryside, with special reference to Cambridgeshire*. Cambridge, CUP (reprinted Ree, 1973).

Morris, H. (1926). 'Institutionalism and Freedom in Education', *New Ideals Quarterly* 2(i).

Morris, H. (1936). 'Rural Civilisation' paper delivered British Association, Blackpool Conference, 15th September (reprinted Ree, 1984).

Morris, H. (1941). 'Post War Policy in Education', paper delivered to the Association of Directors and Secretaries of Education (reprinted Ree, 1984).

Morris, H. (1945). 'Buildings for Further Education' paper delivered Royal Institute of British Architects (reprinted Ree, 1984).

Morris, H. (1946). *Liberty and the Individual*, talk delivered BBC Home Service (script reprinted Ree, 1984).

Nettleship, R. L. (1888). *Memoir of T. H. Green*, in R. L. Nettleship (ed). Collected Works of T. H. Green. London, Longmans.

Nicholson, P. P. (1990). *The Political Philosophy of the British Idealists*. Cambridge, Cambridge University Press.

Palmer, M. (1976). 'Henry Morris', *Education*, 12th March.

Pevsner, N. (1954). *Cambridgeshire: The Buildings of England*. Harmondsworth, Penguin Allen Lane.

Rashdall, H. (1907). *The Theory of Good and Evil: A treatise on moral philosophy*. Oxford, OUP.

Read, H. (1958). *Education Through Art*. London, Faber.

Ree, H. (1973). *Educator Extraordinary: The life and achievements of Henry Morris*. London, Longman.

Ree, H. (1980). 'A Case of Arrested Development', *Times Educational Supplement*, 17th October.

Ree, H. (1984). *The Henry Morris Collection*. Cambridge, CUP.

Robertson Scott, J. W. (1925(a)). *England's Green and Pleasant Land*. London, Cape.

Robertson Scott, J. W. (1925(b)). *The Story of the Women's Institute Movement*. Idbury, Kingham, Oxon, The Village Press.

Robertson Scott, J. W. (1951). *The Day Before Yesterday*. London, Methuen.

Rose, M. (2000). 'If Christ Came to Chicago: The secular faith of the social settlements' in R. Gilchrist and T. Jeffs (eds) *Settlements, Social Change and Social Action*. London, Jessica Kingsley Publishers.

Rowntree, B. S. and Lavers, G. (1951). *English Life and Leisure*. London, Longmans.

Saville, J. (1957). *Rural Depopulation in England and Wales 1851–1951*. London, Routledge and Kegan Paul.

Smith, M. K. (2000). 'Adult Education and the Contribution of the Settlements' in R. Gilchrist and T. Jeffs (eds) *Settlements, Social Change and Social Action*. London, Jessica Kingsley Publishers.

Steele, J. (1994). *Charles Rennie Mackintosh: Synthesis in form*. London, Academy.

Thomas, E. (1920). *Collected Poems*. London, Selwyn and Blount.

Vincent, A. and Plant, R. (1984). *Philosophy, Politics and Citizenship: The life and thought of the British Idealists*. London, Oxford University Press.

Wise, M. (1931). *English Village Schools*. London, Hogarth Press.

I have in my possession a copy of the BBC Home Service broadcast commemorating the life and work of Henry Morris. If you would like a copy please contact the author.

Josephine Macalister Brew

LIVERPOOL JOHN MOORES UNIVERSITY
LEARNING SERVICES

Chapter thirteen

Josephine Macalister Brew: Youth work and informal education

Mark K. Smith

If we are not in youth work because of our love of our fellow men we have no business there at all. This burning love of humanity always meets with response, though not always in the ways we most care for, but nowadays as much youth work is ruined by too much restraint as by too much exuberance. Fear to exert undue influence, fear to assert authority when necessary, conscientious scruples about this and that – are all contributory factors. But young people want to know where they are and they need the friendship of those who have confidence and faith. (Brew, 1957, 112–113)

Josephine Macalister Brew (1904–1957) was an accomplished and innovative educator, whose 'service to the young was unequalled in her generation' (Woods, 1957). She wrote not just one, but three classic books: *In the Service of Youth* (1943); *Informal Education: Adventures and reflections* (1946) – the first full-length exploration of the subject; and *Youth and Youth Groups* (1957). The last started as a rewrite of the first, but ended up a completely different book, 'because we live in a different world' (Brew, 1957, 11). She had an extraordinary ability to connect with people through her writing and speaking. She was also associated with a number of significant innovations in practice including the growing interest in social groupwork at this time in the UK; the development of residentials as an educational form; and the formulation of the Duke of Edinburgh's Award (she wrote much of the programme for young women).

Born on 18 February 1904 in Llanelli, Carmathenshire (and registered as Mary Winifred Brew), the first months of her life were spent in a pleasant house on Park Terrace overlooking a small park near to the centre of the town. She was one of three sisters (Margaret and Betty). Her father, Frederick Charles Brew is listed as a boot salesman on her birth certificate – although later she was to talk of his being in the army. The family appears to have moved a number of times while she was growing up.

She went to the University of Wales at Aberystwyth and graduated in 1925 with a lower second in history. She entered teaching – becoming a history mistress at Shaftesbury High School for Girls, Dorset. According to one of her colleagues (Miss Gilderston Powell), she was a born teacher, but not a teacher in a girl's high school. She looked to the possibilities of the different areas of school life – for example, writing and helping to produce a play for the young women. By this time she was known as Jo. In 1932 she left the school to live with her mother in Cardiff. There she was to write for local papers and to study to attain her doctor of law. It was at this time that she became involved in youth work.

Youth work in Cardiff, Lincoln and beyond

Brew's first encounters with the work had been earlier – probably in Tiger Bay (Chapeltown) in Cardiff.

> *My first introduction to club work at a very tender age was to be sent to a club in one of our most notorious docklands. I was welcomed, if you could call it that, by a harassed leader who hustled me into a roomful of girls, most of them seventeen-year-old girls from dressmakers' and tailors' sweatshops – but of course I did not have even that crumb of information then! 'Well, girls,' said the 'bright' leader, 'here is little Miss – who is going to play you some lovely music.' She then turned to me, and said, 'I'm sorry, but the girl who usually plays for dancing isn't here tonight. I'll come back and do what I can for you later.' That was the last I saw of her until she came back to tell us that the club was closing. In my more cheerful moments I attribute the fact that the class survived the evening to qualities I share with Coleridge's Ancient Mariner, but in moments of grim truthfulness I realize that it was just luck and the fact that even the adolescent shrinks from practising cruelties on the very young and innocent! This may be, one hopes it is, a rare introduction to club work.*
> (Brew, 1943, 82–83; 1957, 190)

At this time it appears that she became involved in work in Chapeltown and the South Wales educational settlements. The latter were linked to initiatives taken by the Society of Friends and drew on the experience of adult schools and other educational settlements such as Woodbrooke, Fircroft and Swarthmore. Strong links were also made with University College, Cardiff, the WEA and with local community leaders such as teachers (see Jones, 1985). Significantly, with the involvement of people like A. D. Lindsay (then Master of Balliol) and Tom Jones (secretary to the cabinet), a coherent philosophy developed, and resources followed. Perhaps the most interesting of the nine settlements established were those pioneered by William and Emma Noble in the Rhondda Valleys (at Maes-yr-Haf from 1927 onwards), and Peter Scott at Brynmawr (near Ebbw Vale). Some of the themes that emerged in her later work can certainly be found running through the activities of these settlements. They were characterized by a focus on democratic control, self-help and cooperative ventures, and a belief in the power of community-based education to change society. 'The principle was always to try to remove the taint of charity by involving local people in practical ways and by developing their skills for the benefit of the community, and to offer educational opportunity as a means of growth' (Jones, 1985, 94). A special emphasis was placed on self-governing clubs, often with club-houses built by members. In the Rhondda Valley there were 52 clubs with a membership of 9,000 men, women and young people that provided, 'warmth, workshop equipment and a chance for people to develop latent abilities (Pitt, 1985). Girls and boys' clubs also formed a significant part of a number of the settlements. In addition, there was a strong emphasis on local investigation and community study, probably the best known being Jennings' study of Brynmawr (see also, Pitt, 1985 for a discussion of this experiment and chapter eleven).

In 1936–37 Brew took up an appointment as the youth officer for Lincoln – one of the first local education authority funded youth work posts. She also became the secretary of the Lincoln Federation of Girls' Clubs. (The 'Macalister' had appeared by this point – from where I do not know!) In Lincoln she was involved in a number of different initiatives including work around community centres and the development of a club for barge children. The latter was located in basic premises but was run with the philosophy that it was the members' club. Brew had the principle that if you break a window it will stay broken until you mend it; if you muck up a wall it will stay like that until you paint it. Through the federation, she became involved with the National Association of Girls' Clubs – serving on the executive committee, and speaking at the secretaries' conference.

With the outbreak of the Second World War there was considerable disruption to the work of the Association, followed by demands that it develop its services. Given widespread interest in the launching of the 'service for youth' there was the need for assistance 'to those who have been called upon at very short notice and often with little preparation and experience to deal with new clubs, youth centres and the like' (Brew, 1940, 10). Brew was asked to edit a number of existing pamphlets into a book, the first under her name, which appeared in 1940: *Clubs and Club Making*. She was also called upon to give talks in various places (many of these talks were later to appear in chapter form in *In the Service of Youth*, 1943). Her career as a writer had really taken off – with various articles appearing in the *Times Educational Supplement* concerning the needs of young people – and provision for them. She moved to Oldham to be the youth officer there but she was encouraged to join the staff of the National Association of Girls' Clubs (by Eileen Younghusband among others). She was appointed education secretary on 1 June 1942 (one of the other candidates for the job was Pearl Jephcott – who also features in this collection).

London and the National Association of Girls' and Mixed Clubs

At NAGMC, Brew joined a very talented group of women including Eileen Younghusband (who was later to write a number of seminal books and reports on social work); Madeline Rooff (author of *Youth and Leisure,* 1935); and later Pearl Jephcott (who had been an organising secretary in Birmingham and Durham, but was later to write a series of important books on the lives of young people, 1942; 1948; 1954; 1967). Brew's work also brought her into contact with key figures around the education world such as Sir John Wolfenden (later to become vice-chancellor of the University of Reading and chair of several royal commissions); and S. H. Woods (an influential senior official in the Board of

Education who became a friend, and who chaired her committee at NAMCGC).

The association's offices moved several times. For a time they rented part of Hamilton House, Bidborough Street, London WC1, shared with the National Union of Teachers, and Brew had a flat close by in Grafton Mansions. Later, the Association moved further away, to Devonshire Street. The people she worked alongside talk of her with great affection. She was friendly – not at all 'stuck-up', committed and talented. However, much of her writing was done at a small desk at Grafton Mansions. Miss Gilderston Powell who was later to share the flat with her, talks about her living on a diet of black tea and cigarettes. She could never persuade her to eat proper food. As Brew wrote, beside her would be a teapot full of stewed tea and a big ashtray full of cigarette ends.

As well as being a period of significant change in her public life, there were major changes in her private life. She had met and apparently married Robin Keene – a relationship that was not to last long for he was killed during the war (although I have not been able to find either a marriage or a death certificate). She talked a little about her husband to colleagues like Vera Mulligan, her secretary for much of the war.

The first few years spent at what became the National Association of Girls' Clubs and Mixed Clubs (then Mixed Clubs and Girls' Clubs) produced two remarkable books: *In the Service of Youth* (1943), effectively the first full statement of 'modern' youth work and *Informal Education* (1946), the first single authored book on the subject. Brew also left us with an array of shorter pieces from this period, for example, those in the various publications and magazines produced by the National Association of Girls' and Mixed Clubs and in the *Times Educational Supplement*.

In the service of youth

Brew's books display her originality as an educational thinker. While her focus was upon young people, she located what she was doing within a view of education that was lifelong. She also recognized the possibilities of learning in social life. As a result, she 'secured for herself a niche in the story of English education comparable with that held amongst an earlier generation of schoolmasters by Caldwell Cook' (*The Times Educational Supplement,* June 7, 1957).

In the Service of Youth, while inevitably a product of its time, was produced at a pivotal moment (see Jeffs, 1979, 13–30; Smith, 1988, 29–47). The youth service had been established by Board of Education Circulars 1486 and 1516 and there had been a massive expansion of youth provision, a change in the social background of both users and leaders, and a fundamental shift in overall character and emphasis. The rhetoric of character building and child saving was pushed to one side. In its place there was an emphasis on enjoyment and recreation, a concern to promote 'cooperation, tolerance, free decision and joint responsibility' (Ministry of Education, 1945, 9). Here I want to note five elements that mark this book out as the first major statement of 'modern' youth work (Smith, 1991, 36–39):

1   *A commitment to community, citizenship and cooperation*

The central vehicle for realizing this was the voluntary association of members – the club. Brew saw in the 'club' a means by which people could freely identify with one another and gain the skills, disposition and knowledge necessary for citizenship.

> *The club at its best creates a society of personalities with a community sense, which is the essence of good citizenship . . . We are not concerned with the making of 'good club members' or 'well-organized youth groups', but with a much wider issue, the making of good citizens. This can only be done in a society where each member is important, where each one is given a chance to contribute something to the life of the group – the leader no more and no less than the member. It is for this reason that self-government is so important in club work. If I had to give the first article of my club credo it would be 'I believe in the club committee'.*
> (Brew, 1943, 12)

The use of clubs in this way was not new and had been articulated most notably within the boys' club tradition by Russell and Rigby (1908). However, Brew was prepared to embrace much looser forms such as the 'in and out' clubs and to engage with ways of organizing which were more of young people's, rather than leaders', making.

2   *A clear focus on process*

One of the striking features of Brew's writing is the attention she gives to the way things are done and what can be learnt from process. 'A youth leader must try not to be too concerned about results, and at all costs not to be over-anxious' (1957, 183). She was later to write:

> *Only by the slow and tactful method of inserting yourself unassumingly into the life of the club, not by talking to your club members, but by hanging about and learning from their conversation and occasionally, very occasionally, giving it that twist which leads it to your goal, is it possible to open up a new avenue of thought to them.*
> (1943, 16)

3   *A recognition of the social and emotional needs of young people*

Brew was a great reader of psychology texts and from those she was well aware of the sea change in understandings of emotional, moral, intellectual and sexual development and the subconscious that had occurred. Her attention to experiences of young people, particularly in relation to their bodies and to sexual activity, is a feature of the progressive girls' club tradition. Much of the basis of her advocacy of mixed clubs lay in this area (1943, 56–63). She displays both a belief in young people's abilities to work things out for themselves, and a concern that workers should not be neutral bystanders in this process. Significantly when she came to re-address these questions in *Youth and Youth Groups* (1957), these sections were altered fundamentally and pulled from the end of the book to the beginning. The nature of adolescence became the starting point rather than youth work or citizenship. The tone had changed and there was less talk of 'the boy' and 'the girl'. She concludes, 'it is probably in the field of promoting healthy personal relationships that the youth group has most to offer to the well-being of the community' (1957, 102–103).

4   *A championing of popular culture as a site for intervention*

Brew displayed an engaging determination to work with the things that young people themselves value. Were she alive today, she would, no doubt, be encouraging sampling and the like. 'The only real sin in all this modern dancing and all this jazz is that it is so frequently shockingly done . . . Start from where your young folks are' (1943, 14). But Brew was concerned to do more than start from where young people are, she did not want to rate activities on some bourgeois notion of value: 'True culture is the appreciation of everything, from a plate of fish and chips to a Van Gogh . . . We must give our young club members a vision, but it must come by way of cooperation through appreciation to creation' (1943, 15).

5   *A recognition of the economic and social context in which work*
takes place

As with many others within the girls' club movement, Brew attended to the economic and social conditions of young people. There are chapters on young people's experience of schooling, housing and work. 'No club on earth will succeed with a programme which bears no relation to the industry, working conditions and economic and social background of the area which it serves' (1943, 69). However, there are limits to her interest. She was not overtly political in her writing, especially when compared with early feminist workers such as Pethick (1898) or campaigners like Montagu (1904).

A sixth element is also discernable in the book, that of youth work as a pioneering form of informal education (1943, 173–74), but more of that later.

Previous writers had, of course, addressed a number of these concerns. What made *In the Service of Youth* special was that Brew managed to bring these elements into a reasonably consistent relationship and to ground this in the daily realities of practice. In describing the approach she was drawing on both her own direct experience of practice and that of several generations of workers within the girls' club movement (e.g. Brooke, 1912). However, what distinguishes her from her contemporaries (e.g. Edwards-Rees, 1943; Armson and Turnbull, 1944) is the sheer fluidity of her writing and her ability to connect quite sophisticated ideas with examples drawn from practice. Much of the significance of this book lies not so much in what is said as in the way things are put. Her tone of voice, and her descriptions of practice and individuals communicate much about her view of relationships between workers and young people; and where workers should focus their attention. Her attention to form and to process in her writing, mirrors that which she expects in workers.

Informal education

Informal Education begins by setting out two contrasting methods of educational approach. The first involved 'serious study' through schools, university extension classes and organisations such as the WEA. The second entailed 'active participation in a variety of social units' (1946, 22). It is the latter with which she was particularly concerned. She argued that education should be taken 'to the places where people already congregate, to the public house, the licensed club, the dance hall, the library, the places where people feel at home' (op. cit.). Much of the book is then focused upon how educators can 'insert' education into such units (discussed in Smith, forthcoming). In particular, she looks to what we might describe now as the process of creating and exploiting teaching moments.

As before, it was not the individual elements of her approach that were new. Each had been recognized by previous generations of educators. Rather it was the way she brought these together in a persuasive and accessible way. Here I want to note five key elements:

1 *Our concern should be with the cultivation of the 'educated man'.*
   The focus of the work, according to Brew, should be people's struggle to gain 'the equipment necessary for the great adventure of living the life of an educated man' (1946, 375). She suggests that probably the best definition of the educated man is that 'he is capable of entertaining himself, capable of entertaining a stranger, and capable of entertaining a new idea' (ibid, 28).

2 *Every human activity has within it an educational value* (1946, 27).
   Brew recognized that the requirement for continuing education could only be met if attention was paid to the experiences, events and settings of everyday life. In *Informal Education,* she explored the educational opportunities that lie in different areas of endeavour. The book is structured around different arenas or approaches where these moments can occur: through the stomach, the feet, the work of the hands, the eyes, the feelings and the ears.

3 *Work with people's interests and enthusiams and, if possible, deal with things quickly and on the spot.*
   'An activity which is so deeply rooted in the hearts of people is obviously a grand jumping-off point for educational programmes' Brew wrote (1946, 96). She argued that often what people needed most is encouragement and that the responses that educators make needed to be unhooked from the notion of subject, course and syllabus. Much educational opportunity is lost because of a desire to encourage people to join classes, she suggested (1946, 32). Things need to be kept simple and be entertaining.

4 *Harness the power of association.*
   Brew talked of the power of activities such as sport to deepen civic consciousness, and of the need to link informal education with such interests, along with 'home interests' such as parent education, and education in other groups and associations. She had no wish 'to turn every association into a solemn conclave for "uplift"', but recognized that there were considerable possibilities for learning in them (1946, 42).

5 *Informal educators need to have a wide cultural background and be lively minded.*
They must be able to engage with themselves, others and ideas, and foster environments where people know belonging and learning. The standards Brew sets for informal educators are high. They have to be educated themselves, 'lively minded, if unconventional', able to relate to people and flexible in approach.

Informal Education was well received (see, for example, the review in *The Times Educational Supplement,* March 8, 1947). As Houle (1992, 285) has subsequently noted, 'beneath its lively and anecdotal surface, the book makes some excellent methodological points'. Kuenstler (1954, 99) describes it as 'a delightfully written account of the new approach needed to educational problems, if the opportunities of youth work are to be fully realised'. It provided a significant number of people with a way of making sense of, and developing their practice. Indeed, over the last 10 years or so, I have talked to a number of former workers for whom it was *the* book that oriented their practice. The book's appeal was strengthened by Brew's commitment to public speaking and the person she appeared to be. As I have argued elsewhere (Smith, forthcoming) in many respects, it is the character of Brew herself that provides a paradigm for the informal educator. Her critical ability and depth of knowledge, her capacity to communicate and encourage, and her spirit and compassion provided both a benchmark by which educators could judge themselves, and the inspiration to do better.

However, one criticism that can be made of the book is its failure to draw upon an explicit or fully worked-through theoretical framework. Brew does not explore the contributions of writers like Dewey, Lindeman and Yeaxlee to the development of thinking about what she talks of as informal education. There is some tension in the way she approaches the notion of informal education. Is it the process of stimulating reflection and active participation (in associations) or is it, more narrowly, the insertion of teaching into different social situations? Brew appears to favour the former but largely focuses on the latter. This said, *Informal Education* was a landmark publication.

The expert in demand

In the later part of the war and after, Brew was much in demand as a writer, an expert on youth work, and as a speaker. Brew became a member of the Central Advisory Council (England) of the Ministry of Education and also of bodies connected with the Ministry of Labour and the Colonial Office. She also made two major foreign trips. Just after the war she went with a government-sponsored advisory group to Australia (there were three other members, one of which was S. H. Woods). They spoke in most of the major cities. Later, in 1950, she and three directors of education went on an advisory trip to west Africa.

She was sought after as a speaker. Brew had that rare ability of being able to connect with an audience, large or small, and to hold it in her hand. In researching this piece I came across a number of people who vividly remembered her performances. As S. H. Woods (1957) wrote, 'no audience could fail to recognize her as an authority on the subjects on which she spoke – and spoke with delicacy and humour'. Something of the quality of her talks and speeches comes through in her writing. Many of the pieces in *In the Service of Youth* were originally given as talks and they were rewritten in *Youth and Youth Groups* (1957). Wolfenden put it this way in his foreword to that book: 'We shall not hear again that precise and lucid speech from the tiny pinched face behind the thick-lensed spectacles. But in every page of this book we *do* hear it.' Yet while Brew possessed considerable 'showmanship', it did not come easily:

> *People used to say isn't she wonderful, but they never knew what it cost her. Before she made these public addresses she was sick as anything, there was a tremendous physical cost. The work was burning her out. A frail body, never strong. When she went into action as it were it was as if a light came on, and afterwards nothing. It is difficult to use the word genius – but she had this extra quality, this something.*

(Gilderston Powell – interview with the writer)

Her physical presence was often commented upon – thin, plantinum blonde, very frail of body – but with an amazing vitality. There was something about her eyes. She wore stylish clothing (often made by herself) and bold colours. One of the many stories that surround her is of a visit to a Belfast youth club dressed in a black suit and a bright red scarf. The week before the young men had been warned about the perils of 'scarlet women' – and her appearance in the club caused a stir. One of them ran to get the leader worried that one of these dangerous women had materialized in their club.

She continued to write for educational journals, but also augmented these with pieces for national papers such as the *Daily Mail* and the *News of the World*. Significantly, she also wrote a number of scripts for the BBC Home Service. She was associated with one series entitled, 'To Start You Talking'. These programmes were designed, as the title suggests, as starters for discussion. Aimed at, and involving, young people, their directness and freshness proved to be both popular and a critical success. Significantly, they picked up a massive audience among adults (see Madge *et al*, 1945, 16) as well as being a focus for a considerable amount of work in youth groups (ibid, 133–62). Brew was heavily involved in the preparation of a number of the 24 programmes (as a guest expert and as a writer of dramatic interludes) designed to stimulate discussion both in the studio and among the listeners. (The experiment is discussed by Brew (1946, 321). Transcripts of nine programmes, including several dramatic interludes written by Brew can be found in Madge *et al*, 1945.)

These dramatic interludes – which have an easy conversational style – flowed from Brew's ability to listen and observe. This was something that she took very seriously. For example, in the manner of mass observation, she went to cafés and public houses to listen to what people were talking about and to look at interactions. She would wear clothes that allowed her to melt into the background – and then take notes about what she had observed. She used similar abilities when visiting clubs and organisations, as the rich vein of stories that permeate her work testifies.

Innovations in practice – youth and youth groups

Josephine Macalister Brew and Miss Gilderston Powell moved from Grafton Mansions near Euston to a beautiful cottage on the edge of Epping Forest (Forest Cottage, Oak Hill, Woodford Green). She acquired a cat, Minnie. At Forest Cottage she was able to relax, to read and to write. She was a great reader. Mrs Ball, their cleaner, used to say: 'Don't let Dr Brew near those books. I dust the books and I come back in half an hour and there she is sitting on the floor reading the first one she's taken out.' Brew's workload continued to be very demanding. She threw herself into life, although she could go very quiet after a period of heavy work. When she let up she was often ill, which always had to be taken into account when planning a holiday.

As the education and training adviser to the National Association of Mixed Clubs and Girls' Clubs she not only designed the Association's training schemes for club leaders and members but was also the founder and director of the Association's 'residential courses for girls working in industry and commerce'. It is this latter area of work, along with her championship of mixed clubs, her involvement in the promotion of groupwork, and her work on the Duke of Edinburgh's Award scheme, that mark out her enduring contribution to the field after *Informal Education*.

Mixing

Brew, along with many other staff members at NAMCGC, was a strong advocate of mixed work: 'Our business is not with the encouragement of boys' clubs, or girls' clubs, but with the welfare of boys and girls, and this welfare is surely best served by the mixed club' (1943, 56). She talked of those who opposed mixing as being either lazy or fearful, and argued that mixed clubs and groups, properly led, contributed to the building of healthy relationships between young women and young men (1957, 151–57). 'The club', she wrote, 'should create in every member a deep natural respect for every human personality, or else it is not doing its work' (1943, 63). In 1947 there was a fierce debate over mixing conducted in the letters column of *The Times* (reported in Bunt and Gargrave 1980, 86–88) between key figures in the boys' clubs movement such as Lord Aberdare and Basil Henriques, and those in the girls' and mixed club movement (including Mrs Walter Elliot and S. H. Woods). Brew argued that boys and girls brought 'different gifts to enrichment of club life' and that mixing did not imply homogenisation but rather the fostering of differing identities (1957, 155–56). She very clearly saw that young men and young women required different opportunities – and that there was a case for some forms of separate provision (see below). However, this was to be within a broad context of mixed provision. (For a review of the mixing debate after the heat of 1947 see Davies 1999, 92–97).

The Girls in Industry programme

Once unfairly described as the 'poor girls' finishing school' (see Allcock, 1988, 23), these NAMCGC courses, designed and directed by Brew, were targeted at young women working in industry and commerce. Young women were released, and usually paid for, by their employers to undertake one of the courses. Based around a residential experience – usually at one of the Association's centres such as Avon Tyrell – the courses used almost stereotypical 'girls' interests' such as homemaking, fashion and beauty and sought to open new vistas. As one person who worked on these programmes put it, Brew wanted to encourage 'adventures of the mind'. In this respect the courses expressed a number of 'Brew themes', for example, starting with a familiar interest and giving it a twist; seeking to expand possibilities and deepen insights; and encouraging people to work together. She had the ability to generate different activities, and to bring people together so that they could work. Part of the impact of the courses lay in their residential nature. 'Perhaps one of the prime necessities of social education,' Brew (1946, 179) wrote, 'is that all of us at least once in our lives should go through the general experience of living in a small group which is not our family, and where we can discover afresh the meaning of social action and shared responsibility.' Some of those working on the courses did not have quite the same vision and facility as Brew, and there was occasionally a tendency to focus on the overt interest rather than the underlying theme. However, the courses, which began in 1952 (Davies, 1999, 94), were innovative and proved to be very popular with their participants. They continued well into the 1970s at NAYC as Macalister Brew Courses (under the direction of Vera Mulligan).

Groupwork

Brew was part of the movement to popularise social groupwork in Britain. Working in and with groups had been central to settlement and youth work since their inception (see Spencer, 1955, 29–48; Young and Ashton, 1956, 223–58), but it was with the work of American writers such as Grace Coyle (1947; 1948), George Homans (1951), and Gertrude Wilson and Gladys Ryland (1949) that it began to gain recognition as a distinctive area of practice and study. Earlier, *In the Service of Youth*, had placed a particular emphasis on working with groups:

> Much of the youth work that we are doing at the moment can only be classified as a brave endeavour to salvage something from the wreck of wartime conditions, but out of that increased tempo . . . there is gradually evolving a new technique – a technique in the imparting of information and instruction, a group technique, a discussion technique, and a new method of training both instructors and leaders.
> (Brew, 1943, 168)

Some 10 years later Brew became a member of the group chaired by Peter Kuenstler that produced 'a first contribution to the literature of social group work in Britain' (Kuenstler, 1955, 7). She argued that the objective of youth work should be that adolescents should be given:

> [O]pportunuties to accept and respect themselves and to pursue any special skills or interests they may have, a sense of belonging and participating in some group or groups, and, finally, as an emotional foundation for all peaceful living, an acceptance of others who have a right to be different and who may nevertheless make valuable contributions to the group.
> (Brew, 1955, 72)

Both *In the Service of Youth* and *Informal Education* explored in different ways, 'the fascinating possibilities of "education through the group"' (Brew 1955, 89). She now bemoaned the tendency in youth work to pay too much attention to individuals rather than groups, and the extent to which group work among adolescents is regarded as a social palliative, rather than as 'a new and exciting form of informal education' (op. cit.).

The Duke of Edinburgh's Award scheme

The idea of a nationwide scheme of awards for young people grew out of an initiative by the Duke of Edinburgh in 1955 (the scheme itself was announced in 1956) (Wainwright, 1966, 89). From the start it was assumed that the girls' award would be different from the boys', and Brew was approached to chair a drafting committee to prepare the syllabus. What emerged in particular was a section, 'design for living', with an emphasis on 'home-making'. Unfortunately, as with the Girls in Industry courses, it was too easy for this to be interpreted in a rather domesticating way by those running the scheme. Dick Allcock described her vision as 'very much to do with giving girls the time, space and skills to make the best of themselves. Those who interpreted this narrowly in terms of face, fashion and food missed the point, which was to aim for a broader, deeper expression of womanhood in every respect' (1988, 24). The pilot girls' award scheme was launched in 1958.

While working on the new award scheme, Brew reworked *In the Service of Youth*. Significantly, the new title was *Youth and Youth Groups* (1957). Given her interest in groupwork this change was not surprising. In the new book she argued that it was in the area of the promotion of healthy relationships that youth groups had the most to offer to the well-being of communities: '[T]he revitalized youth group, far from being an anachronism, can have a very important part to play in the general education of many young people for whom the continuing school pattern is not psychologically satisfying' (Brew, 1957, 103). The interest in democratic living and association remained, but the needs of young people became more clearly, at least in the book's organisation, the starting point for the work.

Youth and Youth Groups takes the themes developed in her earlier work and places them in the context of youth work in the mid-1950s. She also takes the opportunity to incorporate material from her work with Kuenstler *et al* (1955) to reflect on changes in youth work and the situation facing young people since the Second World War, and make some reference to youth work as informal education. Her message was still clearly that the young are not to be patronized:

> [H]owever, informal our approach may be, we must never underestimate the intelligence of young people, their keenness to use their minds as well as their bodies. We tend to constantly water down the milk of education when what is needed is that it should be presented in a vessel of a different shape, in the adult cup instead of the infants's feeding bottle.
> (Brew, 1957, 213)

The book was not to be published until a few months after her death. It was very close to completion before she died and as Sir John Wolfenden wrote in the foreword, 'it gives us the mature fruit of an experience that was unique'. He continued, 'this book makes permanent what might otherwise have faded as ephemeral, her wit, the precise coherence of her exposition, her philosophical mind, and, above all, her abhorrence of what was pompous or pretentious' (Brew, 1957, 9). One reviewer commented on her ability to connect with and to explore the lives of young people.

> She never made the mistake to which, as she says, social reformers are most prone, of projecting herself into other people's lives and imagining that they felt and thought as she did. She got under their skins, understood their thoughts and feelings, and then came back to herself to find out the reasons for it.
>
> (*Times Educational Supplement*, November 29, 1957)

The same reviewer commented that the book showed just how 'devastatingly unorthodox' her conclusions could be, and the extent to which they were 'shocking to conventionally minded people'.

The final days

Not long after Easter 1957 Brew had been very sick on a flight to Northern Ireland. She had not been well for a time, and had put off going to the doctor. This convinced her. She was quickly referred to a specialist who admitted her straight to the Jubilee Hospital in Woodford. Told she had a stomach ulcer (although she feared worse) she knew she required an operation. Brew worked on the foreword to the award scheme in the short time she was waiting in hospital for her operation. She had just learnt that she had been awarded a CBE.

Josephine Macalister Brew died on 13 May 1957. The specialist knew before the operation that what he was looking at was cancer rather than an ulcer – but he didn't want Brew to know. In the end there was little that could be done. Her death certificate records the cause of death as carcinoma of stomach with partial gastrectomy secondaries in the liver. There was a private funeral at the West London Crematorium at Wanstead. Brew did not like gravestones. Miss Gilderston Powell and Mrs Ball walked around the back of Forest Cottage and scattered her ashes.

She was remembered in a memorial service at the St Marylebone Parish Church on 14 June 1957 (which was close by the headquarters of the National Association of Mixed Clubs and Girls' Clubs). A stain glass window was commissioned for Avon Tyrell to commemorate her work. Vera Mulligan found the designer, Stella Gross, who had been working on the stained glass at Coventry Cathedral. It shows the cottage, the cat and pathways linking different areas of her endeavours.

One of Brew's favourite texts was: 'I have come to you and you will have life' – and that is exactly what she had and gave – life. Wolfenden commented that she was 'absolutely unsparing of herself and her energies, and there can be little doubt that it was her burning zeal for young people that burnt her up' (op. cit.). The obituary writer in *The Times Educational Supplement* (June 7, 1957) writes of her 'ceaseless talent for getting human beings to work together', and of her 'notable contribution, both in practical experiment and in writing . . . happily designated in the title of her book *Informal Education*'. He continues, 'as the educationalist grows solemn in his estimate of her work, the quick teasing smile comes back, and perhaps the final memory cherished by so many at home and abroad will be of her gaiety of spirit, her compassion, and her infinite encouragement'. Josephine Macalister Brew wasn't just one of the most able, wise and sympathetic educationalists of her generation, she made a profound contribution to the development of thinking about, and practice of, youth work and informal education.

Acknowledgments

I would like especially to thank Miss Gilderston Powell for sharing her memories of Josephine Macalister Brew. Vera Mulligan and Marjorie Smith also gave me some important insights into her character and work. Thanks also to *Youth and Policy* for allowing me to use some short extracts from articles (1991 and forthcoming) about Brew's work as a writer.

Bibliography

Allcock, D. (1988). *Development Training: A personal view.* Stoneleigh, The Arthur Rank Centre.

Armson, A. and Turnbull, S. (1944). *Reckoning With Youth.* London, Unwin and Allen.

Brew, J. Macalister (1940). *Clubs and Club Making.* London, University of London Press/ National Association of Girls' Clubs.

Brew, J. Macalister (1943). *In the Service of Youth. A practical manual of work among adolescents.* London, Faber.

Brew, J. Macalister (1945). 'Only one living room', 'When should we be treated as grown up?', 'All out for a good time' – dramatic interludes in C. Madge *et al. To Start You Talking. An experiment in broadcasting.* London, Pilot Press.

Brew, J. Macalister (1946). *Informal Education: Adventures and reflections.* London, Faber.

Brew, J. Macalister (1947). *Girls' Interests.* London, National Association of Girls' Clubs and Mixed Clubs.

Brew, J. Macalister (1949). *Hours Away from Work.* London, National Association of Girls' Clubs and Mixed Clubs.

Brew, J. Macalister (1950). 'With young people' in Bureau of Current Affairs *Discussion Method.* London, Bureau of Current Affairs.

Brew, J. Macalister (1955). 'Group work with adolescents' in P. Kuenstler (ed) *Social Group Work in Great Britain.* London, Faber and Faber.

Brew, J. Macalister (1957). *Youth and Youth Groups.* London, Faber and Faber.

Brew, J. Macalister (1968). *Youth and Youth Groups* 2nd edn. revised by J. Matthews. London, Faber and Faber.

Brooke, E. (1912). 'Our Clubs at Home: The Honor Club', *Girls' Club News*, June, 1912.

Coyle, G. (1947). *Group Experience and Democratic Values.* New York, Woman's Press.

Coyle, G. (1948). *Group Work with American Youth.* New York, Harper.

Davies, B. (1999). *From Voluntaryism to Welfare State. A history of the youth service in England, Volume 1: 1939–1979*. Leicester, Youth Work Press.

Edwards-Rees, D. (1943). *The Service of Youth Book*. Wallington, Religious Education Press.

Homans, G. (1951). *The Human Group*. London, Routledge and Kegan Paul.

Jeffs, T. (1979). *Young People and the Youth Service*. London, Routledge and Kegan Paul.

Jeffs, T. and Smith, M. (eds) (1990). *Using Informal Education*. Milton Keynes, Open University Press.

Jennings, H. (1936). *Brynmawr: A study of a distressed area based on the results of the social survey carried out by the Brynmawr community study council*. London, Allenson and Co.

Jephcott, A. P. (1942). *Girls Growing Up*. London, Faber and Faber.

Jephcott, A. P. (1943). *Clubs for Girls: Notes for new helpers at clubs*. London, Faber and Faber.

Jephcott, A. P. (1948). *Rising Twenty*. London, Faber and Faber.

Jephcott, A. P. (1954). *Some Young People: A study of adolescent boys and girls*. London, George Allen and Unwin.

Jephcott, A. P. (1967). *A Time of One's Own: Leisure and young people*. Edinburgh, Oliver and Boyd.

Jones, E. (1985). 'Education as a response to social stress. The South Wales educational settlements' in R. Cann, R. Haughton and N. Melville (eds). *Adult Options. Three million opportunities*. Goudhurst, Weavers Press/Educational Centres Association.

Kuenstler, P. (ed) (1954). *Youth Work in England*. London, University of London Press.

Kuenstler, P. (ed) (1955). *Social Group Work in Britain*. London, Faber and Faber.

Madge, C., Coyish, A. W., Dixon, G. and Madge, I. (1945). *To Start You Talking: An experiment in broadcasting*. London, Pilot Press.

Ministry of Education (1945). *The Purpose and Content of the Youth Service: A report of the Youth Advisory Council appointed by the Minister of Education in 1943*. London, HMSO.

Montagu, L. (1904). 'The girl in the background' in E. J. Urwick (ed). *Studies of Boy Life in Our Cities*. London, Dent.

Pethick, E. (1898). 'Working Girl's Clubs' in W. Reason (ed). *University and Social Settlements*. London, Methuen.

Piaget, J. (1932). *The Moral Judgment of the Child*. New York, Harper and Row.

Pitt, M. R. (1985). *Our Unemployed. Can the past teach the present? Work done with the unemployed in the 1920s and 1930s*. London, M. R. Pitt/Friends Book Centre.

Russell, C. and Rigby, L. (1908). *Working Lads' Clubs*. London, Macmillan.

Smith, M. (1988). *Developing Youth Work: Informal education, mutual aid and popular practice*. Milton Keynes, Open University Press.

Smith, M. (1991). 'Classic texts revisited: In the Service of Youth', *Youth and Policy*, 34, 36–39.

Smith, M. K. (forthcoming). 'Classic texts revisited: Informal Education', *Youth and Policy*.

Spencer, J. (1955). 'Historical development' in P. Kuenstler (ed). *Social Group Work in Britain*. London, Faber and Faber.

Wainwright, D. (1966). *Youth in Action. The Duke of Edinburgh's Award Scheme 1956–1966*. London, Hutchinson.

Wheeler, O. (1945). *The Adventure of Youth*. London, University of London Press.

Wilson, G. and Ryland, G. (1949). *Social Group Work Practice*. Cambridge, Houghton Mifflin.

Young, A. F. and Ashton, E. T. (1956). *British Social Work in the Nineteenth Century*. London, Routledge and Kegan Paul.

Fred Milson

Chapter fourteen

'Youth and Community Work in the 1970s': A missed opportunity?

John Holmes

In 1969 a government review entitled *Youth and Community Work in the 70s* was published. The findings of the Fairbairn-Milson Report, as it was known, were summarised as follows:

> *A youth and community service should be established which will get away from the club-is-the-youth service approach, meet the needs of young people by making contact with them **wherever** they are to be found, and recognise them as part of the community.*

(DES, 1969,1)

When the next government review, *Experience and Participation* appeared in 1980, the focus was back on the youth service and attempts to disconnect the youth service from community work were in train. In 2000, following the establishment of PAULO (named after Paulo Freire, the Brazilian educator) as a National Training Organisation, with the clear brief for youth work to work alongside adult education, community education and community work, there appeared to be a clear commitment from government to link these occupational areas, at least in terms of training. This was apparently an even more ambitious linking than that proposed by Fairbairn-Milson, because this time four occupational areas were involved along with all four administrative regions of the United Kingdom. In the light of these proposals it is perhaps now an opportune time to review the history of the last failed attempt to link community work (or community development) with youth work.

Professionalisation and training

My research undertaken in the late 1970s into the staffing of youth and community work, *Professionalisation – A Misleading Myth* (Holmes, 1981), was commissioned by the Department for Education and Science. The aim of the project was to map the career destinations of those leaving specialist youth and community work courses, and the staffing position of the youth and community service. However, it was seen by many as an attempt to get college-based training courses back on track providing workers for the youth service, as many graduates were taking up posts in community work and non-educational sectors. The research encountered a considerable tension between youth work and community work within college courses. It confirmed that many students were attracted to jobs with young people and adults outside the education-based youth service. However, as the title of the report suggests, these divisions were as much about issues of professionalisation and myths surrounding this trend as about the specific nature of youth work, community work or the youth service.

While this research was limited in a number of respects, not least in failing to foresee the extent to which the Thatcherite Governments would attack local authority services and the professions (in the name of the free market), it does provide a starting point for looking at the potential for occupational groups to work together. The extent to which there are perceived to be core common values and principles; the respect that exists between the partners; the nature of the partnership; and the degree of equality between the partners, would all seem to be key factors in determining the success of the partnership. My argument is that in the 1970s, on all four counts, there were problems which made the attempted 'marriage' between youth work and community work very difficult. This is apart from the influence of politicians who were to undermine the potential of a youth and community service almost as soon as the proposals were published in 1969. However, it remains my belief that the benefits to be gained from related occupational areas such as youth work and community work working together outweighs the disadvantages.

Differences within the Fairbairn-Milson report

Youth and Community Work in the 70s emerged from a partnership of subcommittees. The *Albemarle Report* (Ministry of Education, 1960) had been highly successful in rejuvenating and developing the youth service in the 1960s and as part of this process the Government set up a Youth Service Development Council (YSDC). Denis Howell, Minister for Youth (based within the Department for Education and Science) in the post-1964 Labour Government, served for a time as chairman of the YSDC and encouraged a number of its subcommittees to review various aspects of the youth service. This grew out of the work of previous subcommittees who had reported on young immigrants (Hunt Report, 1967), and part-time training (Bessey Report, 1962). The YSDC also considered work with young people in rural areas, voluntary community service, work with girls and young women, and work with the unattached (Davies, 1999, 118). The aims of the review, which produced *Youth and Community Work in the 70s*, were rather unclear when it was announced in 1967. A number of ad hoc committees were planned but only two materialised (Davies, 1999, 118). The first, chaired by Andrew Fairbairn, was asked to examine the youth service's relationship to schools and further education. The second, chaired by Fred Milson, focused on the relationship with the adult community. It took two-and-half years for these to complete their work. The final consolidated report was delivered to Denis Howell in April 1969 and is generally recognised as two distinct reports stitched together (Smith, 1988, 71).

A fundamental disagreement between the two subcommittees arose over the future role of the youth service. Fairbairn was deputy-director of education for Leicestershire, a local authority committed to the development of community schools and the close integration of schools and adult education. This emphasis on school-based youth work approaches was not surprising in the context of the recently published *Newsom Report* (Central Advisory Council for Education, 1963) on secondary schooling which argued that the 'less able' might positively respond to more informal, less academic approaches. The knowledge of the forthcoming raising of the school leaving age from 15 to 16, long proposed but delayed until 1972 for economic reasons, also fuelled the move to community schools which were seen as likely to be more acceptable to those obliged to stay on.

The Milson half of the report remained sceptical about the extent to which community schools could represent the range of community interests arguing that 'the school should be seen as part of the community rather than that the community should gather round the school' (Davies, 1999, 125). This debate reflects what Jeffs (1987) has described as the mix of utopian and pragmatic thinking surrounding the idea of the community school. The pragmatic basis of combining services to achieve economies of scale (whether school and youth services, or community services and youth services) was clearly promoted in *Youth and Community Work in the 70s* but was linked to more utopian views of the benefits of greater integration for different parts of the community and for professional services.

Theoretical underpinnings

The extent to which one believes more utopian, integrative community views of society are possible partially depends on the theoretical position held. *Youth and Community Work in the 70s* should be commended for making explicit its theoretical base, deriving from Etzioni's view of the *Active Society* (1968). Such an approach combines an emphasis on an increased role for local community groups working alongside the state. This assumes a gradualist liberal view of change which does not fit easily with those who view society as being fundamentally divided by inequality, and the state as primarily a force acting in the interests of those in power. The radical political analysis developed in the 1960s in the Black Power, student and emerging women's movements argued that established power bases had to be challenged in ways that would inevitably lead to conflict if meaningful change was to occur.

While it is unlikely any government review would embrace a conflict-based analysis of society there were some attempts by Fairbairn-Milson to recognise the increased need for a dialogue with older young people, 'The overall purpose of a service for those 16 and upwards should be the critical involvement of young people which is theirs as well as ours' (DES, 1969, 82). It was recognised that this could be divisive because 'there can no longer be an underlying consensus about all the issues that face our society . . . Those who want nothing more than a quiet life should think again' (ibid, 77).

While it was stressed that young people would challenge the status quo, and this would replace views of service providers and receivers, this was done with the aim that the 'great negative of apathy and acquiescence would be replaced by the affirmative of involvement and participation' (ibid, 82). The extent of potential conflict was not recognised fully, nor crucially was the greater extent to which community work (rather than youth work) identified with a conflict view of society. Community work also had a greater recognition of the institutional bases for inequality, and resistance to seeing the state as a benevolent institution. It was to writers who were 're-discovering' poverty and inequality in Western societies (e.g. Harrington, 1963; Townsend, 1967) that community workers were looking as well as to participatory methods of intervention (Gulbenkian Foundation, 1968). The political events of 1968 (anti-Vietnam and Black Power movements in the US, the anti-State Communism movement in Czechoslovakia and the student movements throughout the West) had a big impact on the thinking underlying community work, which came through in what were seen in this sector as the most significant publications of the 1970s (Alinsky, 1969, 1972; Freire, 1972). Neither the Fairbairn nor Milson subcommittee appeared to realise, or maybe wanted to admit, that community development was looking for inspiration to such writers rather than the likes of Etzioni. The reality of conflict came about in the Community Development Project (CDPs) which followed Fairbairn-Milson in 1969. In the CDPs workers critiqued their own funders on the basis of identification with local communities and their analysis of the structural factors influencing deprivation. Among students on the community and youth work courses in the 1970s I found that it was on courses with a strong commitment to community work, and among black and women students that there was a greater resistance to a youth service which was often seen as an agent of a repressive state. Equally there was more resistance to both the concepts of 'career' and 'profession', which were seen as too close to middle-class conformity.

At the time I argued that some of the stances adopted by college students misrepresented the degree of differences between community and youth work. The extent to which either occupation required conformity to the state rather than local people's priorities varied greatly within each and the concept of a profession was significantly different in youth and community work compared to traditional professions (Holmes, 1980). The ability of youth and/or community workers to achieve clear identities, and act collectively to represent their positions was weak in the 1970s, but this capacity was needed as unemployment levels grew, particularly among young people and ethnic minority groups. The potential for community work to politicise youth work, and for youth work to influence community work to act collectively (as a 'profession') was often diminished by the hostile stances adopted between the occupations.

Youth work and schools

It is of course debatable regarding the extent to which more politicised, more collectively vocal occupations would have succeeded in getting their voices heard and also to what extent, if they had, it would have led to them becoming targets for review and reconstruction by the Government. However, the position of youth work within the community schools, so strongly advocated by Fairbairn, provides some evidence of what can happen to a relatively small occupation within an institution dominated by a much larger profession. In Leicestershire from the 1960s onwards youth work was subsumed within the community school structure. Specialist trained youth and community workers did not normally get posts as Burnham conditions applied and qualified teacher status was required to work within the schools. Even the *Albemarle Report* (Ministry of Education, 1960) which had done so much to create a youth work profession advocated movement between the roles of teachers and youth workers. In the 1970s qualified teacher status allowed entry into full-time youth and community work posts and the proportion of teacher qualified entrants rose from one in three to more than 50 per cent by 1978 (Holmes 1981, 223). Specialist qualified entrants fell to only 20 per cent during this period and by the end of the 1970s less than a third of full-time workers were specialist trained (Holmes, 1981, 223). In the early 1970s there were a number of programmes leading to qualified teacher status which ran youth work options but in 1975 five of these converted to two-year full-time specialist youth and community courses. Concern about youth work being subordinated to the larger dominant professional value system in teaching has often been expressed (e.g. Davies and Gibson, 1967; Jeffs, 1987) and it would appear that the Fairbairn model at least in Leicestershire in the 1970s, confirmed these fears.

Community development and social work

The relationship between youth work and schools was particularly difficult in the 1970s but both had common foundations in an educational model of practice. The link to community work and community development, it can be argued, eroded the link to education. Outside of community schools the community development model operated from a wide range of settings, including community centres. However, whatever the setting, it was clearly committed to 'stimulating groups to action' in non-directive ways (DES, 1969, 61–62). This approach means following the interests of, and working with, a range of existing and new groups. While the case was made that the process of community development is inevitably educational for those involved and develops community participation, it is also true that community development was at this time emerging from a social services/social welfare model. Indeed during the late 1970s and early 1980s, some community and youth work courses were able to award dual qualification in youth and community work (JNC) and social work (CQSW). This was the time when the unitary approach to social work was developed (Pincus and Minahan, 1973; Currie and Parrot, 1981) which advocated a 'patch' approach based on the needs and interests of the local community. This approach faded in the 1980s as social work became more specialised, bureaucratic and judged by performance indicators. Such shifts eventually made it impossible to sustain the joint social work and youth and community work qualification.

The concern of social work managers to target those judged as being most in need, and prioritise limited resources accordingly does not easily fit with a community work approach which follows the interests and needs of local groups. Yet the relationship between educational purposes can be argued to be equally strong in both community work and youth work, or similarly vague if a narrow curriculum-based definition of education is adopted. With both it is the process of involvement and participation which is the vehicle for achieving education. Yet, possibly because of the stronger links of community work to social work, the addition of community to youth did appear to lead to a broadening of the role of the worker at this time in ways that could be said to be both vague and confused. *Youth and Community Work in the 70s* summarised the 'exciting possibilities for new partnerships between the service and industry, trade unions, commercial enterprises, the social services and education' (DES, 1969, 2).

Regarding community schools, it has already been argued that this often meant incorporation of the youth service rather than partnership, but even in other areas it could be shown that there was a risk of losing the core identity and purpose of the work.

Youth and community work

In 1970 a joint conference was held between the Community Service Association (CSA) and Youth Service Association (YSA) which led to the creation of the Community and Youth Service Association (the forerunner of CYWU – the Community and Youth Workers Union). A paper was presented which proposed a move to the 'middle ground' in the following way:

The 'Middle Ground'

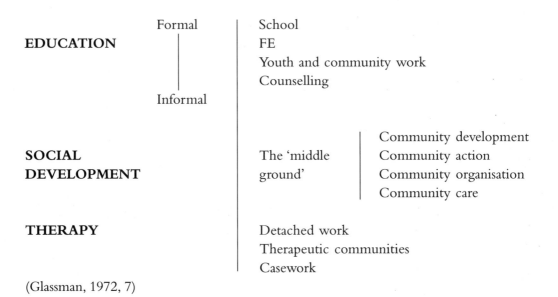

(Glassman, 1972, 7)

This model separates out community work from education, and seems to suggest that therapeutic models needed to be added along with social development. The logic of categorisation of detached work as part of therapy is unclear but may relate to the view that detached work focused on the 'unattached' with social problems (Biven, 1992; Goetschius and Tash, 1967). This model of 'the middle ground' was accepted at the time, with the merger of the two associations, but would seem to be evidence for the criticism that the report was broadening the work but was unclear about the relationship of youth to community. A study of the CYSA during this period (Glassman, 1972) shows that community workers often felt that despite their agreement to the merger they were being incorporated into a larger youth workers' association. This might explain why many left the CYSA shortly afterwards.

The effect of these changes can also be found in documents held within archives of University of Birmingham, Westhill (or Westhill College as it was then). These show the extent to which in the 1970s proposals were being developed for in-service work with education and social services departments, as well as the probation service, churches and voluntary organisations. The proposals reflected the situation where community workers/ youth workers/group workers were finding themselves to be a minority within departments who often did not understand their role (Westhill Papers, 1974–80).

Increasing use of the term 'community' in the 1960s, generally and within a whole range of policy areas, did not help to secure clarity. Davies notes that 'the youth service's educational and developmental traditions – made it rather less preoccupied with pathological versions of the concept than some other services' (1999, 166). This refers to the commonly held view that traditional communities were fragmenting, often as a consequence of housing policies which paid scant regard to existing or future social relationships, and that consequently social policy must try to re-build community, especially in areas exhibiting 'social problems'.

The range of relationships

Within the youth service the debate focused more on the nature of the relationship between youth and community. The model agreed by the new CYSA suggested a separate but complementary service, namely 'youth work and community work'. An alternative model, particularly attractive to the new two-year community and youth work courses which started in 1970, was to link community work more closely to youth work. Other courses, and many in the field, put youth first in youth and community work, emphasising what was for them the primary target group. The term 'youth and community service' also reflected the same priorities, but increasingly in the 1970s youth work was being undertaken beyond the confines of the service. Another formulation adopted by the youth officers' professional body was to try to explicitly hold onto the education link while adding community. The result was a move from National Association of Youth Service Officers (NAYSO) to National Association of Youth and Community Education Officers (NAYCEO).

The compromise view which became increasingly popular as the differences between the above titles (and their different emphasis in priorities) remained unresolved, was youth in community. This again prioritised youth but like the title of the National Youth Bureau house journal at the time – *Youth in Society* – made it clear that youth could not be separated from the communities and wider society. While few would disagree, and many youth workers would argue this had always been so, this formulation did have the effect of marginalising community to the context in which youth work takes place, leaving no clear role for community work or community development

Political context

The retreat from youth and community work, (or one of the other stronger variants) was partly a reflection of the political reception to *Youth and Community Work in the 1970s*. Whatever the failings of the review regarding confusion of purpose and patched-up differences, the timing of its release could hardly have been worse in terms of taking youth work forward. It was noted earlier that Denis Howell, the minister for youth, initiated the work of the two subcommittees which led to the review. At the time he was vague about the status of the review in terms of whether it would be published or even whether it would be considered for policy (Davies, 1999, 118). This suggests there was internal DES opposition from the outset. By the time of publication, the Labour Government was gearing up to an election. They had given no response to the review prior to May 1970 when they left office. The new Secretary of State for Education and Science, Margaret Thatcher, took 10 months to respond before rejecting the review's main proposals including the linking of youth work to community work. While conceding some proposals (around the 14 to 20-year-old age limits, further joint use of premises, local supervision of building projects and some capital funds for experimental work) she expressed her view of the value of the YSDC by abolishing it. The move towards targeting those in 'deprived areas' was emphasised (a policy extended by her Government in the 1980s) via the Urban Programme (Davies, 1999, 130). This period also saw the development of Intermediate Treatment Projects for young offenders which encouraged youth workers to use their skills to target those most at risk. These projects were rapidly taken over by Personal Social Services Departments. This partly reflected the greater power of Personal Social Services, but also a confusion of identity and role in relation to a selective programme based on 'rescue'. Many youth workers committed to the voluntary relationship were suspicious of these projects, particularly when more resources were given to these young people than to those involved in traditional youth work.

Influence of Fairbairn-Milson

Nevertheless, community work and the youth and community service developed along lines which, it can be argued, were influenced by the rejected review. The development of the two-year college-based professional training courses had pre-dated the review, and the merging of the professional association into the Community and Youth Service Association preceded Thatcher's rejection. The merging of services at local authority level, occurred over a longer period of time and the renaming of the officers group to NAYCEO did not take place until 1975. However, those developments did not occur within the context of a positive spirit of moving to a new role; indeed often they were accompanied by considerable acrimony and scapegoating between various interest groups. Economic crises in the 1970s, cutbacks in local authority spending, a new commitment to making Britain more competitive by focusing on improved schooling and vocational training, all tended to marginalise youth work. Governments, both Conservative and Labour, were not that different in their perception of youth work as peripheral. In this context it is difficult to know what difference a united front would have made for youth work but one worker was quoted as saying:

> In the future there would be few government induced changes because the Government thought of this work as peripheral and a luxury. As there was nothing to be gained from the youth and community services, but much to be lost, no government would spend time legislating in this area. Changes pressed for by the profession stood little chance as the profession presented a divided front. Since the Government could not act without antagonising one faction it did not act at all.

(quoted Glassman, 1972, 8)

It is important to try to identify the key areas where the 'marriage' between youth and community went wrong, and thus conversely what principles and contexts were needed for it to have been successful. This, of course, assumes it is necessary to try to build links between related occupations. The main basis for this is the common core that underpins both youth work and community work.

Unresolvable tensions

Bernard Davies identifies four key policy issues 'which have swirled around the service across the decades' (1999, 1). These are:

- Universalism v selectivity;
- Education v rescue;
- Professional v volunteer; and
- Voluntary v the state.

These tensions are not unique to youth work and have been discussed almost endlessly since the development of the welfare state (Jones, Brown and Bradshaw, 1978). Davies rightly holds that these tensions are 'inherent and unresolvable' (1999, 2) and demonstrates in his history how youth work and the youth service have had to work within these tensions. While others such as social workers have had to deal with such tensions, it is striking the extent to which both youth work and community work are defined by being caught by the conflicts they produce. Davies' frustration with how the youth service has developed, particularly since the late 1960s, comes through in his work and could be summarised as an annoyance with the youth service's inability to deal with these tensions in terms of convincing themselves and others (in particular government) that they could manage them. My view of what happened in the 1970s was that there was identification with these ideas as fundamental principles, and stereotyping of other workers, services and trainers in terms of being at the other end of the continuum. Thus these unresolvable tensions became a source of division. The potential marriage between youth and community, while not the only basis for this process of division, was a good example of principles being turned into myths.

Community workers argued both that theirs was the truly universal provision, by not selecting one age group, and also that in comparison to youth work they had a better understanding of the need to work with those subjected to discrimination and oppression. While this did not lead to a view of 'rescue' or 'targeting' as such it did encourage an acceptance of prioritising and a rejection of working with some community groups whose purposes would lead to oppression of others. Community workers saw their work as lying at the volunteer end of the continuum in relation to a professionalised youth service, and of needing to be critical of a state seen as responsible, in part, for upholding a repressive status quo. This was despite the fact that the community work students/ex-students had been through a professional qualifying course and were often working within departments such as the chief executives in local authorities or within voluntary organisations increasingly dependent on contract funding to deliver government targets.

Youth workers were no less likely to be partial in their views of themselves and of community workers. The argument was often that their activities were based on voluntary relationships, open to all young people and offering them the opportunity to be involved in a broad social education. Youth workers often defined themselves as a group against teachers. They saw themselves as more responsive to local conditions but at the same time they were resentful that their activities were not given the same recognition as others. Community workers on the other hand were sometimes seen as political to the extent of not being sufficiently committed to building local and personal relationships and as being too concerned with structural issues.

Conclusion

It comes down to a matter of perception and, in my view, whether workers can be confident enough in their own identity not to feel threatened by somebody coming from a different position. The differences between youth work and community work are much less apparent than the similarities. Because both community work and youth work have origins in a bottom-up *and* a top-down approach, it is not surprising that the four tensions identified by Davies have been central to debates. Neither youth workers nor community workers have been able to resolve them and it is because of this that workers live in an uncertain but relatively independent sector of state welfare intervention. When youth work and community work are compared to areas such as school teaching, social work, probation, careers and police it can be seen that the latter all have origins in both bottom-up and top-down approaches but have moved much more clearly into top-down forms of intervention and to one side or the other in the four sets of issues.

Youth work and community work are also relatively small and powerless occupational groups compared to other forms of 'people work'. While this is in itself a reason for working in partnership one of the key lessons of the 1970s would appear to be that partnership must be based on recognising the distinctive identity of each partner and not trying to subsume one within the other. The potential for the partnership must come from a mutual recognition of the distinctive contribution (or 'added value' to use current terminology) that can be gained. To follow this logic the model of youth work and community work is to be preferred to youth and community work, or community and youth work, or youth in community work. The CYWU formulation came closest to this model in terms of the distinctive identities but did not identify (at least in the documentation published) the basis of commonality, in terms of values and principles and underlying common issues.

This model of partnership would also seem to be closer to that proposed and implemented in Scotland during the 1970s. The report *Community of Interests* (Standing Consultative Council, 1968) was published a year before *Youth and Community Work in the 1970s* and as Davies notes was equally preoccupied with youth service–school and youth service–adult community links (1999, 132). However, in Scotland this was followed through in the Alexander Committee report *The Challenge of Change* (Scottish Office, 1975) which linked together the three separate traditions of adult education, community work and youth work under the overall title of community education. While there is the danger of this analysis suffering from the same perspective exhibited by students in the 1970s who were criticising the youth service, namely 'the grass is always greener on the other side', there does appear to have been established in Scotland a framework for debate and the working out of tensions, without the level of acrimony and division that occurred in England and Wales. This would be just as important as the fact that in Scotland the Government was supporting these developments, whereas in England and Wales the reverse was the case. It must be the job of occupations, or professions, to develop the common identity and policy positions for their collective experience which provides a framework for governments to develop their own policies.

Bibliography

Alinsky, S. (1969). *Reveille for Radicals.* New York, Vintage.

Alinsky, S. (1972). *Rules for Radicals.* New York, Vintage.

Biven, B. (1992). *The Finality of Youth.* Lima, Ohio, Fairway Press.

Central Advisory Council for Education (1963). *Half Our Future (Newsom Report).* London, HMSO.

Currie, R. and Parrott, B. (1981). *A Unitary Approach to Social Work – Application to Practice.* Birmingham, BASW.

Davies, B. and Gibson, A. (1967). *Social Education of the Adolescent.* London, University of London.

Davies, B. (1999). *A History of the Youth Service in England: Vol 1 1939–1979.* Leicester, Youth Work Press.

DES (1969). *Youth and Community Work in the 1970s (Fairbairn-Milson Report).* London, HMSO.

DES (1982). *Experience and Participation (Thompson Report).* London, HMSO.

Etzioni, A. (1968). *The Active Society.* London, Collier-Macmillan.

Freire, P. (1972). *Pedagogy of the Oppressed.* Harmondsworth, Penguin.

Glassman, D. (1972). *The Community and Youth Service Association,* MBA Thesis (unpublished), Cranfield Institute of Technology.

Goetschius, G. and Tash, J. (1967). *Working with Unattached Youth.* London, RKP.

Gulbenkian Foundation (1968). *Community Work and Social Change.* London, Longmans.

Harrington, M. (1963). *The Other America – Poverty in the US.* Harmondsworth, Penguin.

Holmes, J. (1981). *Professionalisation – A Misleading Myth?* Leicester, National Youth Bureau.

Jeffs, T. (1987). 'Youth Work and Community Education'', in G. Allen, J. Bastiani, I. Martin and K. Richards (eds). *Community Education: An agenda for educational reform.* Milton Keynes, OU Press.

Jones, K., Brown, J. and Bradshaw, J. (1978). *Issues in Social Policy.* London, RKP.

Ministry of Education (1960). *The Youth Service in England and Wales (Albemarle Report).* London, HMSO.

Ministry of Education (1962). *Training of Part-Time Youth Leaders and Assistants (Bessey Report).* London, HMSO.

Ministry of Education (1967). *Immigrants and the Youth Service (Hunt Report).* London, HMSO.

Pincus, A. and Minahan, A. (1973). *Social Work Practice: Model and methods.* Itasca, Illinois, Peacock Press.

Scottish Office (1975). *The Challenge of Change (Alexander Report).* London, HMSO.

Social Services (1968). *Report of the Committee on Local Authority and Allied Social Services (Seebohm Report).* London, HMSO.

Smith, M. K. (1988). *Developing Youth Work – Informal education, mutual aid and popular practice.* Milton Keynes, OU Press.

Standing Consultative Council (1968). *Community of Interests.* Edinburgh, HMSO.

Townsend, P. (1967). *International Seminar on Poverty.* University of Essex.

Westhill College (c1974). *In-Service Training Inter Professional Consultation* (Unpublished). Birmingham, Westhill.

Inside a youth club in the 1970s

Chapter fifteen

'Those That I Guard I Do Not Love': A memoir of HM Inspectorate and youth work in the Thatcher era

Tom Wylie

The Victorian legacy

Her Majesty's Inspectors of Schools (HMI) had entered their second century as an institution before they took a serious interest in youth work. From their formation in 1839, HMI reports had reflected the impact of wider social issues on schooling. The first HMI report in 1840 was a wide-ranging enquiry into the state of elementary education in the mining districts of South Wales and also concerned itself with the context of local wage rates, poverty and the custom of paying out miners' wages in public houses (Lawton, 1987). Nevertheless, for most of its first century, HM Inspectors concentrated primarily on formal education – firstly in elementary schools and, as the 20th century opened, in secondary schools and in technical education.

The early years also established the principle that HMI, appointed by Order in Council, were not officials beholden to the policies of the government of the day, but expert professionals giving independent advice, based on inspection. While the primary focus was reporting fairly on what was inspected, a secondary task was always the encouragement of development. As early as 1840 HMI philosophy had been guided by the injunction: 'Bear in mind that this inspection is not intended as a means of exercising control but of affording assistance: that it is not to be regarded as operating for the restraint of local efforts, but for their encouragement' (Kay–Shuttleworth, 1840).

From Butler to Albemarle

As the Inspectorate itself entered the 20th century, youth work was emerging as a distinct form of welfare and education which would eventually find institutional expression in that loose association of organisations and activities known as the youth service. The onset of the Second World War had given impetus to the development of a youth service beyond the long-standing voluntary organisations and also to an increased role for HMI. Two rather general clauses in Butler's landmark Education Act of 1944 were supplemented by Circular 143 of 1947 which required local education authorities to produce plans for the development of their youth services as for other aspects of further education. Some LEAs, notably London County Council, produced expansive plans for youth provision.

By 1949, a specialist youth panel had been designated within HMI's organisational structures, inspections of youth provision in different local authorities were taking place and HMI was offering Whitehall a relatively systematic account of the strengths and weaknesses of post-war youth services.

The weaknesses were more evident than the strengths and pressure from various quarters led to the establishment of the Albemarle Committee, which commenced work in November 1958 and reported in February 1960. An HMI, Ted Sidebottom, was seconded to be its secretary and advice from HMI, visits with HMI by committee members and evidence from inspections contributed substantially to its work. Albemarle set a compelling 10-year development plan for youth services nationwide and also asked that 'a sufficient number of inspectors . . . have this work assigned to them . . . to make certain that the development of the service over the next 10 years is properly assessed and stimulated' (Ministry of Education, 1960).

During the 1960s, HMI played a central role in the development of the post-Albemarle youth service. They advised on the capital building programmes; assessed experimental grants and those to national voluntary youth organisations; advised a series of special enquiries on aspects of youth services and continued routine inspections of youth work. Such reports were usually short but invariably offered pointers for development and were made available to the governing body. One, on a Liverpool youth centre in 1964 concluded:

The good attendance, the range of activities attempted, the variety of links with the neighbourhood and the vigorous life on the club premises indicate the need for a youth centre in this area. Some thought is needed as to how the exuberant spirits of the members might best be canalised into more thriving sections of activity. It might be advisable to build up standards of application and performance in what is already undertaken to provide a firm foundation for future experiment.
(HMI, 1964)

The search for higher standards was to be a continuing refrain in HMI reporting. Reports of this period often had a lyricism which became unfashionable:

To the visitor, the members presented a picture of vigorous, rather unoriented life. They moved like quick-silver about the building, anxious, it sometimes seemed, to find a focus of activity and not over-anxious to become that focus themselves. The girls were especially mobile.
(HMI, 1964)

The development of training was a particular focus for Inspectorate work. Ted Sidebottom was seconded to be the first principal of the National College for the Training of Youth Leaders and, as the routes to professional qualification diversified in the 1970s, HMI made the key decisions on the new locations (using powers for HFE course approval which they retained into the mid-1980s). In the relatively small world of youth services, the work of HMI individually and collectively, was known to the most active national players, often through participation in summer courses held in Salisbury. But, in common with many other sectors, until the early 1980s much of the great enterprise of education was a secret garden, dimly remembered from childhood, known in detail only to those still directly involved. HMI reports were not published and inspectors' advice glimpsed only through closed doors. The Inspectorate's activities and their judgements on youth work were similarly hidden from public view. This position was to change utterly as the 1980s unfolded.

The youth policy context of the 1980s

The 1980s saw a heightened profile for youth work within the Inspectorate[1]. The causes were two-fold: first, an increased interest in the youth service within the Department of Education and Science (DES) and second, pressure for more published reporting by the Inspectorate overall. Increased interest in youth service provision reflected a number of public concerns about what was happening to young people. Such concerns ebbed and flowed often in a set of moral panics, and had found particular expression in the early 1980s arising from urban disturbances in Bristol, Liverpool and elsewhere, and in the sharp increase in youth unemployment. These led, in time, to a set of government initiatives, notably the Youth Opportunities Programme orchestrated by the Manpower Services Commission – seen by many in the education service as a powerful predator.

Specialist youth HMI, although relatively few in number, were often at the sharp end of intelligence-gathering for the Inspectorate and department about street-level, community-based activity designed to ameliorate youth issues, including unemployment. Such activity often went well beyond the responsive capacity of most formal educational institutions, whether schools or FE. There was, potentially, a major task for the country's youth service with its diverse, if unbiddable, organisations.

Youth work itself had had little national policy direction for most of the 1970s. The Fairbairn-Milson report of 1969 (*Youth and Community Work in the 70s*) had lacked the authority of the *Albemarle Report*. Fairbairn-Milson was, moreover, an uneasy and often contradictory, compromise document stitched together from reports by two working groups of the Youth Service Development Council (DES, 1969). Pushed along by Denis Howell, Labour's Minister of Youth, the report landed on the desk of the incoming Conservative Secretary of State, Margaret Thatcher, and was eventually rejected by her. The Youth Service Development Council was also disbanded. Her decision, long delayed, had not prevented a number of local authorities and HE institutions, engaged in professional training, from anticipating a favourable outcome. Many had accepted the Milson-Fairbairn philosophy, vague as it was, and retitled their services or courses. Such localised, often idiosyncratic, decision-making intensified the difficulty caused by the absence of a national policy rudder.

Various parliamentary attempts to clarify the statutory basis and role of the youth service eventually smoked out of the DES a commitment to review the youth service. Inevitably, the department established a review group, chaired by a recently-retired DES deputy secretary, Alan Thompson, with the customary secretariat support from serving and retired HMI, notably Edwin Sims. In 1982, the review group produced a thoughtful and humane document in the best traditions of liberal social democracy (DES, 1982). But the department cherry-picked its recommendations. Some useful initiatives were set in train but the most important youth service needs identified by Thompson – notably for a clearer statutory basis – were not addressed and in due course the agenda of the formal education bureaucracy re-asserted itself.

Meanwhile, the cadre of specialist HMI with substantial youth work assignments had been increased in number to 14, to reflect the new demands. In no small measure this increase reflected the sympathy and recognition of Eric Bolton, later senior chief inspector (SCI), for the contribution of youth specialists to the overall work of the Inspectorate. Some non-specialist HMI also continued to take an interest in youth provision within their districts just as youth HMI were expected to contribute to the generality of FE inspection work. Into the HMI youth team came specialists with substantial backgrounds in youth and community work, and leadership of the specialist team also returned unequivocally into specialist staff inspector hands (David L. Rees, 1982–84; Tom Wylie, 1985–90 and Bryan Merton, 1990–92).

For the wider educational world the arrival of Sir Keith Joseph as Secretary of State for Education in 1981 had marked an important change of gear in matters other than his eventual curt dismissal of the key elements in the *Thompson Report*. As Eric Bolton later observed:

> As the arch-monetarist, less government more self-help guru of what was beginning to be called Thatcherism, his agenda was to reduce public expenditure on education and minimise the influence of bureaucrats and professionals. He also wanted to raise levels of achievement and make what went on in education at all levels more relevant and useful to the worlds of making and spending; and generally to bring the education service more in line with a market place characterised by informed consumers choosing from among competing providers.
> (Bolton, 1998)

Publish and be damned?

Sir Keith Joseph also set about a review of HM Inspectorate. There were fears for its survival but in the event, decisions on this scrutiny concluded that the Secretary of State regarded the Inspectorate's work as indispensable to the process of making educational policy. Furthermore, the concept of informed consumers making choices between schools for their children also underlined the need, in ministers' view, for HMI's reports on individual educational institutions as well as on broad educational themes, to be published. Joseph decided that they would do so from 1 January 1983.

At first an unwelcome demand to some HMI, publication sharpened the role and raised the profile of youth and community specialists. They were drawn into inspecting and contributing evaluative paragraphs about youth services in published reports on the overall work of LEAs (e.g. on Coventry, Sheffield and Cornwall); to thematic reports, including, for example, the *Response of the Educational Service to Youth Unemployment*; on health education and to the annual reports on LEA expenditure (HMI 1986(a)(c), 1987(b), 1991(b)). They brought a youth work perspective to inspections of FE colleges and of young offender institutions but attempts to work on school inspections were less successful, generally because of the dominance of subject specialisms in the school context.

The traditional mode of HMI inspection and reporting was of the individual school or college or, by extension, youth club[2]. In preceding decades HMI had carried out numerous 'full inspections' of individual youth clubs or centres but their reports were only made available to the governing body and, of course, to the Ministry or Department of Education. In the early days of published reporting, a few HMI youth reports continued this tradition. One of the first, for example, was highly critical of work in three Lambeth youth clubs which it had inspected in the autumn of 1982 (HMI, 1982(b)).

There was no prospect of the Inspectorate ever making full inspections of all schools, still less of youth projects. In any event, the primary purpose was to inform central government about standards. Accordingly, the national HMI youth team soon decided it was not worthwhile to concentrate on publications about individual youth centres or projects. Instead it deployed its limited resources on inspecting and reporting on overall youth service provision made by an LEA, or a national voluntary youth organisation or on specific forms of youth work practice, for example, detached work. Such reports – over 50 by the end of the decade – still based their judgements on the work observed by HMI in individual youth clubs or projects but it was hoped that such an approach would both inform policy and resonate widely, and thereby disseminate good practice. Another focus was on the inspection of training, especially initial qualifying training for youth and community work which was reflected in a series of reports on all the relevant HE courses including those at Westhill, YMCA, Leicester and Manchester and which were drawn together into an overview report in 1990 (HMI 1985, 1986(b), 1987(d), 1988(b), 1990).

A seminal report *Effective Youth Work* (HMI, 1987(a)), in the 'Education Observed' series, sought to characterise the distinctive values and educational methodology of youth work. It emphasised personal and social development as the principal raison d'être of youth work and, in a set of case studies, exemplified how various activities could be used as the means to this end. It suggested that the goals of personal development were being achieved when young people:

> . . . *begin to show an increasing ability to cooperate with others; to lead and respond to leadership; to exercise choice; to make decisions both alone and with others; to start, maintain and end relationships; to find appropriate expression for anger and frustration, love and affection; to deal with success, disappointment and conflict; and to adopt or reject ideas and viewpoints.*

(HMI, 1987(a))

HMI inspected youth work in the mushrooming variety of settings and projects – on the streets as well as in buildings, in the voluntary as well as the maintained sector. Such inspection activities challenged, widened and deepened HMI's inspection methodology: how were judgements to be reached on the performance of street-based or arts youth workers, of crime prevention programmes, of the totality of a local authority's youth provision? The honing of collective judgments and a greater measure of 'inter-rater reliability' became imperative as reports were now public documents and, properly, open to critical commentary. One external commentary, based on evaluating the first half dozen or so published youth specialist reports, had identified some apparent differences of emphasis between inspection teams (and had also suggested that HMI were constantly disappointed with the quality of the youth work they observed!) (Ritchie, 1986). In the days before HMI codified their criteria for judgement and put them explicitly into the public domain, the strength of HMI's approach lay in collegiality – the testing out of perceptions and judgements with colleagues who brought a range of nationwide inspection experience into the evaluation of a particular piece of youth work or of an LEA's overall service including its resourcing and, especially, its management – an enduring focus for HMI concern.

The growing diversification and targeting of youth work across the country was captured and encouraged in a series of published Inspectorate reports, e.g. on the National Federation of Young Farmers' Clubs; youth work on urban housing estates; school-based youth and community work; and more controversially, youth work responses to the needs of young women (HMI 1987(c), 1988(a), (d), (e), 1991(a)). Not all of these reports passed straight-forwardly through the Inspectorate's editorial command: some senior FE colleagues found it difficult to understand that HMI were reporting on the work of an education service with young prostitutes or young drug users as they did, in *Developmental Approaches to Youth Work in Wirral* and in *Responsive Youth Work* (HMI, 1988, 1990(b)). But most reports made it into print, albeit with tempered messages. *Responsive Youth Work*, an overview document, took the national story on from 1987. It helped to legitimate a range of practice, including harm minimisation approaches to drugs and work with gay and lesbian young people. It offered also an embryonic model for calculating staffing formulae.

Reports were complemented by specialist courses within the Teachers (sic) Short Course programme and by HMI support for a variety of field-based networks and national bodies such as the National Youth Bureau and the Council for Education and Training in Youth and Community Work. Such roles enabled HMI to contribute their national perspective and inspection evidence. HMI was generally designated an 'assessor', a role stronger than observer but not having management responsibility in a governing body. In the absence of specific directions from central government and lacking a professional institute, these loose arrangements often helped to sustain, however imperfectly, a sense of agreed purpose in a diverse sector and contributed to the development of a profession whose members were often isolated, structurally and temperamentally, within LEA departments.

British experience of youth work routinely gained international interest from the 1950s, especially within Europe. The Council of Europe committee for cultural cooperation established a misleadingly named 'European Youth Centre' (it was more a conference and training venue) and HMI served on its governing body and helped with its symposia and other events. Youth services had their own extensive network of international contacts and activities – many youth organisations are international in character. The Council of Europe in 1985 began to develop a pattern of European youth ministers' conferences. HMI attended these accompanying the junior Ministers of Education who held the youth services portfolio. They were, by and large, rhetorical events with little practical outcome, and much DES briefing encouraged ministers to be defensive (not that one of them, Bob Dunn, needed much encouragement). The department's line was thus rarely in tune with UK youth interests, not least in resisting any opening of links with Eastern Europe which was pioneered by several British youth bodies. Not for the first time, DES policy struggled to keep up with the innovative practice of youth organisations and thus failed to gain credit in European youth circles for the quality and enterprise of British youth work. More productive international work was done behind the scenes where specialist HMI, probably unknowingly, got on with the business of helping to reshape the roles and functioning of the Council of Europe's youth bodies and to play a part in developing some transnational associations, for example, in respect of youth information services.

The smack of firm government?

Policy command of youth work remained with the department. Here it was anchored in the shifting sands of ministerial and official interest. Some initiatives pressed by HMI captured political support. One such was a youth work apprenticeship scheme crafted by Janet Paraskeva, then an HMI, sold by senior HMI to Kenneth Baker, and designed to bring a new, younger cohort of peer educators into youth work practice. The *Thompson Report*, too, had identified various possibilities for action – including the creation of the Council for Education and Training in Youth and Community Work and of a National Advisory Council for Youth Service. Specialist HMI invariably supported such bodies as giving the possibility of greater field influence on policy-making. Departmental officials generally disliked them for the same reason. The time needed to build consensus in such a diverse field generally ensured a slow start and thus offered a good excuse to terminate them at a convenient moment. Moreover, if they were genuinely representative of the youth work field, they could be relied upon to be critical of government policy towards young people and youth services. So it proved again with NACYS: a departmental official, against HMI advice, persuaded the minister to bundle it into touch in 1989 just when it was getting into its stride with a series of useful reports.

In any event, the department now had other ambitions for the governance of the youth service. These were expressed in three major administrative actions. The grant scheme for National Voluntary Youth Organisations was recast to tie funding to specific programmes which would be closer to governmental priorities. Although some HMI jibbed at this, it was hardly exceptional given the climate of the times and HMI, in a version of their original

1839 task, continued to assess the work of these bodies against the overt grant criteria. Secondly, in 1990, the department decided to withdraw most of its funding from the National Youth Bureau (NYB), the Council for Education and Training in Youth and Community Work (CETYCW), the British Youth Council (BYC), the National Association of Young People's Counselling and Advisory Services (NAYPCAS) and the National Council for Voluntary Youth Services (NCVYS). Instead, it would create a National Youth Agency (NYA) as the central focus for youth work in England. In its grand design this was a far-sighted proposal but the details and implementation were flawed. At the heart of the difficulty was the decision to create the NYA as a non-departmental public body (a 'quango' in popular speech) with the membership of its governing body appointed by the Secretary of State and its activities and services largely determined by the DES on pain of withdrawing the grant on which NYA would depend for its existence. HMI counselled against this model but officials pressed on. The NYA was created (its first director was Janet Paraskeva, who had moved from HMI to become director of NYB) but BYC, NAYPCAS and NCVYS, determined to maintain an independent voice for their respective constituencies, sought funds from elsewhere and survived as independent bodies to await a turning DES tide[3].

The most ambitious of the department's activities by the late 1980s was an attempt to identify a 'core curriculum' for the youth service. This had echoes of the national curriculum for schools set out in Kenneth Baker's 1988 Education Reform Act. As with the creation of the NYA, the department's goals were not wholly misguided. The cold climate for public expenditure was requiring services of all kinds to be clearer about their outcomes and benefits and a sprawling youth service was particularly vulnerable. HMI agreed with the department's analysis – indeed their inspection reports contributed to it.

But the attempt to produce a consensus across such a wide field of endeavour – both LEA and voluntary sector – and in a form which would be genuinely useful was doomed from the start. It was made worse, in the view of HMI, by the failure to offer clarity about the meaning of the very word 'curriculum': HMI considered themselves the guardians of educational philosophy! The department's great project was also handicapped by the generally hamfisted management of the tortuous process of a series of ministerial conferences by an alliance of DES officials and the newly-formed, and still mistrusted, NYA. Since HMI were known to be sceptical, they were kept at a distance. The result pleased no-one. The department blamed the field for its failure to answer the questions correctly and an incoming official ordered 'full speed astern' and changed the compass bearing from dirigisme to laisser-faire.

The long day closes

By then it was becoming clear that HMI's specialist knowledge, advice and professional judgment were welcomed on specific matters such as the department's grants, now to over 70 national voluntary youth organisations, on grant programmes for in-service training, or on the development of specific initiatives, such as youth work apprenticeships in the inner cities. It was less welcome when HMI raised questions about the department's overall stewardship of youth service, in particular its unwillingness to give unequivocal statutory underpinning and a consistent policy and resourcing framework to a diversifying sector. The much enhanced inspection activity, both across the country and across the range of needs, which the youth service was endeavouring to meet had exposed the feebleness of Government's policy and funding for youth work. This was not a comfortable message for HMI to convey. HMI's heightened profile in the field, its involvement as assessors on a range of national youth-related bodies, its short course programme and willingness to speak, however judiciously, on public platforms all risked illuminating tensions between the department and the professional advice its Inspectorate offered on policy development (or its lack).

However, HMI's relationships with ministers and DES officials in the youth field were only a small part of a much larger picture. Within a few years the publication of reports on individual schools was prompting the question of how a national inspectorate could possibly report on all 26,000 schools within any reasonable timescale if consumers were to be informed at the point of choice for their children. Moreover, quite apart from individual institutions, HMI was publicly and heavily involved in inspecting, reporting and advising on policy and its implementation across the whole of the education service.

As Eric Bolton, the SCI at the time, was later to comment:

It had become accepted that all that inspection effort would lead to publication and, given HMI's remit to report without fear or favour, there were many tensions and differences with ministers and officials, opposition spokesmen on education, local politicians, chief education officers, heads' and teachers' associations and unions as well as with the heads and staff of individual institutions.

In short, almost everything that was concerning the education service in the late 1980s stemmed from Government policy and its implementation. While that meant that the Government and its officials were increasingly dependent on inspection-based information and advice about the effectiveness of their policies, they were becoming increasingly irritated that most of it went public, especially as some was very critical, and little, if any, ever wholly congratulatory.
(Bolton, 1998)

In such a context the relatively minor, if emblematic, flurries of disagreement between DES officials in its youth policy branch and specialist HMI were, by 1992, to be swamped by the political waves which would overwhelm HM Inspectorate as a whole[4].

Footnotes

[1] The organisational structure of HM Inspectorate in the 1980s consisted essentially of: chief inspectors, led by a senior chief inspector, responsible for the coordination of the Inspectorate's overall work; staff inspectors responsible for subjects, aspects or phases of education such as primary education and the territorial deployment of inspectors; HM Inspectors covering a subject or phase within a particular territory and working nationally as required. In January 1985 there were 460 HMI in England of whom 14 had a major responsibility for youth work and were led by a staff inspector who operated within the FE command of the Inspectorate.

HMI had no direct responsibility for educational management and few powers except the right of access to institutions and the duty to inspect on behalf of the Secretary of State for Education. There were similar arrangements in Scotland, Wales and Northern Ireland and specialists from these Inspectorates regularly attended HMI England 'youth' committees.

[2] The authorship of inspection reports was not disclosed but they were never the work of a single HMI; they were based on a team approach with the deployment of HMI resource, the management of processes leading to collective judgements and the eventual drawing together of a report coordinated by a designated 'reporting inspector'. Drafts were, in turn, cleared with the team and through the Inspectorate's own chain of command, not by the DES. By a century-old tradition, any suggested amendments had to be acceptable to the reporting inspector.

[3] The tide did turn. By the early 1990s the DES was again paying grants to BYC, NAYPCAS and NCVYS, though not at the same level. And, by 1995, following a change of departmental official and another review of NYA, the department ended NYA's 'quango' status, its core funding responsibility was picked up by the local government associations and the governance of the agency became democratically accountable to a range of nominating bodies representative of youth work. Most of the HMI reports on youth work published since 1983 are available from the NYA's Information Service.

[4] The (unexpected) return of a Conservative Government in the general election of 1992 enabled it to implement its plans to establish a Funding Council for FE, with its own inspection arm, and a new inspection body chiefly for schools – the Office for Standards in Education (Ofsted). The existing cadre of youth specialist HMI fragmented: some retired or went freelance; a few went to the FEFC and a few to Ofsted, whose professional core retained the title 'HMI' and could still inspect youth work since Ofsted had inspection duties in aspects of FE, such as adult education and youth work, which were outwith FEFC's responsibilities. By 1998, Ofsted had three HMI with a youth work specialism.

Bibliography

Ministry of Education (1960). *The Youth Service in England and Wales*, The Albemarle Report. London, HMSO.

Bolton, E. (1998). *'HMI – The Thatcher Years'*, in Oxford Review of Education Vol 24, No 1, pp 45–55.

DES (1969). *Youth and Community Work in the 70s* (The Fairbairn- Milson Report). London, HMSO.

DES (1982). *Experience and Participation* (The Thompson Report). London, HMSO.

HMI (1964). *Victory Memorial Youth Centre, Liverpool* (unpublished).

HMI (1982). (a) *'Education Service Provision for the Young Unemployed: September 1978– December 1979'*. DES, London.

(b) *'Three Lambeth Youth Clubs'*. DES, London.

HMI (1985). *'Westhill College Birmingham Initial Training for Community and Youth Work'*. DES, London.

HMI (1986). (a) *'Aspects of the Youth and Community Service in Sheffield'*. DES, London.

(b) *'YMCA National College Two Year Certificate Course in Youth and Community Work'*. DES, London.

(c) *'Youth Service in Cornwall'*. DES, London.

HMI (1987). (a) *'Effective Youth Work'*. DES, London.

(b) *'Youth Work in Coventry'*. DES, London.

(c) *'Youth Work in Eight Inner City Areas'*. DES, London.

(d) *'Manchester Polytechnic Initial Qualifying Training in Youth and Community Work'*. DES, London.

HMI (1988). (a) *'Survey of the National Federation of Young Farmers' Clubs'*. DES, London.

(b) *'Aspects of provision at Leicester Polytechnic'*. DES, London.

(c) *'Developmental Approaches to Youth Work in Wirral'*. DES, London.

(d) *'Youth Service Responses to the Needs of Young Women in Selected LEAs'*. DES, London.

(e) *'Youth Work on Urban Housing Estates'*. DES, London.

HMI (1990). (a) *'Initial Training for Professional Youth and Community Work'*. DES, London.

(b) *'Responsive Youth Work'*. DES, London.

HMI (1991) (a) *'A Survey of School Based Youth and Community Work'*. DES, London.

(b) *'Standards in Education 1989–90'*. DES, London.

Kay-Shuttleworth, J. (1840) cited in Blackie, J. (1970). *Inspecting and the Inspectors.* London, Routledge and Kegan Paul.

Lawton, D. (1987). *HMI.* London, Routledge.

Ritchie, N. (1986). *An Inspector Calls.* Leicester, NYB.